FEMINIST
INTERPRETATIONS
OF
BENEDICT SPINOZA

RE-READING THE CANON

NANCY TUANA, GENERAL EDITOR

This series consists of edited collections of essays, some original and some previously published, offering feminist re-interpretations of the writings of major figures in the Western philosophical tradition. Devoted to the work of a single philosopher, each volume contains essays covering the full range of the philosopher's thought and representing the diversity of approaches now being used by feminist critics.

Already published:

Nancy Tuana, ed., *Feminist Interpretations of Plato* (1994)
Margaret Simons, ed., *Feminist Interpretations of Simone de Beauvoir* (1995)
Bonnie Honig, ed., *Feminist Interpretations of Hannah Arendt* (1995)
Patricia Jagentowicz Mills, ed., *Feminist Interpretations of G. W. F. Hegel* (1996)
Maria J. Falco, ed., *Feminist Interpretations of Mary Wollstonecraft* (1996)
Susan J. Hekman, ed., *Feminist Interpretations of Michel Foucault* (1996)
Nancy J. Holland, ed., *Feminist Interpretations of Jacques Derrida* (1997)
Robin May Schott, ed., *Feminist Interpretations of Immanuel Kant* (1997)
Celeine Leon and Sylvia Walsh, eds., *Feminist Interpretations of Soren Kierkegaard* (1997)
Cynthia Freeland, ed., *Feminist Interpretations of Aristotle* (1998)
Kelly Oliver and Marilyn Pearsall, eds., *Feminist Interpretations of Friedrich Nietzsche* (1998)
Mimi Reisel Gladstein and Chris Matthew Sciabarra, eds., *Feminist Interpretations of Ayn Rand* (1999)
Susan Bordo, ed., *Feminist Interpretations of René Descartes* (1999)
Julien S. Murphy, ed., *Feminist Interpretations of Jean-Paul Sartre* (1999)
Anne Jaap Jacobson, ed., *Feminist Interpretations of David Hume* (2000)
Sarah Lucia Hoagland and Marilyn Frye, eds., *Feminist Interpretations of Mary Daly* (2000)
Tina Chanter, ed., *Feminist Interpretations of Emmanuel Levinas* (2001)
Nancy J. Holland and Patricia Huntington, eds., *Feminist Interpretations of Martin Heidegger* (2001)
Charlene Haddock Seigfried, ed., *Feminist Interpretations of John Dewey* (2001)
Naomi Scheman and Peg O'Connor, eds., *Feminist Interpretations of Ludwig Wittgenstein* (2002)
Lynda Lange, ed., *Feminist Interpretations of Jean-Jacques Rousseau* (2002)
Lorraine Code, ed., *Feminist Interpretations of Hans-Georg Gadamer* (2002)
Lynn Hankinson Nelson and Jack Nelson, eds., *Feminist Interpretations of W. V. Quine* (2003)
Maria J. Falco, ed., *Feminist Interpretations of Niccolò Machiavelli* (2004)
Renée J. Heberle, ed., *Feminist Interpretations of Theodor Adorno* (2006)
Dorothea Olkowski and Gail Weiss, eds., *Feminist Interpretations of Maurice Merleau-Ponty* (2006)
Nancy J. Hirschmann and Kirstie M. McClure, eds., *Feminist Interpretations of John Locke* (2007)
Penny A. Weiss and Loretta Kensinger, eds., *Feminist Interpretations of Emma Goldman* (2007)
Judith Chelius Stark, ed., *Feminist Interpretations of Augustine* (2007)
Jill Locke and Eileen Hunt Botting, eds., *Feminist Interpretations of Alexis de Tocqueville* (2008)

FEMINIST INTERPRETATIONS OF BENEDICT SPINOZA

EDITED BY
MOIRA GATENS

THE PENNSYLVANIA STATE UNIVERSITY PRESS
UNIVERSITY PARK, PENNSYLVANIA

Library of Congress Cataloging-in-Publication Data

Feminist interpretations of Benedict Spinoza / edited by Moira Gatens.
    p.   cm.—(Re-reading the canon)
Includes bibliographical references and index.
Summary: "A collection of essays on the metaphysical, political, theological, ethical and psychological writings of Spinoza. Examines the ways in which his philosophy presents a resource for the re-conceptualization of friendship, sexuality, politics and ethics in contemporary life"—Provided by publisher.
ISBN 978-0-271-03515-4 (cloth : alk. paper)
ISBN 978-0-271-03516-1 (pbk. : alk. paper)
1. Spinoza, Benedictus de, 1632–1677.
2. Feminist criticism.
I. Gatens, Moira.

B3998.F28 2009
199'.492—dc22
2008045147

Copyright © 2009 The Pennsylvania State University
All rights reserved
Printed in the United States of America
Published by The Pennsylvania State University Press,
University Park, PA 16802-1003

It is the policy of The Pennsylvania State University Press to use acid-free paper. This book is printed on stock that meets the minimum requirements of American National Standard for Information Sciences—
Permanence of Paper for Printed Library Material, ANSI Z39.48-1992.

Contents

Preface   vii
   Nancy Tuana

Acknowledgments   xi

List of Abbreviations and Notes on Translations   xiii

Introduction: Through Spinoza's "Looking Glass"   1
   Moira Gatens

1   Dominance and Difference: A Spinozistic Alternative to the Distinction Between "Sex" and "Gender"   29
   Genevieve Lloyd

2   Autonomy and the Relational Individual: Spinoza and Feminism   43
   Aurelia Armstrong

3   Spinoza on the Pathos of Idolatrous Love and the Hilarity of True Love   65
   Amelie Rorty

4   Spinoza and Sexuality   87
   Alexandre Matheron

5   Reason, Sexuality, and the Self in Spinoza   107
   David West

6   What Spinoza Can Teach Us About Embodying and Naturalizing Ethics   125
   Heidi Morrison Ravven

7	Adam and the Serpent: *Everyman* and the Imagination Paola Grassi	145
8	The Envelope: A Reading of Spinoza's *Ethics*, "Of God" Luce Irigaray	155
9	Re-reading Irigaray's Spinoza Sarah Donovan	165
10	The Politics of the Imagination Moira Gatens	189
11	Law and Sovereignty in Spinoza's Politics Susan James	211
	Further Reading	229
	List of Contributors	231
	Index	233

Preface
Nancy Tuana

Take into your hands any history of philosophy text. You will find compiled therein the "classics" of modern philosophy. Since these texts are often designed for use in undergraduate classes, the editor is likely to offer an introduction in which the reader is informed that these selections represent the perennial questions of philosophy. The student is to assume that she or he is about to explore the timeless wisdom of the greatest minds of Western philosophy. No one calls attention to the fact that the philosophers are all men.

Though women are omitted from the canons of philosophy, these texts inscribe the nature of woman. Sometimes the philosopher speaks directly about woman, delineating her proper role, her abilities and inabilities, her desires. Other times the message is indirect—a passing remark hinting at women's emotionality, irrationality, unreliability.

This process of definition occurs in far more subtle ways when the central concepts of philosophy—reason and justice, those characteristics that are taken to define us as human—are associated with traits historically identified with masculinity. If the "man" of reason must learn to control or overcome traits identified as feminine—the body, the emotions, the passions—then the realm of rationality will be one reserved primarily for men,[1] with grudging entrance to those few women who are capable of transcending their femininity.

Feminist philosophers have begun to look critically at the canonized texts of philosophy and have concluded that the discourses of philosophy are not gender-neutral. Philosophical narratives do not offer a universal perspective, but rather privilege some experiences and beliefs over others. These experiences and beliefs permeate all philosophical theories whether they be aesthetic or epistemological, moral or metaphysical. Yet this fact has often been neglected by those studying the traditions of philosophy. Given the history of canon formation in Western philosophy, the perspective most likely to be privileged is that of upper-class white males. Thus, to be fully aware of the impact of gender biases, it is imperative that we re-read the canon with attention to the ways in which philosophers' assumptions concerning gender are embedded within their theories.

This series, Re-reading the Canon, is designed to foster this process of reevaluation. Each volume will offer feminist analyses of the theories of a selected philosopher. Since feminist philosophy is not monolithic in method or content, the essays are also selected to illustrate the variety of perspectives within feminist criticism and highlight some of the controversies within feminist scholarship.

In this series, feminist lenses will be focused on the canonical texts of Western philosophy, both those authors who have been part of the traditional canon, and those philosophers whose writings have more recently gained attention within the philosophical community. A glance at the list of volumes in the series will reveal an immediate gender bias of the canon: Arendt, Aristotle, Beauvoir, Derrida, Descartes, Foucault, Hegel, Hume, Kant, Locke, Marx, Mill, Nietzsche, Plato, Rousseau, Wittgenstein, Wollstonecraft. There are all too few women included, and those few who do appear have been added only recently. In creating this series, it is not my intention to rectify the current canon of philosophical thought. What is and is not included within the canon during a particular historical period is a result of many factors. Although no canonization of texts will include all philosophers, no canonization of texts that excludes all but a few women can offer an accurate representation of the history of the discipline, as women have been philosophers since the ancient period.[2]

I share with many feminist philosophers and other philosophers writing from the margins of philosophy the concern that the current canonization of philosophy be transformed. Although I do not accept the position that the current canon has been formed exclusively by power relations, I do believe that this canon represents only a selective history of the tradition. I share the view of Michael Bérubé that "canons are at once the location, the index, and the record of the struggle for cultural representation; like any other hegemonic formation, they must be continually reproduced anew and are continually contested."³

The process of canon transformation will require the recovery of "lost" texts and a careful examination of the reasons such voices have been silenced. Along with the process of uncovering women's philosophical history, we must also begin to analyze the impact of gender ideologies upon the process of canonization. This process of recovery and examination must occur in conjunction with careful attention to the concept of a canon of authorized texts. Are we to dispense with the notion of a tradition of excellence embodied in a canon of authorized texts? Or, rather than abandon the whole idea of a canon, do we instead encourage a reconstruction of a canon of those texts that inform a common culture?

This series is designed to contribute to this process of canon transformation by offering a re-reading of the current philosophical canon. Such a re-reading shifts our attention to the ways in which woman and the role of the feminine are constructed within the texts of philosophy. A question we must keep in front of us during this process of re-reading is whether a philosopher's socially inherited prejudices concerning woman's nature and role are independent of her or his larger philosophical framework. In asking this question attention must be paid to the ways in which the definitions of central philosophical concepts implicitly include or exclude gendered traits.

This type of reading strategy is not limited to the canon, but can be applied to all texts. It is my desire that this series reveal the importance of this type of critical reading. Paying attention to the workings of gender within the texts of philosophy will make visible the complexities of the inscription of gender ideologies.

Notes

1. More properly, it is a realm reserved for a group of privileged males, since the texts also inscribe race and class biases that thereby omit certain males from participation.
2. Mary Ellen Waithe's multivolume series, *A History of Women Philosophers* (Boston: M. Nijoff, 1987), attests to this presence of women.
3. Michael Bérubé, *Marginal Forces/Cultural Centers: Tolson, Pynchon, and the Politics of the Canon* (Ithaca: Cornell University Press, 1992), 4–5.

Acknowledgments

For permission to use previously published materials I am grateful to the following: Cornell University Press, for Chapter 1, "Dominance and Difference: A Spinozistic Alternative to the Distinction Between 'Sex' and 'Gender,'" an abridged and edited version of chapter 5 of Genevieve Lloyd's *Part of Nature: Self-Knowledge in Spinoza's Ethics* (Ithaca: Cornell University Press, 1994); Amelie Rorty, for permission to reprint Chapter 3, "Spinoza on the Pathos of Idolatrous Love and the Hilarity of True Love"; Alexandre Matheron and the *Giornale Critico della Filosofia Italiana*, for permission to publish a translation of "Spinoza et la sexualité," from *Giornale Critico della Filosofia Italiana* 8, no. 4 (1977): 436–57, which appears as Chapter 4, "Spinoza and Sexuality"; David West and Polity Press, for permission to reprint Chapter 5, "Reason, Sexuality, and the Self in Spinoza," which is a revised version of a section of chapter 4 of *Reason and Sexuality in Western Thought* (New York: Polity Press, 2005); Cornell University Press, for permission to reprint Chapter 8, "The Envelope: A Reading of Spinoza's *Ethics*, 'Of God,'" from Luce Irigaray's *An Ethics of Sexual Difference*, translated by Carolyn Burke and Gillian Gill (Ithaca: Cornell University Press, 1993); and Cengage Learning (formerly Taylor and Francis), for permission to use in revised form sections from chapters 8 and 9 of Moira Gatens's *Imaginary Bodies: Ethics, Power, and Corporeality* (London: Routledge, 1996) in Chapter 10, "The Politics of the Imagination."

I am greatly indebted to Paul Patton, Genevieve Lloyd, Rosalyn Diprose, Simon Duffy, John Burnheim, Tim Fitzpatrick, Linnell Secomb, and Lisa Trahair for their invaluable assistance and constructive criticism at various stages of this project. I am grateful to colleagues in the Department of Philosophy at the University of Sydney for providing a vibrant and supportive environment for research. Warmest thanks to Jeremy Bell and Amanda Hickling for their research assistance and to Romaine Perin for rigorous copyediting. I appreciate the patience shown by my contributors when the gap between the expected and actual publication date of this volume kept getting wider. I would like to acknowledge the important support for this research provided by the Australian Research Council (DP0665045). I am also grateful to the Wissenschaftskolleg zu Berlin for providing a peaceful environment in which to bring this project to completion. Finally, Nancy Tuana and Sanford G. Thatcher deserve recognition and thanks not only for conceiving the Re-reading the Canon series but also for the grace, wisdom, and patience with which they continue to produce it.

Abbreviations and Notes on Translations

References to the five parts of Spinoza's *Ethics* are given in parentheses in the body of the chapters. The translation used (unless otherwise stated) is *The Collected Works of Spinoza*, edited and translated by Edwin Curley, volume 1 (Princeton: Princeton University Press, 1985). The abbreviations follow.

Ax	Axiom
D	Definition
E	*Ethics*
Exp	Explanation
L	Lemma
Pref	Preface
Prop	Proposition
Schol	Scholium
Cor	Corollary
Dem	Demonstration
Def Aff	The Definition of the Affects at the end of Part III of the *Ethics*
Appen	Appendix

Thus, E, III, Prop 16, Schol refers to the *Ethics*, Part III, Proposition 16, Scholium.

TdIE	*Treatise on the Emendation of the Intellect*

References to Spinoza's *Tractatus Theologico-Politicus* are given in parentheses in the body of the chapters. The translation used (unless otherwise stated) is Baruch Spinoza, *Theological-Political Treatise*, translated by Samuel Shirley, second edition (Indianapolis, Hackett, 2001). Citations provide the chapter number and page number.

TTP *Theological-Political Treatise*

Thus, TTP, XIX, 214, refers to the *Theological-Political Treatise*, Chapter 19, page 214.

References to Spinoza's *Tractatus Politicus* are given in parentheses in the body of the essays. The translation used (unless otherwise stated) is Baruch Spinoza, *Political Treatise*, translated by Samuel Shirley (Indianapolis: Hackett, 2000). Citations provide the chapter number and page number.

TP *Political Treatise*

Thus, TP, VIII, 101, refers to the *Political Treatise*, Chapter 8, page 101.

Introduction

Through Spinoza's "Looking Glass"

Moira Gatens

I have taken great care not to deride, bewail, or execrate human actions, but to understand them.
—Spinoza, *Political Treatise*

Spinoza and Feminism

Some Spinoza scholars may be surprised by the assumption that underlies this volume, namely, that feminist scholarship can offer new interpretative insights into the notoriously difficult philosophy of Benedict Spinoza. I hope that, for these readers, the surprise will be a pleasant one. The exclusion of most women from the historical development of philosophy has meant that, until recently, certain questions, preoccupations, and points of view were left out of consideration. This exclusion has meant that the philosophical treatment of issues important to us all have been conceived in an unbalanced, or partial, fashion.[1] While it is certainly the case that a philosopher of either sex might use the considerable resources of Spinoza's philosophy, the particular questions and concerns that feminist philosophers bring to this venture adds a further, enriching, interpretative dimension. Questions to do with power, with the gendered distribution of the benefits and burdens of social and political life, and with the "naturally dependent" status of some individuals—to name just a few of the issues central to recent feminist scholarship—all take on a specific resonance when posed from the standpoint of those who were all but barred from participation in philosophical thought.[2]

As the essays in this volume show, when feminist concerns are brought to bear on Spinoza's philosophy, themes that otherwise may not appear in Spinoza scholarship are highlighted or developed in novel ways. Examples of this include using Spinoza's mind-body thesis to challenge the sex-gender distinction, developing his views on "sensual love" to question the grounds of normative heterosexuality, and exploring the role of the imagination in determining how "difference" is configured in sociopolitical contexts. But, as the contributors to this volume also demonstrate, the relationship between Spinoza's philosophy and feminist scholarship is a two-way street. Just as feminist research has brought new insights to Spinoza's philosophy, his thought, in turn, has allowed feminist theorists to approach recalcitrant problems—for example, the mind-body and culture-nature dualisms—from a new nondualistic angle. Despite the formidable character of Spinoza's philosophy, many of his ideas and concerns are strikingly modern.[3] Spinoza's appeal to modern sensibilities might be explained, in part, by his commitment to an immanent, naturalistic worldview that is amenable to the human understanding through "scientific" explanation. Indeed, some contemporary theorists have argued that it is only in recent times that the acuity of much of his philosophy has fully been appreciated.[4] What is it about Spinoza's life and the contours of his thought that makes his philosophy "untimely," in the Nietzschean sense?[5]

Spinoza's Life and Thought

Baruch Spinoza was born on November 24, 1632, in Amsterdam, to a Jewish family of the merchant class. From the late sixteenth century, the comparatively tolerant city had been a refuge for those of the Jewish faith who were forced to flee the Inquisitorial horror that had swept Spain and Portugal. Some of those fleeing persecution were known as *conversos* (or *marranos*), that is, Jews who were compelled to adopt the Christian faith on pain of death. Although compliant with Christian values, and outwardly observant of Christian rituals, some *conversos* continued to practice their Jewish faith in secret, thus leading a double life. Spinoza's parents were descendents of Portuguese *conversos* and many commentators argue that an understanding of this ethnoreligious background is necessary in order adequately to grasp Spinoza's philosophy.[6]

The tendency for Spinoza to use terms common in medieval and early modern philosophy in new ways—most strikingly, his (re)definition of Substance (God *or* Nature)—is taken by some to indicate the esoteric character of his writing. The idea that Spinoza led a "double-life," and wrote in a "dual-language," that only the "initiated" could understand, is not without merit.[7] In his time, the open questioning of religion or of the authority of theologians was a dangerous business, even in Amsterdam.[8] Spinoza repeatedly made clear that he did not want his writings to be read—and inevitably misconstrued—by "the common people" or by those whose judgment was blinkered by religious dogma.[9] However, it is contentious to assert that this amounts to duplicity or deceit, rather than mere prudence or cautiousness, on Spinoza's part.[10] Besides, the charge of duplicity does not sit easily with the fact that Spinoza was formally ostracized from the Jewish community in 1656, when he was only twenty-four years old, with the pronouncement of a particularly harsh *cherem* for his "monstrous deeds" and "abominable heresies."[11] Although this writ includes the directive that "no one should communicate with him, not even in writing, nor accord him any favor nor stay with him under the same roof nor [come] within four cubits of his vicinity," Steven Nadler rebuts the common misconception that Spinoza lived the lonely and isolated life of an outcast.[12] The ban was binding on practicing Jews only, and Spinoza, in fact, enjoyed rich friendships and lively intellectual exchange with a group of "free-thinkers" and religious dissenters.[13] It was after his exclusion from the Jewish fold that Spinoza adopted the Latinized version of his name: Benedict (which, like Baruch in Hebrew, means "blessed"). In addition to a small annuity, he made his living from lens grinding. Spinoza was known for making fine lenses for telescopes and microscopes, a particularly fitting pursuit for one whose distinctive worldview extends from the microlevel of the simplest bodies (*corpora simplicis-*

sima) to the macrolevel of the single, indivisible, and unique Substance (*Deus sive Natura*). Tracing the movement of his thought in the *Ethics*—from the account of Substance, in Part I, to that of the simplest modes; then on to complex bodies; and concluding, in Part V, with a return to (a now radically transformed conception of) God—one can imagine oneself seated next to Spinoza, looking at life through his carefully prepared glass. The occupational hazard of producing lenses—the inhalation of the fine particles of glass—no doubt exacerbated the consumption from which he died in 1677, aged forty-four.

In some ways the *cherem* served to free Spinoza from the constraints of his community of birth and gave him free rein to study and develop the diverse philosophical and theological ideas available to him. These intellectual influences were exceptionally eclectic. As well as having a thorough grounding in Judeo-Islamic thought (especially that of Maimonides and Gersonides), Spinoza was influenced by Stoic and Aristotelian thought.[14] He also enjoyed a comprehensive knowledge of contemporary philosophy, one of his early works being an exposition of Descartes' *Principles of Philosophy*.[15] As even the novice of Spinoza studies will know, Spinoza's philosophy is usually explained by way of contrast with the tenets of Cartesian thought. Whereas Descartes posits substance dualism (thought and extension), Spinoza is a substance monist; whereas Descartes sought to explain free will in terms of the soul, Spinoza dismissed free will as a fiction; and whereas Descartes conceives God as a transcendent power, separate from that which he creates, Spinoza's God is the immanent cause of all that exits.

The *Ethics*

The *Ethics* is regarded as Spinoza's magnum opus. It was composed over many years; according to Edwin Curley, "Spinoza was occupied with writing this work, off and on, for most of his adult life."[16] An eccentric text by contemporary standards, the posthumously published *Ethics* is composed of five parts and is presented in "geometric order," with all the paraphernalia—propositions, scholia, demonstrations, axioms, and definitions—of its paradigm: Euclid's *Elements*.[17] As one contemporary commentator has observed, the *Ethics* "touches on almost every major area of philosophy: metaphysics, theory of knowledge, philosophy of mind, philosophical psychology, moral philosophy, political philosophy and the philosophy of religion."[18] According to Spinoza, we cannot know what we are—our limits, our powers, or our "good"—unless we have an understanding of the whole of which we are merely a part.[19] This is why the *Ethics* begins with defining and explicating Substance (God *or* Nature). His ethical stance is fully integrated within nature and cannot be grasped independently of his account of metaphysics and physics. It is necessary to reject the doctrine of "final causes" (the Aristotelian notion that things exist for a reason, and have an aim or *telos*, toward which they tend) if we are to cease imaginatively projecting onto nature our own desires and preferences, or as Spinoza put it, if we are to escape from "the sanctuary of ignorance" (E, I, Appen). The god of the *Ethics* has not arranged reality to satisfy any end or aim—not even the admirable aim of serving human convenience—and on Spinoza's view, the acquisition of adequate philosophical knowledge depends on giving up the anthropomorphic image of the god of traditional religion.

It follows from Spinoza's substance monism that the human mind is not an individual substance. Rather, mind and body are conceived as modifications of the *attributes*—thought and extension—of the unique Substance (God or Nature). Far from taking the attributes to be creations of an omnipotent God, they are better understood as "aspects" or "essences" of God. In some sense, God *is* Nature, and Genevieve Lloyd draws out an important implication of this view: "The divine attributes cease to be properties of a transcendent god and become instead ways in which reality is construed, articulated, or expressed."[20] Some have seen this aspect of Spinoza's philosophy as the "divinizing" of Nature (or pantheism) but it may just as well be interpreted as the "naturalizing" of God. This interpretation is consistent with Spinoza's assertion that we "acquire a greater and more perfect knowledge of God as we gain more knowledge of natural phenomena" (TTP, IV, 50). As cryptic as this might seem to those unfamiliar with Spinoza's metaphysics, this conception of Substance dispenses with many of the problems that plagued Descartes' philosophy: the problem of God's veracity, the existence of other minds, and the mind-body relation are all dissolved through this shift in metaphysical perspective. Likewise, there is no place in Spinoza's deterministic philosophy to pose the problem of free will; this is another of the fictions produced by the imagination because of its partial grasp on reality: the imagination experiences affects without understanding their causes. Perhaps surprisingly, the rejection of free will does not entail the denial of freedom. Spinoza defines freedom as self-caused activity. Strictly speaking, only Substance (God or Nature) is truly free because nothing external to it exists. Hence, no external cause exists that could affect it. The distinct freedom, or power, of human beings lies in our capacity to form adequate ideas and enhance our understanding of nature: "I call him free who is led by reason alone" (E, IV, Prop 68, Dem). Freedom, put differently, is not the capacity to will whatever I desire but rather the ability to understand the causes that determine all things, including my desires. It is through Spinoza's second kind of knowledge, reason, that reality can be adequately understood. Along with the third kind of knowledge, intuition, Spinoza's account of how we come to be reasonable is both developmental and dynamic. The three kinds of knowledge that compose Spinoza's epistemology should not be understood in purely cognitive terms. Human activity, under the attribute of thought, always implies a correlative bodily activity, under the attribute of extension. For Spinoza, "knowledge is more a mode of being than of having, not something we possess but something we *are* or *become*."[21]

Although no one is born rational, with luck and the right kind of environmental conditions—a good education, good health, and so on—everyone can become reasonable. The greatest obstacle to becoming free is the passive affects, especially fear and hope. They enervate our power to act and experience joy; and this, in turn, encourages the formation of hostile relations with others. Parts III and IV of the *Ethics* provide an analysis of the origins of the human affects, or emotions, and what we can do to transform our passive and debilitating feelings into those actively affirmed emotions that characterize a life of understanding and harmonious sociability. Spinoza's ethical vision does not encourage the renunciation, or repression, of pleasure. On the contrary, he says: "Nothing forbids our pleasure except a savage and sad superstition" and "no deity, nor anyone else, unless he is envious, takes pleasure in my lack of power." The wise person is not a dour person but rather will enjoy his or her pleasures, whatever they may be, so long as these pleasures do not cause "injury to another" (E, IV, Prop 45, Cor 2).

Spinoza's ethics, then, cannot be understood in terms of a fixed moral code: a list of "thou shalt nots." Rather, "the *Ethics* is necessarily an ethics of joy: only joy is worthwhile, joy remains, bringing us near to action, and to the bliss of action. The sad passions always amount to impotence."[22] The dynamic character of Spinoza's version of individuality derives, in part, from his definition of the "actual essence," or *conatus* of an individual thing. The *conatus* is that "striving by which each thing strives to persevere in its being" (E, III, Prop 7). Such striving determines what each body shall judge to be "good" or "bad," life enhancing or debilitating (see E, III, Prop 9, Schol and E, IV, Pref and Def Aff 1 and 2). The *Ethics* presents a set of arguments that endeavor to correct the mistaken theological link between piety and virtue, on the one hand, and feelings of sadness, on the other. It is "common notions" that provide the hinge to connect the joyful passions of the imagination with adequate knowledge and reason. Common notions arise when one body encounters another with which it is compatible and so experiences joy. Although such encounters initially arise through chance—and so the cause of joy is external to the body that experiences it—the desire to repeat the joyful experience necessarily involves striving to understand the cause of the joy: the drive to repeat the joyful experience promotes reflection upon what it is that bodies have in common. If a notion can be formed of what is common between the two then that notion will be an adequate idea (see E, II, Prop 38). Even though she or he who forms the common notion was not the (sole) cause of the joyful feeling, she or he will be the cause of the formation of the adequate idea. An understanding of adequate ideas involves an understanding of Spinoza's physics of bodies. The formation of common notions is the first step on the path to becoming the active cause of one's encounters, a path that leads to an increase in our freedom through an increase in our understanding of ourselves, others, and broader nature.

Spinoza dissolves a number of dichotomies that have dominated Western philosophy: he does not oppose mind to body, reason to emotion, or freedom to necessity. Rather, his fundamental contrast is between passivity and activity, and it is our position on the passivity-activity spectrum that will determine the shape of our ethical lives. Far from freedom being opposed to necessity, it is the very condition of our liberty: "freedom does not remove the necessity of action, but imposes it" (TP, II, 42). The more we understand necessity, the more active we become, and the more active we become the more we express our freedom, or power, or essence. Our power, our freedom, our virtue and our *conatus* all begin to converge, and by Part V of the *Ethics*, these terms are all but indistinguishable. The notoriously opaque thesis of "the eternity of the mind," along with that of the "blessedness" arising from the contemplation of God by the third kind of knowledge (intuition), have generated a good deal of discussion and debate in Spinoza scholarship.[23] However, what is clear is that Spinoza's philosophy culminates in an affirmation and celebration of *this* life and seeks to promote human empowerment, joy, and harmony through understanding and friendship. However, it would be a mistake to characterize his ethical theory as utopian or naive. Spinoza had no delusions about the difficulty of *becoming* a reasonable and active individual or of forming a sound democratic polity. The *Ethics* closes with the observation that "what is found so rarely must be hard" and "all things excellent are as difficult as they are rare" (E, V, Prop 42, Schol). Spinoza's experience of the deep irrationality of the sad and destructive passions of his fellow citizens supplied ample materials to demonstrate just how difficult is the establishment, and maintenance, of a good polity. The political context in Holland in the mid- to late seventeenth century provided grounds for both hope and fear, optimism and pessimism, for those who promoted human "enlightenment." One event, in 1672, shook the equanimity of even the normally serene Spinoza. The already conflicted relations between the conservative Orangist and the Republican political parties had been intensified by the war with France.[24] The Republican brothers Johan and Cornelius de Witt, falsely accused of crimes against the state, were murdered by an unruly mob and their bodies torn to pieces. Spinoza, a supporter of the defeated Republican regime, on hearing of their murders, had to be restrained from placing a sign at the scene of the carnage that read: "Ultimi barbarorum." Had he not been restrained, his intended act could well have led him to suffer a similar fate.[25] Little wonder, then, that he writes in the *Ethics*: "The mob is terrifying, if unafraid" (E, IV, Prop 54, Schol).

Tractatus Theologico-Politicus and *Tractatus Politicus*

Edwin Curley suggests that Spinoza may well have put aside his work on the *Ethics*, in 1665, because he judged that the time "was not yet ripe" for its publication.[26] Rumors about Spinoza's "atheism" and the strong hostility various theological authorities expressed towards him might have encouraged the thought "that another work was required which could help to prepare the way for the *Ethics* by freeing people from their reliance on scripture."[27] As Curley notes, in fact, the publication of the resulting text in 1670—the *Tractatus Theologico-Politicus*—had exactly the opposite effect and Spinoza found himself more reviled than ever.

Spinoza's low opinion of the "vulgus" (the masses, or the common people, or the uneducated) derives from their imaginative and superstitious disposition. This disposition is not peculiar to the *vulgus*: on Spinoza's account, it is the natural condition of all human beings. "All men are by nature liable to superstition," he writes, and it is the passion of fear that "engenders, preserves, and fosters superstition" (TTP, Pref, 2). Superstition is fertile ground for the development of religion and there are those—tyrants and cunning leaders—who will take advantage of the gullibility of the masses. In a scathing attack on despotism, Spinoza wrote that "the prop and stay" of the despot "is to keep men in a state of deception, and with the specious title of religion to cloak the fear by which they must be held in check, so that they will fight for their servitude as if for salvation" (TTP, Pref, 3). Nevertheless, he does not underestimate the possible advantages of religion and its power to bind together a people. Nor does he rule out the existence of benevolent rulers.[28] For example, in the *Theologico-Political Treatise* Spinoza writes of Moses as both wise and benevolent: although he taught obedience rather than understanding, his laws aimed to benefit the whole Jewish people rather than serve his self-interest. Religion can be a powerful instrument of socialization because its simple parables are accessible to people of little learning. Reasonable states, no more or less than reasonable persons, can emerge only through time and experimentation. Spinoza does not propose a radical rupture between the "state of nature" and theologicopolitical life. Rather, organized forms of political collective life, based on (more or less) reasonable principles, can emerge only gradually and will retain elements of the earlier historical, theological forms that always lie at their origin.

The state of nature, according to Spinoza, "is prior to religion in nature and in time"; it is a condition "without religion and without law, and consequently without sin and without wrong" (TTP, XVI, 181). Thus, each state—within natural limits—will make its own distinctive laws and construct its own distinctive religion and morality. Although on Spinoza's account of (human) law obligation is always an a posteriori construction, his account of law is nevertheless a thoroughly naturalistic one. Religion, law, and morality develop according to the invariant principles of nature, including human nature. This produces variability because (human) law and morality develop under specific conditions and in particular times and places. The variety of factors involved introduces a certain contingency into the way different peoples, states, and laws will develop.²⁹ An understanding of the particular character of any given people, or nation, requires attending to its history, that is, to the conditions of its emergence in Nature. As Spinoza stresses, the Law of Moses "was specially adapted to the character and preservation of one particular people" and has no "universal application" (TTP, IV, 51). Nature does not supply ready-made citizens (TP, V) or subjects but only individuals who happen to share a common history and who, over time, will take on a "particular character," a "particular mode of life," and a "particular set of attitudes" that will define their collective identity (TTP, XVII, 200) or what we might call their "second nature."

The normative lives of distinct peoples will necessarily differ. Spinoza is undoubtedly a contextualist, on this point. Each state will institute and regulate its own particular construction of religion, of law, and of moral norms. Just as with other individuals then, the character of a state will reflect the type of power and the kind of knowledge possessed by the ruler and the ruled, and this character will, in turn, affect the historical development of a distinctive "second nature." A state that rules exclusively by threats, fear, and punishment shows its lack of power (see TTP, XIX) because it fails to understand that to enhance the capacities of its subjects/citizens also would enhance the power of the state to endure and thrive.

From his earliest writings, Spinoza linked the achievement of our "highest good" with the collective human endeavor to form the kind of society that would allow "as many as possible" to perfect the intellect and to attain this good.³⁰ In the *Theologico-Political Treatise*, as well as in the *Ethics*, this "highest good" consists in the increase in our knowledge of god or nature. The best and most powerful kind of state, then, is one that recognizes the human power of thought and that constitutes itself in a way that facilitates the fullest expression and development of this power by the greatest possible number. Democracy "comes closest to the natural state" (TTP, XX, 228) because it recognizes and promotes "that freedom which nature grants to every man" (TTP, XVI, 179). While it is true that Nature does not forbid "strife, or hatred, or anger, or deceit" (TTP, XVI, 174), Parts IV and V of the *Ethics* present an argument for why a philosophical understanding of God or Nature, and the nested place of human nature within it, necessarily entails the desire for mutual aid, friendship, honor, and justice.

Until relatively recently, many students and scholars would have read Spinoza's *Ethics* without paying much attention to his political writings.

However, Spinoza's political writings have played a central role in recent appraisals of his philosophy. A distinctive feature of much recent Spinoza scholarship is the way it treats his writings—ethical *and* political—as an integrated whole. The chapters in this volume (both reprinted work and specially commissioned pieces) reflect this integrated approach and range across Spinoza's entire corpus. It is a virtue of the collection that most of the contributors draw on both "Continental" and "Anglo-American" approaches to Spinoza's philosophy. Indeed, many of the essays, in a manner typical of much contemporary feminist philosophy, show the constructive way in which these two traditions have cross-fertilized.

The traditional philosophical account of human nature in relation to the rest of nature is that the capacity for reason—which both transcends the natural world and is the means through which "man" dominates nature—is the locus of human privilege. Those who are deemed to be closer to nature (for example, women, the "uncivilized," the untutored, those who labor with their bodies) and farther from nature are conceived as forming a "natural" hierarchy where "the man of reason" rightly rules over nature and his "natural" subordinates.[31] The free human will is here conceived as transcending nature over which it exercises its powers. On this Cartesian view, as Genevieve Lloyd explains in Chapter 1, "we dominate nature in the very act of knowing it." Spinoza's rejection of Descartes' substance dualism presents new possibilities for conceiving of knowledge and the mind-body and culture-nature relations. It is in these relations, after all, that many feminists have located the philosophical justifications offered for the dominance of men over nature, the body, and women. On Spinoza's account the mind and body are not two different substances but two different expressions, or manifestations, of the one Substance (God or Nature). The mind is, he tells us, the idea of an "actually existing body." Where there is no body there can be no mind, and vice versa. On Spinoza's account, the fissure between mind and nature is seen as the consequence of a fundamental misapprehension about ourselves as well as our place in nature. Human life, no more and no less than all else that exists, is a part of nature. Although this approach does not entirely give up the picture of the human dominance of nature (for example, Spinoza endorses the "right" of humans to exploit animals), the grounding of that privilege has shifted. If humans have greater "right" than animals this is because they enjoy powers superior to theirs. Although there are certainly differences between the differing powers and pleasures of human beings, these differences are not as significant as the differences in power between different species. The commonality of human powers and joys is what constitutes a human "moral community" from which animals are excluded. Human commonality is based not only in our peculiar powers but especially in the shared capacity for reason. But, as Lloyd explains, for Spinoza this capacity does not transcend nature; rather "reason is just the mind's power of acting, expressed in the striving for understanding." Contrary to the Cartesian view, Spinoza holds that the mind, as "the idea of an *actually existing body*" must reflect the powers and capacities specific to that body. So, does this mean that the idea of a male body is "masculine" and that of a female body, "feminine"? This question goes to the heart of contemporary feminist theory: does the sex of a body affect the gender identity of an individual? Is "sex" the "cause" of "gender"? On Spinoza's account no causal relation can be posited between body and mind because they are modal expressions of the *one* Substance, though expressed differently through the attributes of thought and extension, respectively. As Lloyd cautions, one should not leap to conclusions. For example, would we maintain that the mind of a large body is therefore also large? Although it will follow that the "ideas of female bodies will be, trivially, female" it does not therefore follow that "there is any underlying essence of femaleness which they all have in common."

Although the issue of sexual difference was of little concern to Spinoza, Lloyd shows that he nevertheless considered men and women to be alike, that is, "to agree in their nature." It may be puzzling then to realize that in his political writings he excludes women from government. Rather than seeing this exclusion as permanent, or inevitable, Lloyd argues that this exclusion is consistent with Spinoza's views on the interconnections between the ability to realize one's rational capacity and one's actual social context. A body excluded from full social participation will not develop its capacities to the full. "If human powers are enriched by the operation of good forms of social organization, it is to be expected that they will be impeded by bad ones." The position of women in seventeenth-century Europe was not, by and large, likely to promote the flourishing of their reason. And here another important difference between Spinoza and Descartes may be noted: Spinoza's mind-body theory can take seriously the ways in which social and political power affects the kinds of bodies and minds we become. Lloyd's application of Spinoza's thought to the contested relation between sex and gender opens a new path of inquiry into how sex difference is lived at different times and places. She offers an alternative to the dominant Cartesian picture where a sexless mind (or soul) is conjoined to a sexed body, a picture that has encouraged the contemporary notion of "a biologically given sex and a socially constructed gender." A Spinozistic approach allows the affirmation of bodily differences, and their corresponding powers and pleasures, without thereby implying an essential sexual difference. Spinoza, suggests Lloyd, can help chart a constructive course between the polarized "equality" versus "difference" feminisms. Rather than seeing sex difference as being either pure social construction or a biological essence, Lloyd's reading of Spinoza allows us to entertain a more complex understanding of sexual difference where "there are no facts of the matter other than those produced through the shifting play of the powers and pleasures of socialized, embodied, sexed human beings."

Human dependence, independence, and interdependence are crucial to a consideration of how feminists should value ideals of autonomy. The historical, and present, greater involvement of women with child care, and care for the aged and the infirm, are often taken to indicate the unfair gendered distribution of the benefits and burdens of familial and social life. In Chapter 2 Aurelia Armstrong deploys a Spinozistic perspective in order to develop a notion of autonomy that does not deny the essentially relational nature of identity. Spinoza offers a fresh perspective from which to rethink the "entrenched dichotomies between independence and dependence, self and other, individual and society, separation and connection" that underpin contemporary approaches to autonomy. Why do many feminist theorists take a skeptical stance toward the ideal of autonomy? In the first part of her chapter Armstrong rehearses some common feminist arguments against a conception of autonomy conceived as individual self-governance—an approach typified by the dominant ideal of the masculine rights-bearing individual of the liberal tradition. Recent feminist attempts to go beyond this ideal have stressed that the achievement of autonomy needs to be understood in relational terms that acknowledge "the social dimensions of selfhood and the relational contexts within which agents develop their capacities." Feminist reconceptualizations of autonomy have had to chart a course between the freestanding preferences of the robust individual of liberal philosophies and the valorization of the "encumbered" and "embedded," constitutively social, self of communitarianism. Repudiating the dichotomy between individual autonomy and relationally conceived identity,

Armstrong sees the task of feminist theorists of autonomy as being to show that these are "interconnected rather than opposed" conceptions.

Turning to Spinoza's famous explanatory letter about how parts relate to the whole (Letter 32 to Oldenburg), Armstrong uses Spinoza's analogy of "the worm in the blood" to explore an alternative conception of self, relations with others, and the relation of all to wider nature. On this interpretation of Spinoza's philosophy the growth of self-understanding encourages the movement from a self-centered, imaginative perspective, where each self (part) struggles to assert itself against all others, toward a more adequate grasp of the self as part of a harmonious whole. Spinoza's rejection of an atomistically conceived individual, along with his skepticism about the "free" will, allows him to develop an understanding of the connections between human beings (and human beings and the rest of nature) "that suggests a close association between the development of the capacity for autonomy and the endeavor to promote harmonious forms of sociability." Far from undermining the notion of autonomy through insisting on the mutual determination of the "parts" composing the "whole," Spinoza's account allows us to conceive of individuals as "reciprocally determining rather than opposed."

It is in Spinoza's theory of the affects (or emotions) that Armstrong locates the true worth of his philosophy for the feminist project of reconceiving autonomy along relational lines. On his account the relative complexity of the human body gives rise to the capacity of the individual to both affect and be affected in a multiplicity of ways. The "receptivity" of human beings to a range of encounters should not be viewed, Armstrong insists, as "the mark of passivity in the face of the external forces of nature, but is itself a power, and a power which increases our power of acting." Although Spinoza's conception of the individual is both dynamic and "permeable" it is nonetheless a fully-fledged self or individual. However, it is not coherent to see the Spinozistic individual as the sole source of its own identity. The identity of any given individual necessarily is "a function of that particular causal and affective history of interactions that determines an individual's present capacity to affect and be affected." Spinoza does not underplay the negative, sad, or otherwise destructive passions, and any account of autonomy to be developed from his philosophy must acknowledge this. Armstrong points out that autonomy, on this interpretation, needs to be understood in terms of Spinoza's views on the determination of our affects. We cannot ever be entirely free from the affects, but what we can do is endeavor to understand their causes and thereby transform their debilitating features into knowledge about them. For Spinoza, "freedom is a function of adequate knowledge of oneself and one's emotions."

Armstrong warns against the too swift conclusion that Spinoza, after all, subscribes to a notion of a "free" or "self-determined" will that could become master of its emotions: human beings, like all else, can never be free from causal determination. Knowledge of the affects does not contract the "sphere of selfhood" to "the (personal) will"; rather, the sphere of selfhood is expanded because "the gradual effort to understand the causes of one's emotions requires attending to the complex history of one's causal and affective interactions." This "effort to understand" oneself inevitably connects us to our context. Thus, "autonomy and sociability are related." Insofar as "Spinoza's individual is constitutively rather than merely incidentally social" his conception of autonomy "must be conceived as a social process, that is, an effort to build and maintain mutual, reciprocal relationships with others that support and foster this striving for all concerned."

Love, in its various forms, has long been a contested subject in feminist theory. Firestone, for example, said of love that it "is the pivot of women's oppression today" and that an analysis of it "*threatens the very structure of culture.*"[32] De Beauvoir, by contrast, looked forward to a time when the free man and "the independent woman" would enjoy "a reciprocal relation of amity."[33] In Chapter 3, Amelie Rorty offers an engaging account of Spinoza's theory of the passions in order to present a kind of love that is an expression of wisdom and mutual flourishing. Rorty begins by explaining the "particularism" of Spinoza's account of individuals. By way of telling an imaginative and engaging story about two lovers—named Ariadne and Echo—Rorty offers us a thread to follow through the labyrinthine twists and turns of the "everyday" understanding of reality to a scientific account of the individual, her passions, her struggle for knowledge, and her ultimate understanding of her place within an interconnected complex unified system. Closely tracing Spinoza's account of love and feelings of elation (and their reversals) in Part III of the *Ethics*, Rorty unravels Ariadne's and Echo's experiences of the passive emotions, such as jealousy, hatred, and envy, to arrive at the attainment of self-knowledge.

Highlighting Spinoza's view on the mind-body, Rorty explains that emotions, or "affects," are "ideational indicants of bodily thriving or declining." One of the great difficulties in maintaining a love relation is the necessarily dynamic and relational nature of the passions. For the love between Ariadne and Echo to remain a happy one they will have to achieve a balance and harmony not only between the passions they feel for each other but also between themselves as a "composite body," or couple, and the broader context within which their love is expressed and lived. The likelihood of achieving and preserving this harmony are, unfortunately, slim. This is, in part, because love for a particular individual is inevitably "idolatrous," that is, "fetishistic and partial" and bound to be the source of "ambivalence and frustration." However, this is not the end of the story. Ariadne's natural striving to express and enhance her powers (her *conatus*), coupled with her luck in having enjoyed a good education, lead her to reflect on how and why Echo can be the source of her feelings of both elation *and* dejection. Ariadne comes to realize that not only are she and Echo "complex, constantly changing, compounded entities," they are also embedded within webs of relations with "other equally historically conditioned, dynamic individuals" who will affect their love relation. When Ariadne comes to realize that neither she nor Echo are "closed and bounded entities" she begins to follow the thread that will help her find her way through the labyrinth. The revelation of the interconnectedness of all things takes the pressure off Echo as the sole source of Ariadne's elation or dejection and the sad passions often associated with love—fear, envy, jealousy—are transformed through this new knowledge. Ariadne's inadequate ideas (her passions) are transformed into adequate ideas (knowledge and active emotion).

The story of love, in its commonsense form, belongs with an inadequate and imaginative grasp of who and what we are. The "scientific understanding" that positions the particular within the vast interconnected causal webs of reality tells a different story. The "common notions of mathematical physics" take Ariadne beyond the imagination and even "beyond psychological and historical insight." Ariadne now comes to see herself as a particular body-mind inserted within the determined order of extension and the "system of interrelated ideas." Having achieved an understanding of who she is, and her relation to all that exists, does Ariadne now turn up her nose at the mere passion of love for a "particular" (namely, Echo)? Or can this love, too, be understood in terms of "adequate ideas"? Making innovative use of Spinoza's third and highest kind of knowledge—intuition (*scientia intuitiva*)—Rorty explains how love for the particular is not necessarily lost in the quest for adequate knowledge. Rather, Ariadne's love for Echo has been totally transformed.

In loving Echo Ariadne now "loves Echo-as-a-particular-expression-of-the-vast-network-of-individuals that have affected him; through him, she loves all that has made him." Lovers who are not dominated by the bondage of passive emotions, suggests Rorty, make "wise lovers" who "are not only more joyous, but more effective and beneficent than unenlightened lovers."

In Chapter 4, Alexandre Matheron offers an analysis of the ten passages in Spinoza's works where Spinoza directly considers women and sexuality, and Matheron admits that, superficially at least, they do not paint a flattering picture. However, Matheron reads each passage in its broader textual, historical, and ethicopolitical context and offers a deeper, and surprisingly contemporary, interpretation of Spinoza's views on "sensual love." Taking as his focus Spinoza's account of lust—"the desire for and love of joining one body to another"—Matheron shows that because love is "joy associated with an external cause," and joy itself is defined as an "increase in our power to act" then lust can be understood as "good" to the degree that it enhances our power of action, or *conatus*. Of course, as with any joyful passion, lust easily may turn from joy into sadness, and the more excessive is the love of "joining bodies" the more likely it is to end in disaster. However, on Spinoza's account, the desire for and love of sexual union simply "is joyful through and through." Why, then, does Spinoza caution against the immoderate or excessive nature of lust? For the same reason that he cautions against any excessive passion: the excessive and obsessional nature of gluttony, avariciousness, ambition, and so on all suffer from the same problems. Lust is not singled out in this context. Rather, it is the fixation on any passion that Spinoza sees as problematic because an *idée fixe* blocks the development and flourishing of the whole person and, especially, the development of reason.

On Matheron's reading of Spinoza, lust, when excessive, is no more or less damaging than other obsessional desires. Sexuality itself is not singled out as "sinful" or "taboo." On Spinoza's nonjudgmental account, there is no "natural" object of desire: sexuality, says Matheron, "is no more *intended* to ensure the perpetuation of the species than eyes are made for seeing or teeth for chewing." Sexual taboo can find no purchase here, because "nothing prohibits . . . nongenital sexuality" and Spinoza's philosophy admits an "infinite diversity of conceivable sexual behaviors." How, then, can we explain the dominance of one form—monogamous heterosexuality—over all others? Matheron observes that although Spinoza takes the perspective of a man—he writes of the love and desire *of* men *for* women—there is no reason to think that what he says in the *Ethics* cannot be expressed equally well from the woman's point of view: the love and desire *of* women *for* others, including men. This is precisely the point at which Matheron locates the *political* element in relations between the sexes. Despite their equal claim to the capacity for reason, women "find themselves always and everywhere in a position of inferiority" and their affects and preferences therefore are of less practical importance.

By Matheron's lights, Spinoza rightly sees that the "sexual drama, essentially, *plays out between males*." Spinoza's theory of the "imitation of the affects"—the tendency to desire what others desire—coupled with the exclusive nature of sexual love, leads to combative and competitive relations between men. Caught in a dilemma of his own making, the man suffering from obsessive sexual desire *both* desires that other men desire the woman he loves *and* demands that other men acknowledge his sole possession of her. In the absence of external constraint, this dilemma, according to Matheron, renders the competition between men "inescapable and inexpiable." Hence, excessive sexual desire leads to two bad outcomes: it blocks the flourishing of the whole person and is the cause of discord between men. Each of these bad outcomes, however, is amenable to transformation. First, a collective solution to the problem of discordance: men may make laws that "'democratically' divide the women." Matheron's reading of Spinoza on sexuality in a collective setting provides a rough sketch of a possible genealogy of patriarchal political societies. But what about the other problem, namely, by what means might we ensure the flourishing of the individual? In addition to sketching a sexual politics Matheron considers what Spinoza may contribute to a sexual *ethics*.

In the absence of reason, bodies politic will supply constraints on passion, even if these constraints, in the form of law, are themselves biased toward the passions and interests of those who formulate them, namely, men. But where does this leave relations between individual men and women who live, at least mainly, by reason? Free men and women, Spinoza says, will together seek to increase their knowledge, will endeavor to promote the mutual development of their bodies and minds, and will seek those things that promote social harmony. Provided they understand the debilitating effects of sexual passion, they will also pursue sexual pleasure in whatever form and manner is consistent with a reasonable and flourishing life. Such a life may involve raising children within a heterosexual marriage but it also admits myriad other forms of pleasure to be had through the "mixing of bodies" and the nurturance of others.

Spinoza's rejection of the Christian notion of a "free will" puts a new slant on Western notions of "the fall," sexuality, and sin. In Chapter 5 David West explores some implications of Spinoza's departure from a tradition that reaches from Plato, through Augustine and Aquinas, to the present. West argues that there are two major branches in the Western tradition of the development of ideas concerning reason, self, and sexuality: the idealist and the hedonist traditions. The idealist conception can be traced to Plato's philosophy and gave rise to "ascetic idealism" where the true, higher rational self is valued over a disparaged body and its sensual pleasures. The hedonistic conception of self is most readily associated with Jeremy Bentham, and with materialists such as Hobbes and Hume, and can be traced back to the ancient Epicureans. West argues that Spinoza's philosophy offers us an account of reason, sexuality, and the self that is neither idealist nor hedonist. In particular, Spinoza's thoroughgoing monism "is systematically resistant to the Western tradition's habitual reductions of self and sexual experience to *either* mind and reason *or* the body and its desires."

Spinoza's direct attack on mind-body dualism, coupled with his repudiation of teleology in nature, act to subvert Christian attitudes to the body and the idea that sexuality has the "natural" aim of procreation. Although Spinoza views the self as part of a wider social and natural whole, this does not imply that all individuals are identical or driven by identical needs and desires. Stressing the particularity of each individual's essence, or *conatus*, West shows how Spinoza avoids any commitment to "universal and potentially oppressive norms of human behavior." Rather, on his view "each individual is free to realize its own essence in its own way." Insofar as much contemporary sexual morality is derived from the Christian heritage, Spinoza's insightful critique of religion, superstition, and biblical taboo is a useful resource for those who seek a more reasonably grounded ethics of sexual conduct. Spinoza's antiteleological understanding of sexuality does not, however, reduce to mere hedonism. As West demonstrates, Spinoza is critical of love and sexual passion that is likely to become obsessive, harmful to individual well-being, and socially disruptive.

West's interpretation of the relevance of Spinoza's philosophy to contemporary sexual ethics offers a positive view of both homosexual and heterosexual relationships. The Spinozistic conception of nature as being without ends allows the separation of sexuality and sexual reproduction because the "purpose" of sexual intercourse cannot be procreation. Sexual intercourse has no a priori purpose, no inbuilt teleology. Hence, as West argues, "men and women need not be defined first and foremost according to their complementary roles in sexual reproduction." A great strength of Spinoza's account of the individual is that he "is able to recognize without essentializing the actual differences and multiple possible relationships amongst individuals."

Despite Spinoza's attractiveness to those who seek a nonoppressive and nonjudgmental sexual ethics, West wonders about the degree to which Spinoza remains within a basically rationalistic framework that tends to devalue particular and personal attachments in favor of the "contemplative life of reason." As we have seen, Amelie Rorty, in Chapter 3, argued that Spinoza's third kind of knowledge (intuition) can be understood in terms that allow love for the particular to fully be part of "the life of reason." On West's interpretation of Spinoza's philosophy, this remains a moot point.

In Chapter 6, Heidi Ravven proposes that Spinoza's "naturalistic" ethics provides a rich alternative to the standard Western accounts that are "theologically driven" and express "an unacknowledged Christian cultural provincialism." Ravven argues that although feminist moral philosophy has been critical of standard ethical views, Spinoza's approach offers an even deeper critique because of the rival, suppressed sources he deploys, namely, Judeo-Islamic thought. Spinoza's alternative ethical stance should be of great interest to feminist theorists because of their shared concerns: "the search for an embodied and situated kind of thinking, a non-reductive materialist perspective that can overcome dualisms." Islamic and Jewish philosophers, whose work was "outlawed and vilified" by medieval Christian theologians, have much to offer contemporary thought. Ravven's ambition is to promote an intellectual project that would bring together Spinoza scholars, feminist scholars, and Jewish and Muslim philosophers to explore common concerns that have been marginalized since the thirteenth century.

A central plank of Christian anthropology is the notion of free will, a notion that has given rise to a "human ideal of an absolute mastery over the self and the world." This notion not only "mis-describes the human person," it "also has negative personal, social, and public policy consequences" insofar as it "suggests that all solutions are individual rather than primarily social and systemic." Whereas the Western religious-philosophical tradition "embraced the reconciliation of Greek and Jewish thought in a miraculous doctrine of free will," many scholars now agree that most Islamic and Jewish medieval scholars did not. Thus, Jewish and Islamic traditions were expurgated from the European community of thought. Spinoza, argues Ravven, is the direct heir of Judeo-Arabic naturalism, which in turn was indebted to Aristotelian-Stoic determinism. Descartes and Kant, by contrast, are here seen to be the philosophers who helped to integrate the Platonic-Christian view into the early modern Western scientific framework. Spinoza's expulsion from the Western canon can be viewed as a consequence of his self-aware rejection of this dominant theoretical trajectory in the West, along with its Christian roots. As Ravven asserts, "Mainstream philosophy, unbeknownst to itself, is still fighting ancient theological battles with Islam and Judaism and also still engaged in a battle to repudiate Greek naturalism."

Ravven's foregrounding of the suppression of Jewish and Islamic philosophy allows her to argue against influential analyses of the inadequacy of contemporary ethics such as that offered by Alasdair MacIntyre.[34] On Ravven's account, MacIntyre's claim that "philosophical ethics is dysfunctional because its attempt at universalism rendered it no longer able to grasp the homogenous cultural setting" mistakes cause for effect. On her view the problem centers on philosophy's past, and continuing, suppression of its "Christian presumptions and origins." In other words, universalism is not the problem; rather, philosophical ethics "is too provincially Christian!" Moreover, the doctrine of free will, central to contemporary ethical theory, and derived from Platonized Christianity, "is simply wrong." Spinoza's determinism and naturalism cannot make an exception for human being. His philosophy offers the contemporary theorist "a non-moralistic ethics" that is, a "mature ethical stance without praise and blame." Although Spinoza's ethical philosophy is "nonpunitive" it is "neither naive nor relativistic." In concluding, Ravven urges the pursuit of a cooperative theoretical program that would combine the marginalized views of Spinoza, Judeo-Islamic thought, and feminist thought in order to develop a more adequate ethical philosophy based not in a moralistic blaming but on the endeavor to promote "social harmony and individual joy." Her own contribution to this enterprise presents an invaluable foundation for this effort.

The two short chapters that follow Ravven's contribution provide sharply diverging interpretations of some theological themes in Spinoza's work. In Chapter 7, Paola Grassi reads Spinoza's appraisal of the story of Adam and Eve and "the fall" as providing a "paradigm of knowledge." Whereas Grassi sees Spinoza's philosophy as offering a rapprochement between man and woman, in the following chapter, Luce Irigaray reads Part I of the *Ethics* as a continuation of the long history of conceiving of man-woman and mind-body in terms of an oppositional hierarchy. These two chapters, then, provide contrasting feminist readings of Spinoza's philosophy of religion. Unlike Irigaray's essay—which treats Part I of the Ethics in isolation from the rest—Grassi connects Spinoza's account of Adam's "fall" with the whole of his corpus. Rather than reading the story of Adam as the genesis of "sin," Grassi argues that Spinoza means us to understand Adam's fate as an allegory: "an expression of the emancipation of the *human* by means of knowledge."

Spinoza's account, according to Grassi, turns on a positive appropriation of the power of the imagination that is seen as a *virtue* rather than a vice of human nature. In a manner that resonates with Ravven's arguments in Chapter 6, Grassi stresses the important influence of Jewish thought on Spinoza's account of the imagination and the role it plays in developing knowledge about the world. Spinoza transforms the opposition between imagination and intellect, drawn by Maimonides—along with the role of the former in "sin"—into a naturalistic account of the development of human knowledge in history. Spinoza's positive stance toward affectivity is, in part, what allows him to reassess the role of imagination in human life. Imagination, in Spinoza's epistemology, is the first and lowest kind of knowledge: it tells us more about how things in the world affect us than it does about the things themselves. In other words, imagination does not adequately understand *causes* but rather is a register of effects, namely, our affects. Nevertheless, it is what Grassi calls the *drive* to imagine that forces us out of ourselves and onto the path of knowledge about others and the world.

Grassi explains that it is the encounter with the other—for Adam, the encounter with Eve—that breaks one's initial entrapment in the imaginary. The "agreement" between male and female natures is what brings both to sociability. It is only in concert with others of "our own kind" that human power can be truly developed and enhanced. In the *Ethics* Spinoza provides "a science of the imaginary," which he puts in the service of human flourishing, joy, and self-determination. The analysis of the imagination provided by Spinoza is linked with the demystification of the theologicopolitical and with an increase in our independence from the sad, superstitious passions encouraged by traditional religious accounts of "sin" and "the fall." On Grassi's reading of Spinoza, it is Eve who "exculpates" Adam: the mutual recognition between man and woman saves both from passivity and merely chance joys. The knowledge they gain together leads both to a more autonomous existence. The "problem of the other," Grassi argues, "is a problem of the imagination" and it is only through the other that human beings can extend the power to imagine and so gain adequate knowledge.

In Chapter 8, Irigaray offers a reading of Spinoza's metaphysics through the image of "the envelope." Quoting extensively from Part I of the *Ethics*, Irigaray ventures the view that Spinoza's "unique and necessary" god may be understood in terms of a "self-sufficient" being "which is its own place for itself," or a being that "provides its own envelope." Human beings, by contrast, conceived as neither necessary nor self-sufficient, lack our own "place," our own "envelope." However, insofar as woman provides man with an envelope—his mother's womb, a "sheath" for his manhood, and a womb for his children—she is left without "place" and without "envelope." Where does this leave the sexual relation? Irigaray argues that for there to be a sexual relation there must be "two bodies, two thoughts" and "a relation between the two." Adopting a contentious reading of Spinoza's mind-body parallelism, Irigaray argues that because Spinoza's monism disallows mind acting on body, or body acting on mind, "thinking is unable to limit the body, or vice versa" and so "no sex act is possible." Understanding Spinoza's immanent monism in dualistic terms, Irigaray argues that the theory of parallelism encourages "insane thinking" and constructs women and children (those who fall on the side of the body) as beings without language or place.

On this understanding of parallelism, Spinoza's philosophy "prevents the maternal-feminine from being inscribed in duration as causes and effects." Irigaray presents Spinoza's metaphysics as one that forecloses the existence of a genuine relation between the sexes. His conception of god not only injures woman—leaving her without a "place" or a "language"—it also injures man because it encourages his desire "to be master of everything." However, this desire is self-defeating and succeeds only in making man "the slave both of discourse and of mother nature."

In Chapter 9, Sarah Donovan offers an alternative reading of Spinoza's metaphysics and suggests that his philosophy—understood as a whole—shares some surprising affinities with important features of Irigaray's project. Donovan argues that Irigaray's reading of Spinoza "glosses over" important components of the *Ethics*. Most important, perhaps, Donovan suggests that Irigaray fails to note that Spinoza offers an alternative position to the substance dualism of Descartes. Highlighting the similarities between Irigaray's broad project and Spinoza's philosophy, Donovan notes their agreement on three crucial points. First, both wish to revalue extension and nature (broadly understood). Second, both Spinoza and Irigaray challenge the traditional notion that the body has no, or only a negative, role in acquiring knowledge. Finally, Donovan emphasizes the affinity between Irigaray's view of the repressed "imaginary" and Spinoza's account of the imagination.

Working through the implications of Part I of the *Ethics* for Spinoza's philosophy taken as a whole, Donovan not only shows where some productive points of similarity between the two thinkers have been overlooked, but also indicates how these similarities might be developed. She concludes by urging a reconsideration of Spinoza's philosophy and its utility for feminist epistemological, ethical, and political theory.

The chapter that follows Donovan's explores the contribution that Spinoza's conception of the imagination—in its social dimension—can make to a feminist critique of traditional theories of politics and law. Moira Gatens first offers an outline of Spinoza's philosophy of the body as presented in the *Ethics*. The more complex a body is, the more complex will be its mind. Spinoza's account of the human mind-body yields a nonjudgmental ethical stance. Virtue, for Spinoza, cannot be about mind disciplining the body and passion. Rather, virtue concerns the power of the individual to act, to understand, and to flourish. As previous chapters in this volume have shown, however, human flourishing is never simply a matter of individual striving. Human flourishing necessarily assumes a social and political context that does not thwart the reasonable striving of each to increase her or his powers of action. Different forms of sociability and different kinds of body politic may act to constrain or enable the development of the capacities of their constituent members. Spinoza's theologicopolitical theory makes clear that the qualities, attributes, and capacities of subjects or citizens are determined, in large part, by the laws and customs of the social body in which these capacities develop.

In the *Tractatus Theologico-Politicus* Spinoza contrasts natural (or divine) law and civil (or human) law. The former cannot be broken or disobeyed, because, adequately understood, it is simply the law of nature. It is only civil (human) laws that can be broken or disobeyed. The Christian idea that divine law is law decreed by God is a product of the imagination that grasps God as a lawgiver and judge. Reason reveals to us that the laws of nature are *intrinsic* to nature; they do not act on nature from without as does a decree. Unlike the unvarying laws of nature, an analysis of civil laws reveals the historical particularity of any given body politic. How does it understand itself? Does it imagine that its organization was divinely decreed? Are the principles underlying its laws for the benefit of all or for the few? Gatens argues, on Spinoza's view, no matter what the "self-image" of a given body politic is, there are limits to what a sovereign can oblige its subjects to do because the beliefs of its subjects cannot be coerced. A sovereign may be able to coerce its subjects to refrain from certain *acts* through fear of punishment but it cannot control what they think or believe. Spinoza, in other words, is an early proponent of freedom of speech and thought. Wise sovereigns, on this interpretation of Spinoza's political theory, understand that their rule is better secured when founded not only on fear and awe but also on the love and respect of their subjects. The most virtuous (for Spinoza, this always means the most powerful) sovereign understands that the ultimate purpose of the state is to enable those under its rule to develop their capacities in safety. Inspired by Gilles Deleuze's innovative reading of Spinoza, Gatens asks, what kind of political body would be capable of endeavoring to realize the capacities of all people—women as well as men, "black" as well as "white"? And what role does the social imaginary play in enhancing or depleting the powers of socialized bodies? Gatens suggests that the tension in Spinoza's thought between the drive to democratize sovereignty, on the one hand, and the fear of the destructive imaginings and passions of the masses, on the other, is a productive one. This productive tension in Spinoza's political theory can contribute to understanding the ways in which some citizens of contemporary democratic polities suffer an unfair burden imposed by imaginaries that demean them. Such understanding, in turn, provides a starting point for transforming destructive imaginaries in order that the well-being of each person receives fair representation in the body politic.

In the final chapter, Susan James, while commending recent feminist interpretations of Spinoza's theory of the imagination and its productive role in politics and law, nevertheless questions whether these interpretations capture the full complexity of Spinoza's thought. By placing Spinoza's thought in its historical context, and noting its affinities with Hobbes's political theory, she demonstrates that Spinoza's commitment to a consensual image of government is, at best, ambivalent. Spinoza also held that the power of the sovereign to make and enforce law should be absolute. When Spinoza's indebtedness to Hobbes's views on law and sovereignty are fully appreciated, the extent to which these issues are enmeshed within fierce theological and political debates in Spinoza's own time emerges. Insofar as Spinoza's account of Substance (God or Nature) eliminates anthropomorphic understandings of natural (or divine) law, it also eliminates the idea of natural law as command. Although Hobbes's and Spinoza's theories of law differ in the detail, both assert that "only human agents can transform either the law of nature or the moral law into commands."

Spinoza's theory of the imagination adds a distinctive touch to his understanding of the role of prophecy in lawmaking. Prophets are people with especially powerful imaginations as well as powers of persuasion. They can convince others to accept their narratives and visions as true descriptions of God's wishes and of our obligations. Moses, for example, possessed the power to rule because he had the power to bind together individuals as one people, with one story, and one law. The success of a prophet-ruler does not, however, alter the fact that his representation of God as legislator rests on a misconception. The basis of a state thus formed confirms that the imagination can engender constructive (as well as destructive) social outcomes.

Spinoza's critique of prophecy, and the role of the imagination in sociability, served to undermine the theological arguments of his contemporaries in two ways. First, reason exposes the imaginary character of grasping divine or natural law on the model of command. God is not a judge and the truth of natural law cannot depend on his will or decree. Second, Spinoza's account of the firm hold of the imagination over our everyday consciousness allows us to understand the remarkable resilience of the beliefs and commitments of those who are under its spell. The upshot of James's argument is that law is "always something that humans have to use their reason and imagination to construct." This understanding of Spinoza's critique of the "theological illusion" in the context of law and sovereignty puts his insistence on the absolute power of the sovereign in a new light. A sovereign who is unable to construct and enforce law cannot realize the ultimate aim of sovereignty: to protect its subjects and promote their freedom. James's meticulous reconstruction of Spinoza's complicated views on law and sovereignty both deepens our appreciation of the role of the imagination in the political realm and explains why the sovereign's ability to negotiate with its subjects necessarily involves an absolute limit.

The essays presented in this volume attest to the evocativeness of Spinoza's philosophy as well as to the ingenuity of feminist interpretations of its capacity to enable thought and action committed to the promotion of human flourishing.

Notes

1. Two early and influential feminist texts that argued along these lines are Sandra Harding and Merrill Hintikka, eds., *Discovering Reality: Feminist Perspectives on Epistemology, Metaphysics, Methodology, and Philosophy of Science* (Dordrecht: Reidel, 1983), and Alison Jaggar, *Feminist Politics and Human Nature* (Brighton: Harvester Press, 1983).

2. A good example of this kind of feminist theorizing is Carol Gilligan, *In a Different Voice: Psychological Theory and Women's Development* (Cambridge: Harvard University Press, 1982). Gilligan's work was important to the development of "standpoint feminism."

3. Two clear and accessible introductions to Spinoza's thought are Genevieve Lloyd, *Spinoza and the Ethics* (London: Routledge, 1996) and Steven Nadler, *Spinoza's Ethics: An Introduction* (Cambridge: Cambridge University Press, 2006). See also Gilles Deleuze, *Spinoza: Practical Philosophy*, trans. Robert Hurley (San Francisco: City Lights, 1988).

4. See, for example, Antonio Damasio, *Looking for Spinoza: Joy, Sorrow, and the Feeling Brain* (New York: Harcourt, 2003), who argues that Spinoza anticipated aspects of contemporary neurophysiology and psychology.

5. I mean to suggest that Spinoza's philosophy may be seen as "untimely" in Nietzsche's sense, that is, "acting counter to our time and thereby acting on our time and, let us hope, for the benefit of a time to come." Friedrich Nietzsche, "On the Uses and Disadvantages of History for Life," in *Untimely Meditations*, trans. R. J. Hollingdale (Cambridge: Cambridge University Press, 1983), 60.

6. See Yirmiyahu Yovel, *The Marrano of Reason*, vol. 1 of *Spinoza and Other Heretics* (Princeton: Princeton University Press, 1989), especially 28–39. See also Leo Strauss, *Spinoza's Critique of Religion* (New York: Schocken Books, 1965) and *Persecution and the Art of Writing* (Chicago: University of Chicago Press, 1980), especially chap. 5.

7. See Yovel, *The Marrano of Reason*.

8. See Steven Nadler, *Spinoza's Heresy: Immortality and the Jewish Mind* (Oxford: Oxford University Press, 2001).

9. See Spinoza's preface to the *Theological-Political Treatise*, 8.

10. Recall the motto on Spinoza's signet ring: *Caute* ("Caution," or "Be careful").

11. For a full account of the *cherem*, or writ of ostracism, see Nadler, *Spinoza's Heresy*.

12. Nadler, *Spinoza's Ethics*, 6.

13. See ibid., 10–11.

14. See Nadler, *Spinoza's Heresy*, chap 5. On the influence of Stoic thought on Spinoza's philosophy, see Moira Gatens and Genevieve Lloyd, *Collective Imaginings: Spinoza, Past and Present* (London: Routledge, 1999), chaps. 2, 3; Susan James, "Spinoza the Stoic," in *The Rise of Modern Philosophy*, ed. Tom Sorel (Oxford: Clarendon Press, 1993), 289–316.

15. The title of Spinoza's work on Descartes, published in 1663, is *Parts I and II of Descartes' Principles of Philosophy Demonstrated in the Geometric Manner*.

16. *The Collected Works of Spinoza*, ed. and trans. Edwin Curley, vol. 1 (Princeton: Princeton University Press, 1985), 405.

17. See Edwin Curley, *Behind the Geometrical Method: A Reading of Spinoza's Ethics* (Princeton: Princeton University Press, 1988).

18. Nadler, *Spinoza's Ethics*, ix.

19. See Genevieve Lloyd, *Part of Nature: Self-Knowledge in Spinoza's Ethics* (Ithaca: Cornell University Press, 1994).

20. Lloyd, *Spinoza and the Ethics*, 31.

21. Yovel, *The Marrano of Reason*, 159; emphasis in the original.

22. Gilles Deleuze, *Spinoza: Practical Philosophy*, trans. Robert Hurley (San Francisco: City Lights, 1988), 28.

23. For an introduction to this debate, see Lloyd, *Spinoza and the Ethics*, chaps 4, 5; Nadler, *Spinoza's Ethics*, chap. 9. See also Steven B. Smith, *Spinoza's Book of Life* (New Haven: Yale University Press, 2003).

24. For a fuller account of the political context in Holland at this time, see Jonathan Israel, *The Dutch Republic: Its Rise, Greatness, and Fall* (Oxford: Oxford University Press, 1995).

25. For a fuller account, see Steven Nadler, *Spinoza: A Life* (Cambridge: Cambridge University Press, 1999).

26. For a more detailed account of Spinoza's political writings than that offered in the present section, see Moira Gatens and Genevieve Lloyd, *Collective Imaginings: Spinoza, Past and Present* (London: Routledge, 1999), chaps. 4, 5. See also Steven B. Smith, *Spinoza, Liberalism, and the Question of Jewish Identity* (New Haven: Yale University Press, 1997); Etienne Balibar, *Spinoza and Politics*, trans. Peter Snowdon (New York, Verso, 1998); Douglas Den Uyl, *Power, State, and Freedom: An Interpretation of Spinoza's Political Philosophy* (Assen: Van Gorcum, 1983).

27. *Collected Works of Spinoza*, 350.

28. For an argument in favor of this "mixed" account of origin of political life, see Den Uyl, *Power, State, and Freedom*.

29. Of course, for Spinoza, nothing is really contingent, because "all things have been determined from the necessity of the divine nature." If things appear to be contingent this is because we lack the knowledge of their causes. See E, II, Prop 29.

30. For example, see *The Emendation of the Intellect*, ed. and trans. E. Curley, in *Collected Works of Spinoza*, §13, §14, 10–11.

31. See Genevieve Lloyd, *The Man of Reason: "Male" and "Female" in Western Philosophy* (London: Methuen, 1984).

32. Shulamith Firestone, *The Dialectic of Sex* (St. Albans: Paladin Frogmore, 1973), 121; emphasis in the original.

33. Simone de Beauvoir, *The Second Sex*, trans. H. M. Parshley (Harmondsworth: Penguin, 1975), 727.

34. Alasdair MacIntyre, *After Virtue* (Notre Dame: University of Notre Dame, 1981).

1

Dominance and Difference

A Spinozistic Alternative to the Distinction Between "Sex" and "Gender"

Genevieve Lloyd

Knowledge and Dominance

Human beings, as has often been remarked, occupy an ambivalent position in nature, an ambivalence that philosophers have tried to resolve by an emphasis on—even an exultation in—the distinctive human capacity for knowledge. We may, as Pascal summed it up in his *Thoughts*, be the weakest reeds in nature. But we are thinking reeds.[1] Poised though we are between the two abysses of nothingness and infinity, we can draw comfort from the fact that, even though it may need only a drop of vapor to kill us, we are still nobler than the whole universe. For we know that we are dying and the advantage the universe has over us, of all of which the universe knows nothing. We may be unable to know nature in all its infinite extent. We do not know it all, but that we know at all makes us superior to the rest of nature, which is not only ultimately unknowable but unknowing.

Pascal's theme of our superiority as knowers over the rest of nature reverberates through modern philosophy. For him the ambivalence of our position in nature is only ambivalently resolved through our self-esteem as knowers. Nature is, after all, unknowable as well as unknowing. Descartes, as was his wont, thought the ambivalence could be resolved by turning it into a dualism. Our bodies are parts of nature; our minds transcend nature. It is only as composites of mind and body that our position is ambivalent. And if we are careful to keep separate what pertains to mind, to body, and to the intermingling of the two, the way is clear to a form of knowledge which will make us—far from being nature's weakest reeds—its lords and masters.

The theme of dominance is central in Descartes' theory of knowledge; and it is reinforced by the notoriously sharp distinction he draws in the Second Meditation between mind and matter. If mind is superior to matter, and if—as his theory of knowledge demands—there is nothing mind-like in the material world, that world becomes inferior to the mind that knows it. With mind now completely withdrawn from matter, its superiority becomes the basis for a new privileged position in relation to the rest of nature. Knowledge was once the understanding of intelligible principles, which were integrated with matter in substantial unities. The knowing intellect was seen as superior to matter but had as its object mind-like forms, which shared that superiority over mere matter. The withdrawal of the forms from matter opens up a conceptual space in which knowledge can be seen as an enactment of the mind's position of dominance, transcending the merely natural. And since the will is central to Descartes' theory of knowledge, this transcendence can be seen as not a simple superiority in status, but an exercise in control. The traditional superiority of form over matter is absorbed into the idea of mind's superiority to produce a new twist to the idea of human dominance: we dominate nature in the very act of knowing it.

Ambivalences have a way of reasserting themselves, undercutting the neat resolution of dualisms. The enticing clarity of the model of knowledge which comes from the separation of mind from matter becomes more opaque with their intermingling, in the fuller picture of human knowers which Descartes goes on to offer in the Sixth Meditation. With mind and matter intermingled, it is difficult to be clear what is to count as "us" and what as the "nature" we come to know. In reaction against what he sees as the inadequacies of the Cartesian approach, Spinoza's treatment of minds and bodies opens up the possibility of a very different way of looking at knowledge and its connections with human dominance. Reading it in our own context also opens up possibilities for different ways of conceptualizing some related issues of sexual difference and its connections with power.

For Spinoza, although we are both minds and bodies, human nature is not an uneasy intermingling of two kinds of thing that are in principle separable. To think of mind and body together is, for him, to think of the same reality in two distinct ways. And, what is more, we cannot think of ourselves as minds without thereby thinking of body. Because the mind is the idea of the body, to think of mind and body together is just to think body reflectively. This means that being knowers does not separate human beings out from the rest of nature. Rather, it makes us aware of our integration with it. As the idea of a body which is what it is, and does what it does, only through its insertion into wider totalities, reaching up to the universe as a whole, we are ourselves part of nature, with no privileged position that would allow us to claim exemption from its necessities.[2] We are not, in Spinoza's phrase, located in nature as "a kingdom within a kingdom." We are not, as Descartes thought, its "lords and masters."

Despite his rejection of any metaphysically privileged status for human beings in nature, Spinoza's philosophy continues to stress the appropriateness of human domination. His stress on a relation of integration rather than separateness between human beings and the rest of nature does not yield any repudiation of the exploitation of animals. He dismisses such concerns as "unmanly" pity. In relation to the animals, we should consider our own advantage, use them at our pleasure, and treat them as is most convenient for us (E, IV, Prop 37, Schol 1). But this approval of dominance is very differently based from Descartes'. And the view of knowledge that accompanies it is very different from the one founded in Descartes' ideal of control of nature through the autonomous rational will.

Despite the common view of him as obliterating individuality in an all-encompassing unity, Spinoza's version of dominance is, like the rest of his philosophy, strongly centered on the recognition of difference. For

Descartes, the exclusiveness of the human moral community was justified by our possession of a rational soul that transcends body, and hence transcends difference. For Spinoza, in contrast, it rests simply on the differences between the powers of human and animal bodies. It is not lack of feelings that excludes the beasts from the moral considerations appropriate within the human species. What excludes them is the difference between their feelings and ours. We are separated from the beasts by the distinctive character of our emotions, by the affective affinities that bring human beings together. In knowing an individual we know its characteristic joys and pains. Our pains and pleasures define us, and human virtue is nothing but human power—the striving by which we endeavor to persist in being. "So the more each one strives, and is able to preserve his being, the more he is endowed with virtue" (E, IV, Prop 20, Dem).

Different kinds of body involve different kinds of power and virtue. Differences between the powers and pleasures of horses and humans make for differences in soul. And within the human species differences in pleasure express differences in soul. The pleasures of a drunk are different from those of a philosopher (E, III, Prop 57, Schol). (The pleasures of a drunken philosopher, Spinoza does not discuss.) Our individual striving is greatly strengthened by collaboration with others who share our range of affective responses. This is the basis for the exclusion of nonhumans from the moral community. Other species have their own joys, their own lusts. And this means that they cannot collaborate with human beings in a shared pursuit of self-preservation. "Any singular thing whose nature is entirely different from ours can neither aid nor restrain our power of acting, and absolutely no things can be either good or evil for us, unless it has something in common with us" (E, IV, Prop 29).

So the law against the killing of animals, Spinoza suggests, is "based more on empty superstition and unmanly compassion than sound reason." We have the same rights against them as they have against us. Indeed, because the right of each one is defined by his virtue, or power, "men have a far greater right against the lower animals than they have against men" (E, IV, Prop 37, Schol 1). Out of all this there emerges a very different picture of human dominance from the Cartesian one. Our "rights" against other species remain grounded in reason, but not in any privileged position for human beings within nature. The cultivation of human reason, although it has crucial significance for human beings, does not give us any grand metaphysically privileged position. Reason is an expression of human nature, and it arises from the complexity of bodily structure that distinguishes human bodies. It strengthens human powers, especially when pursued in collaboration with other rational beings. But it is circumscribed by human needs, by the demands of human self-preservation. Nature, Spinoza says in the *Theologico-Political Treatise*, is not bound by the laws of human nature, which aim only at man's true benefit and preservation. Humanity is "but a particle" in the infinitely wider limits that have reference to "the eternal order of the whole of nature" (TTP, XVI, 174). And in the *Ethics* he stresses that there is no hierarchy of degrees of perfection. We cannot judge the good of other things by reference to ourselves. The perfection of things is to be reckoned only from their own nature and power. A horse is destroyed as much if it is changed into a man as if it is changed into an insect. And perfection in general is just "the essence of each thing insofar as it exists and produces an effect" (E, IV, Pref).

Spinoza's ethics is human-centered. But the belief in human superiority on which it rests is different from the Cartesian picture of the transcendence of the mind. On that picture, our minds, being purely intellectual, transcend the limitations of mere unknowing nature, powerful though its force may be over our bodies. Cartesian minds rest their self-esteem on that transcendence and the prospects of control which go with it. Spinozistic minds rest their self-esteem on knowing their status as ideas of bodies of a sufficiently complex structure to allow the formation of the common notions of reason. They esteem themselves for the capacity this brings to understand their interdependence with other things and to strengthen their powers by collaboration with the minds of similarly structured bodies. Such minds, like their Cartesian counterparts, would see themselves as superior to other parts of nature. But it is a superiority without transcendence. Collectively we exert a force that can temporarily resist or overcome other natural forces that will ultimately destroy us, mind and body alike. It is a strength that comes from the understanding of necessities—not from thinking ourselves exempt from them. We remain part of nature. But that does not mean that we have no right to exert our temporary power over the rest of it. The importance of reason is circumscribed by the needs, desires, and pleasures of a speck in the universe. But its power and importance in relation to that speck are none the less for that.

Spinoza puts human advantage first, just because we, who have an interest in the matter, are human—not because we occupy, from some disinterested standpoint, a privileged position. He refuses to extrapolate from the inevitable human-centeredness of our interests to an anthropocentric view of the world. Things are to be judged with regard to their own well-being and perfection, not ours. His approach takes seriously the sentience and the thriving of other species, and acknowledges that reason itself rests on human "interests," as we might now put the point. Here reason is not at odds with nature, pulling against it and trying to subdue it. Reason is just the mind's power of acting, expressed in the striving for understanding. And the very contrast between conscious reason and unconscious nature, so sharp in the Cartesian view, is blunted here. What makes human beings distinctive is not their possession of a rational soul, utterly different in kind from other parts of nature, but rather the affinities and commonalities that allow them to collaborate with one another and thus strengthen their individual powers.

Sexual Difference

Spinoza's way of stressing the commonalities of human nature avoids the Cartesian abstraction from differences that has become such a strong element in ideals of a human nature, common to all, transcending all merely bodily differences of race or sex. It is interesting to see what happens when we attempt to develop Spinoza's very different way of thinking of sameness and difference in relation to questions of sexual difference—an area that was of course marginal to the concerns of both philosophers.[3] Like Descartes, Spinoza grounds the life of reason in the sameness of human minds. Insofar as human beings are torn by the passions, they disagree in nature, whereas insofar as they live "according to the guidance of reason," they always agree in nature (E, IV, Prop 35). Reason is in all human beings the same. But Spinoza conceptualizes this sameness very differently.

For Descartes, all souls are equally endowed with the capacity for thought, and reason occurs whole and entire in them. All minds must be essentially the same, because they transcend body. And the natural light of reason is supposedly equal in all. The power of judging well and of distinguishing the true from the false, which is properly called "good sense or reason," he says at the beginning of the *Discourse on Method*, is naturally equal in all men. "The diversity of our opinions does not arise because some of us are more reasonable than others but solely because we direct our thoughts along different paths and do not attend to the same things."⁴ By implication, although he does not make it explicit, reason must be naturally equal also in men and women. Sexual difference cannot reach into Cartesian minds. Descartes can nonetheless allow that differences in bodily structure can be associated with differences in intellectual functioning or capacity. Mind's causal transactions with the world must be mediated through different bodies. But those differences are extraneous to the mind; they cannot properly be attributed to the mind itself. So the picture is of minds, which are themselves undifferentiated, intermingling, and causally interacting with, and through, sexually differentiated bodies.

It is a model that lingers in contemporary ideas of sexless minds and sexed bodies intermingling in an uneasy realm of socially constructed "gender." For Spinoza, in contrast, since the mind is not a separate intellectual substance but the idea of body, sexual difference can reach right into the mind, although its attribution to bodies still has a certain conceptual priority. Minds could not be sexually differentiated independently of the bodies of which they are ideas. Spinozistic minds, after all, cannot be differentiated at all independently of the bodies of which they are ideas. So difference in mental functioning does not have to be treated, as it is by Descartes, as an effect of an extraneous intermingling with body, from which the true nature of the mind could be extricated. Spinoza's view of the mind-body relationship opens up conceptual space for the possibility that minds are sexually differentiated—a possibility that Descartes' view of the mind closed off. Does this mean that a Spinozistic way of thinking of mind-body relations would commit us to thinking of minds as "male" or "female"? The answer is not straightforward. Why should the idea of a male body be male, we may ask, any more than the idea of a large body is large? This does seem a blatant fallacy from within a Cartesian way of thinking of ideas as modes of an intellectual substance, utterly different in kind from bodies. But there is a way of taking it which is not ludicrous. The idea or mind of a large body is a mind whose nature reflects the "powers and pleasures," in Spinoza's phrase, of a large body. There are distinctive powers and pleasures associated with different kinds of bodily structure. And our minds enact in thought those powers and pleasures. To the extent that the powers and pleasures of human bodies are sexually differentiated, it will then be quite appropriate for a Spinozist to speak of "male" and "female" minds. A female mind will be one whose nature—and "gladness"—reflects its status as idea of a female body. The powers and pleasures of such a body will of course be partly the same as those of a male body. But there will also be differences that cut across other differences and similarities between human bodies.

Because Cartesian minds are simple, transcending all bodily differences, the answer to the question "Are the minds of women the same as those of men?" has to be categorically that they are the same. However complex bodies might be, their differences are transcended in the simplicity of minds. Spinozistic minds, in contrast, reflect the multifacetedness of bodies. They can be alike in some ways, different in others, reflecting the sameness and differences of the bodies of which they are ideas. This suggests that there need not be any specifiable content to what it is to be a "female" or "male" mind. All ideas of female bodies will be, trivially, female. But that does not mean that there is any underlying essence of femaleness which they all have in common. What content they have as minds is determined by the powers and pleasures of the bodies of which they are ideas, and that cannot be known in advance.

This brings us to another important point of contrast between Cartesian and Spinozistic reconstructions of sex and gender. There is for Spinoza continuity between the natural body and the socialized body. The powers of individual bodies are enriched by good forms of social organization which foster the collective pursuit of reason, which enhances human powers and enriches human pleasures. "It is impossible for man not to be part of nature and not to follow the common order of nature. But if he lives among such individuals as agree with his nature, his power of acting will thereby be aided and encouraged. On the other hand, if he is among such as do not agree at all with his nature, he will hardly be able to accommodate himself to them without greatly changing himself" (E, IV, Appen 7). Among singular things, "we know nothing more excellent than a man who is guided by reason." So we can show best how much our skill and understanding are worth by "educating men so that at last they live according to the command of their own reason" (E, IV, Appen 9).

So much for the men of reason. What of the women? There is little explicit discussion of sexual difference in the *Ethics*. In Part IV, Spinoza makes a passing reference to the Genesis story of Adam and Eve, in which he implies that there is no difference between male and female in respect of rationality. The man, having found a wife who "agreed completely with his nature," knew that there could be nothing in nature more useful to him than she was. But, after he came to believe the lower animals to be like himself, he immediately began to "imitate their affects," and to lose his freedom (E, IV, Prop 68, Schol).

Spinoza's concern here is not with sexual difference but with the relations between freedom and the knowledge of good and evil. His political writings make it clear that, whatever women may be like in the state of nature—if that is how we should describe the location of the Genesis paradise—in the state of society their capacity does not match that of men. They are accordingly excluded from the responsibilities of government.

Sexist though this may appear from our perspective, it is only what we should expect from Spinoza's treatment of reason and nature and his emphasis on the social dimensions of reason. He stresses the interconnections between the life of reason and forms of social organization that enhance freedom. If our natural powers are enriched by the operation of good forms of social organization, which foster the collective pursuit of reason, it is only to be expected that groups excluded from full participation in that shared pursuit of reason will miss out on the full flourishing of their natural powers and pleasures, leading distorted, mutilated lives. If human powers are enriched by the operation of good forms of social organization, it is to be expected that they will be impeded by bad ones, and this state of obstruction is of course the actual position of women, even amidst the good forms of social organization he outlines in the *Theologico-Political Treatise*. Being female in the conditions of that society sets severe restraints on human powers, pleasures and virtue.

This much of what emerges as a Spinozistic view of sexual difference could be accommodated in a Cartesian framework. The same Cartesian reason must find its way out from the soul into the realm of intermingling with body through more circuitous paths in the case of women. The same mental capacity has a rather more difficult time when intermingled with a female body, and the mind in which it inheres can be expected to achieve rather less in the enterprise of becoming a "lord and master" of nature. But if we take seriously the implications of Spinoza's theory of mind, we must say also that female minds are formed by these socially imposed limitations on the powers and pleasures of female bodies. Differences in male and female experience of the shared social world will mold the minds of women, making them different *as minds* from those that are the ideas of unimpeded male bodies. The bodies of which we are aware, the bodies of which our minds are ideas, have had their powers affected not only by our own "natural" development, but by the social forms that provide a context for that development. Spinozistic bodies are socialized bodies, and our minds reflect that socialization of bodies.

Social arrangements, for better or worse, modify the powers of bodies and, hence, on Spinoza's theory of mind, our awareness of ourselves. There is more to being a male or female body than anatomy. It is a matter of how we move, of posture and gesture, and of the kind of activity we can perform as socialized bodies. Our minds reflect that socialization. In this way a Spinozistic theory of the mind, in contrast to the Cartesian, can be seen as taking seriously both sex differences and power. Sex differences for Spinoza apply to minds no less than to bodies. But that need not involve the affirmation of any male or female content, existing independently of operations of power.

For Spinoza our minds are not insulated, as they are for Descartes, from the operations of power enshrined in social forms. On this view of the mind, sexual difference is not merely bodily. But this does not mean that there must be some specific content to our awareness of our socialized bodies as male or female. What content this has at any time will reflect the social organization of sex differences—the way collective social power has structured the powers of bodies. But the powers of bodies can in principle always be extricated from the contingent social wholes in which they are embedded, to form new social wholes that may better enhance their powers—as well, of course, as creating ever new possibilities of suppression or oppression. Something remains in all this of the ideal of a shared human nature that transcends difference. But the sameness here, unlike the Cartesian version, is not an already existing metaphysical status, but an ideal of a wholeness to be achieved. Rather than asserting an already existing sameness of soul, underlying the extraneous accretion of bodily differences, the Spinozistic ideal aims at achieving commonalities. The participants in such social wholes carry their differences with them. Those differences can be set aside as irrelevant in specific contexts. But they are not minimized, negated, or subsumed under an idealized sameness.

There is of course a biological basis for the formation of such social wholes. Bodies have affinities and dissonances, which allow for some forms of social integration and exclude others. Such possibilities and impossibilities, compossibilities and incompatibilities may not be determinable in advance. They are revealed by what bodies can do and are experienced as pleasure or pain, feelings of affinity or disharmony. Sameness of human nature arises from the fact that different bodies have shared affinities that allow their differences to be transcended in the realization of common pleasures. It is a sameness that expresses neither a common higher intellectual nature nor an underlying, circumscribed biological one. Sex differences come out as different ways of experiencing the commonalities of human life, and there is of course more involved in this than the physical differences of male and female bodies. The differences reflect also the influence of social roles and expectations. To pursue Spinoza's example, the physical differences of men and women might not of themselves make all that much difference in the way human beings experience the pleasures of getting drunk or doing philosophy. But the powers and pleasures involved in getting drunk or doing philosophy in seventeenth-century Netherlands society may, for all that, come to something very different for the ideas of male and female bodies.

Such an approach allows us to say that bodily differences have mental ramifications. Sex differences apply to minds just as much as, and because, they apply to bodies. But, again, this does not mean that we must be able to prescribe any definite content for the differences. To be a male or female mind is to be the idea of a male or female body. Sometimes, in some contexts, being the awareness of a female body will amount to something very different from being the idea of a male body. At other times, and in other contexts, the differences will be minimal. Traits related to sexual difference are changeable, and always, for some minds, the differences will be more important than for others.

The Cartesian way of thinking of minds and bodies—reason transcending mere nature—lingers in contemporary thought of sexless minds and sexed bodies and in an uneasy realm of intermingling, of socially produced gender, which seems unable to engage with either. A Spinozistic way of thinking of sex differences might help resolve some of the impasses that have arisen in contemporary debate about the relations between supposedly biologically given sex and socially constructed gender. Such an approach would take seriously the ramifications of bodily differences without affirming any specifiable content for "true" femininity or masculinity. It could continue to affirm the ideal of a shared human nature, differently sexed though we undoubtedly are, without falling into the Cartesian model of a supposedly already existing sameness of soul. The idea of a shared human nature, on this way of looking at it, would become an ideal of a range of commonalities that can be achieved, not an expression of an already existing sameness.

Such commonalities amidst difference are achievable precisely because our bodies are socialized bodies. The ideal, and the psychic distortions and mutilations it opposes, are made possible by the same fact: that the bodies of which our minds are ideas, are formed, for better or worse, through the operations of collective human power. This conception of the powers of bodies as modified through social power might open up more fruitful ways of articulating some contemporary feminist aspirations. It could repudiate the spurious "unsexed soul" that has, with reason, been criticized by some feminists as masking real, socially imposed differences under an idealized sameness. A Spinozistic approach would here take seriously the idea that bodily differences do have ramifications for the minds and selves that we are. But it could do this while avoiding some of the hazards of contemporary feminist affirmations of difference.

Feminist affirmation of difference, in reaction against the idea of gender as transcending sex, and hence malleable almost without limit, has been accompanied by a rejection of the philosophical assumptions implicit in the idea of a free-floating gender, especially Descartes' model of the mind-body relationship. The idea of mind as transcending sexual differences has been seen as contributing to a spurious ideal of sameness, to the disadvantage of women. The future is then seen to lie in taking seriously the fact that, as embodied human beings, we are embodied as different sexes. But, in the lack of an alternative way of conceptualizing the relations between mind and body, such affirmations of difference risk "naturalizing"—and hence rationalizing and perpetuating—some of the content of existing sexual stereotypes.

A Spinozistic approach to these issues allows us both to take seriously the role of body in our understanding of sex difference and to recognize the contributions of social power to the content of our sexual stereotypes. It allows us to take body seriously, while yet seeing gender as socially constructed all the way through, as it were, rather than as resting on a preexisting and unchangeable base of biological sex difference, in an uneasy causal relationship with gender. It allows us to see our awareness of ourselves as male or female as responding to the experienced facts of bodily sex difference—difference, however, that reflects the operations of social power no less than it reflects biology. On this way of looking at sex difference, there is no sexless soul waiting to be extricated from socially imposed sex differences. But nor is there any authentic male or female identity, existing independently of social power. It allows us to see that, with regard to sexual difference, there are no facts of the matter other than those produced through the shifting play of the powers and pleasures of socialized, embodied, sexed human beings.

Notes

1. Blaise Pascal, *Pensées*, trans. Alban J. Krailsheimer, Brunschvig ed. (Harmondsworth: Penguin, 1966), fragment 347, 95.

2. I discuss the implications of Spinoza's philosophy for environmental ethics in "Spinoza's Environmental Ethics," *Inquiry* 23 (1980): 293–311.

3. The ideas in this section draw on my paper "Woman as Other: Sex, Gender, and Subjectivity," *Australian Feminist Studies* 10 (Summer 1989): 13–22. I discuss the "maleness of reason" further in *The Man of Reason: "Male" and "Female" in Western Philosophy*, 2nd ed. (London: Routledge, 1993) and in "Maleness, Metaphor, and the 'Crisis' of Reason," in *A Mind of One's Own*, ed. Louise Antony and Charlotte Witt (Boulder, Colo.: Westview Press, 1993), 69–84.

4. R. Descartes, *Discourse on Method*, in *The Philosophical Writings of Descartes*, ed. John Cottingham, Robert Stoothoff, and Dugald Murdoch, 3 vols. (Cambridge: Cambridge University Press, 1985–91), vol. 1, III.

2

Autonomy and the Relational Individual

Spinoza and Feminism

Aurelia Armstrong

Should contemporary Western feminism champion the cause of women's autonomy? To even ask this question seems to betray a shameful ignorance of the political struggles and goals that have been central to feminism. If, as some feminists claim, however, the concept of autonomy is bound up with assumptions about individuality and agency that can be shown to be metaphysically, politically, and ethically problematic from a feminist perspective, then there would seem to be strong grounds for treating it with suspicion. Yet despite reservations about the modern ideal of autonomy and its value for women there has been a widespread reluctance on the part of feminist moral and political theorists to give up entirely on a concept that many feel has a significant role to play in feminism's efforts to understand oppression and agency. Thus, rather than abandoning the concept of autonomy, recent feminist theory has called for its reconfiguration from a feminist perspective.

A key challenge faced by feminists seeking to rethink the concept of autonomy is how to negotiate the various conceptual dualisms that inform traditional conceptions of autonomy. Feminists seeking to reconfigure autonomy as a capacity of desiring, feeling, and embodied selves, not only the property of the rational will, have been forced to confront the deeply ingrained conceptual polarization between authentic selfhood, mind, reason, and masculinity on the one hand and embodiment, affectivity, and femininity on the other. Similarly, feminists investigating the possibility of combining a strong notion of individual autonomy with a view of the self as a fundamentally socially embedded and relational entity face the issue of how to think through entrenched dichotomies between independence and dependence, self and other, individual and society, separation and connection.

It is in relation to the issue of how to think through, and perhaps beyond, the tacitly assumed oppositions that structure prevailing approaches to autonomy and individuality that Spinoza's philosophy can be assessed for its potential contribution to the feminist project of rethinking autonomy. Spinoza's treatment of the themes of individuality and autonomy has itself been subjected to radically different interpretations. There are those who see Spinoza's position as profoundly individualist in orientation, while others claim that it is best understood as envisaging the expansion of the boundaries of individuality to the point of their ultimate dissolution. For some commentators the coexistence of these two perspectives points to a "deep incoherence" in Spinoza's philosophy.[1] For others, however, the judgment of incoherence itself is an indication of the difficulty readers have in understanding a philosophical perspective that calls into question the basic antinomies of classical metaphysics and ethics.[2] Thus, according to this latter school of interpretation, the challenge posed by Spinoza's philosophy consists in the way in which it twists free of the dualisms that form the conceptual infrastructure of post-Cartesian Western thought.

The following discussion pursues the interpretive possibilities opened up by this perspective with a view to exploring some of the ways in which Spinoza's account of individuality may contribute to feminist efforts to criticize and revise dominant conceptions of individual autonomy. I will argue that Spinoza's *Ethics* is particularly relevant to recent feminist efforts to rethink the autonomous individual in a way that adequately incorporates recognition of the irreducibly social character of selves, since its fundamental concern is with the possibilities for autonomy of an individual conceived in a profoundly relational way.

To consider the ways in which Spinoza's relational view of individuality may contribute to feminist efforts to revise canonical conceptions of individual autonomy we need some appreciation of the grounds for the feminist ambivalence toward these conceptions. In the first part of this essay I briefly outline the core feminist objections to traditional conceptions of autonomy, which converge in the charge that the individualistic and rationalistic bias of these conceptions represents a failure to do justice to the socially embedded and embodied nature of the self. I suggest that feminist efforts to reconfigure autonomy on the basis of a social conception of selves require and entail a complex negotiation of the dichotomy between individuality and autonomy on the one hand and sociability and the collectivity on the other. It is this dichotomy that Spinoza's philosophy takes issue with. In the second part of the chapter I argue that Spinoza's definition of the individual in terms of its power to affect *and* be affected contains a powerful alternative to a tradition of "abstract individualism" that has tended to confuse autonomy with atomic isolation.

Feminism, Autonomy, and the Social Self

Feminist critiques of prevailing conceptions of autonomy generally target the type of individualism with which autonomy has been linked in the popular and philosophical imagination. The ideas of self-governance and authenticity that are the core of such concepts of autonomy are clearly reflected in the value that is invested, at least in modern liberal democracies, in the notions of having control over one's life and being true to oneself. In taking issue with this culturally dominant conception of autonomy, feminists have pointed to the historical association of these values with masculine models of selfhood and masculine character ideals. They have suggested that this association can be clearly discerned in the caricature of the autonomous individual as potentially or ideally "self-originating, self-sufficient, coldly rational, shrewdly calculating, self-interest maximizing" and, in general, independent from the influence of others and the wider social context.[3] Feminists have argued that the power of this caricature in shaping Western ideals of autonomous individuality is especially evident in the ideology of liberal individualism, with its "deeply ingrained sense that individual autonomy is to be achieved by erecting a wall (of rights) between the individual and those around him."[4]

It is this broadly liberal conception of autonomy that is the focus of the majority of feminist critiques. Some of these critiques target the metaphysical assumptions about individuality that underpin mainstream conceptions of autonomy and question the plausibility of these assumptions. Others take issue with traditional accounts of autonomy on normative grounds and raise concerns about the value accorded to substantive independence, self-sufficiency, and separation from others in these accounts. Still others target the character ideal of the autonomous individual and one or other of the traits typically associated with it.[5] At the heart of these various critiques is a shared concern about the extent to which a certain conception of atomic individuality has inflected prevailing ideals of autonomous agency. The grounds of this concern are most clearly articulated in the feminist ethics of care. According to care critiques, the reliance of traditional ideals of autonomy on a conception of individuality that is defined in opposition to dimensions of subjectivity conventionally coded as feminine—embeddedness, embodiedness, affectivity, connection to others, and interdependency—sets up a serious conceptual and practical conflict between, on the one hand, the feminist project of revaluing interpersonal capacities that have historically been central to many women's lives and identities, and on the other hand, the project of promoting women's autonomy.[6]

In response to this dilemma many feminists have called for autonomy to be rethought, starting from an alternative, richer conception of the self. Recent work by feminist moral and political theorists on the notion of relational autonomy represents an attempt to rethink autonomy in terms that recognize the social dimensions of selfhood and the relational contexts within which agents develop their capacities, including their capacity for autonomy. Against the prevailing conception of autonomous individuality as the ability to govern oneself uninfluenced by others and the wider social context, the emphasis in relational accounts is on developing a model of autonomy capable of acknowledging the social embeddedness of selves. The term *relational autonomy* refers to a range of related perspectives united by a commitment to the view that "persons are socially embedded and that agents' identities are formed within the context of social relationships and shaped by a complex of intersecting social determinants. . . . The focus of relational approaches is to analyse the implications of the intersubjective and social dimensions of selfhood and identity for conceptions of individual autonomy and moral and political agency."[7]

Feminist efforts to revise the conception of self that underpins the traditional view of autonomy raise the issue of how to do justice to the social nature of selves, while simultaneously upholding the value of self-determination. This way of describing the challenge faced by proponents of relational autonomy suggests that these approaches occupy the conceptual space between the (broadly conceived) traditions of classical individualism, which prioritizes the freedom of the individual, and communitarianism, which emphasizes communal sources of identity. Insofar as relational approaches seek to preserve and promote some of the capacities for autonomous agency championed by liberalism, they seem to remain within the orbit of a broadly liberal perspective. However, insofar as such approaches raise various objections to the hyperindividualism of traditional liberal theories and insist on the fundamentally social nature of selves and their identities, they appear to be allied with communitarian perspectives.

In fact, relational approaches may be fruitfully understood as seeking to combine elements of each of these traditions in order to avoid undesirable features of both. By insisting that an adequate conception of autonomy must incorporate recognition of the essentially social nature of the self, relational approaches seek to preserve the value attached to the capacity for autonomous agency in the liberal tradition while rejecting this tradition's atomistic conception of individuality. Feminist philosophers have claimed that any theory of individual autonomy that fails to give due recognition to the role played by social relations, practices, and institutions in the development and exercise of the capacity for autonomy is misguided.[8] As a corrective to overly individualistic models of autonomy, which present it as the capacity of the isolated, rational agent to transcend social influences and act on "his" authentic desires, proponents of relational autonomy emphasize the need to "think of autonomy in terms of the forms of human interactions in which it will develop and flourish."[9] This insistence on the importance of acknowledging the positive contribution made by interpersonal relationships to the realization of autonomy also reflects feminist concerns about the normative implications of theories that fail to mention the role played by social relationships in fostering autonomy. Feminists have argued that these theories serve to valorize the life of the separated and self-sufficient individual at the expense of those, typically women and the marginalized, whose lives do not conform to such an ideal.[10]

Some feminists have claimed that an ambivalent attitude toward the social is apparent even in those philosophical theories that *are* attentive to the effects of socialization on individuals' capacities for autonomy. For example, in their analysis of procedural accounts of autonomy, Catriona Mackenzie and Natalie Stoljar argue that while these accounts admit that "our values, beliefs, and desires, as well as our characters and life plans are inevitably shaped by socialization, autonomy tends to be represented as the quest to shape an identity for oneself in the face of, or against, this influence."[11] In other words, social influence is recognized as a necessary but *negative* condition of autonomy. It is what must be resisted or overcome if authenticity is to be realized and autonomous selfhood achieved. Feminist philosophers have interpreted this largely negative attitude toward the social as reflecting and expressing an uncritical acceptance of entrenched conceptual dichotomies between autonomy and sociability, independence and dependence, separation and connection, self-sufficiency and social embeddedness. They have argued that this predominantly negative view of the social sources of selfhood has served to block adequate consideration of the highly complex relation between the capacities and skills required for exercising autonomy and the social relationships that may *both* hinder and foster them.[12]

Feminist critiques of autonomy thus converge in the rejection of any theory or ideal of autonomous individuality that identifies the autonomous self with the socially unencumbered self. This rejection of atomistic and asocial conceptions of individuality has led a number of feminists to suggest the possibility of an alliance between feminist and communitarian perspectives on the basis of their convergence on these points.[13] But while feminist proponents of relational autonomy take inspiration from the communitarian insistence on the social nature of the self, they are wary of endorsing a communitarian view of the constitutively social self. Within a communitarian framework the notion of the constitutively social self acquires normative force as an ideal of agency in which shared ends and values are endorsed as the guiding sources of action. On this view an individual's identity, aspirations, and values are constituted by her communities of origin, such as family, neighborhood, and nation, and agency that flows from embracing these constitutive, shared ends and values is considered more valuable than autonomous agency, understood as action proceeding from the self's strongest desires or preferences. The communitarian repudiation of autonomy in favor of a vision of the common good is thus grounded in a belief in the value of inherited social roles and identities and the social traditions and institutions that sustain them. Although feminists endorse the descriptive claim that our identities are socially determined, they draw very different conclusions from this insight, especially about the value of autonomy. From a feminist perspective, the fact that identity is socially and historically constituted is a liberating insight to the extent that it opens up possibilities for the *autonomous* reconstitution of these inherited identities and roles. Whereas communitarians reject the cultural ideal of autonomy and the political value attached to this ideal within a liberal perspective on the grounds that the exercise of autonomy has the potential to disrupt shared values and ways of life, feminists have (warily) embraced this disruptive potential as the condition for questioning oppressive social relationships and structures.[14] Indeed, a key feminist motivation for insisting on both the possibility and the value of autonomy is the role that it plays in enabling women to challenge and reject the oppressive and exploitative practices and relationships characteristic of many traditional communities.[15]

Although feminists raise distinct criticisms of the treatment of autonomy within the traditions of liberal individualism and communitarianism, the grounds of these criticisms converge in concerns about the assumption, common to both, that there is an unresolvable tension between individual autonomy and the relational ties that bind us to others in community. It is this assumption that feminism must find a way to negotiate if it is to explain the disruptive potential of autonomy without falling back on the view that interpersonal relationships and autonomy are mutually exclusive. Some feminist proponents of relational autonomy argue that in order to challenge this assumption successfully we need more than an instrumental conception of community as external support for (or hindrance to) the realization of autonomous individuality, since this does not in itself serve to contest the conflation of autonomy with separation from others and aggressive independence. Feminists have argued that to detach the ideal of autonomous individuality from its association with independence, self-sufficiency, and separation, less individualistic ways of thinking selfhood are required. In the following discussion of Spinoza's conception of individuality I aim to contribute to these efforts by demonstrating the way in which it rethinks autonomy and relationality as interconnected rather than opposed, but without denying that the striving for autonomy may at times involve severing some of the relational ties that bind us to others.

Relational Individuality and Autonomy in Spinoza

In Letter 32 to Oldenburg, in answer to a query on the relations between parts and wholes within his philosophy, Spinoza uses the analogy of a worm in the bloodstream to illuminate the peculiar characteristics of the human individual's perception of itself and its place relative to others in the surrounding environment. Spinoza asks his correspondent to conceive

> that there is a little worm living in the blood which is capable of distinguishing by sight the particles of the blood, of lymph, of chyle, and the like, and capable of observing by reason how each particle, when it encounters another, either bounces back, or communicates a part of its motion, and so on. Indeed, it would live in this blood as we do in this part of the universe, and would consider each particle of the blood as a whole, not as a part. Nor could it know how all the parts of the blood are restrained by the universal nature of the blood, and compelled to adapt themselves to one another, as the universal nature of the blood requires, so that they harmonize with one another in a certain way.[16]

In the first part of this passage Spinoza suggests that, because of the perspectival nature of our view of the world, we are, like the worm, prone to imagining ourselves as self-contained wholes interacting with other clearly bounded wholes through relations of collision and rebound. Toward the end of the passage Spinoza seems to indicate that if we could expand the horizons of our knowledge, we would be able to adjust our understanding of our status and see ourselves as parts of a more encompassing, internally integrated, and harmonious whole.

When considered as viewpoints that the human individual may adopt in regarding herself, these two perspectives correspond to very different types of relation between self and other. From our worm's-eye view we are prone to viewing ourselves and those "particles" with which we "collide" as self-contained and independent wholes more or less in conflict.[17] Under the influence of such a view I will be led to locate my individuality in those aspects of my character whereby I differ from others and that thus seem to constitute my distinctive or idiosyncratic identity. When this conception of the self as a whole distinct from and opposed to differing others is combined with the related belief that each such whole is intent on asserting her own particular interests, it results in the accentuation of conflict and ambivalence in interindividual relations. Since I define myself in opposition to others, on the basis of perceived differences, I will tend to cling to those differences rather than seek out commonalities and grounds for agreement and cooperation. And because I imagine other individuals as atomized egoists bent on self-interest, I am more likely to regard them as a threat to my integrity and autonomy and, thus, to adopt an embattled stance toward them.

To view the part as a whole, like the worm, is to imagine it not only as self-contained and independent, but also as self-controlling or self-caused. The structure and source of these two errors is essentially the same. We conceive ourselves in isolationist terms by abstracting ourselves from the network of relations in which we are inserted. And we view ourselves as freely self-determining because we are conscious of our actions and appetites yet ignorant of the causes by which they are determined (E, II, Prop 35, Schol). Awareness of action and appetite combined with ignorance of their causes leads us to believe that we can govern ourselves uninfluenced by "alien" causes. This misunderstanding of our identity and agency—which results from viewing the individual in isolation from its conditioning causal environment—is not simply false. Rather, it is limited or, in Spinoza's terminology, "inadequate." It is, Spinoza argues, a partial and fragmented grasp of reality that gives rise to the related illusions of free will and self-contained independence. What especially concerns Spinoza about these fictions is not so much their epistemological status as their impact on human flourishing. As we have seen, Spinoza suggests that the more I imagine myself and others as independent sites of free causation, the more likely it is that my relationships will be marked by conflict and antagonism. And the greater the degree of conflict and antagonism between individuals the less likely it is that they will be able to develop an adequate grasp of their interrelatedness.

Spinoza's alternative to will-based accounts of autonomy turns on this understanding of interrelatedness in a way that suggests a close association between the development of the capacity for autonomy and the endeavor to promote harmonious forms of sociability.

In his letter to Oldenburg, Spinoza suggests that we may amend the inadequacy of this view of ourselves and others as discordant wholes by recognizing that we are, like the worm, parts of a larger whole related to other parts according to laws that determine our more or less harmonious interaction. This adjustment to our original perspective involves attending to the laws of interconnection that determine our nature and our interactions with surrounding others. As Spinoza explains: "By the coherence of the parts . . . I understand nothing but that the laws *or* nature of the one part so adapt themselves to the laws *or* nature of the other part that they are opposed to each other as little as possible. . . . I consider things as parts of some whole insofar as the nature of the one so adapts itself to the nature of the other that so far as possible they are all in harmony with one another."[18] Parts, then, are mutually adapted to other parts and are defined by reference to the kind of causal connections interrelating them, rather than by their distinctive characteristics.[19] To the extent that we adopt the perspective of a part, we conceive ourselves and others as connected through relations of agreement or concordance insofar as we are all alike dependent for our self-identity on the nature of, and laws governing, the whole in which we participate.

Although Spinoza's meditations on the worm in the blood appear to endorse the view that our self-conception becomes more adequate to the extent that we view ourselves as parts of a more encompassing whole and thus as determined by and dependent on a common order, it would be a mistake to see this as a denial of the reality of individuality and the possibility of autonomy. This conclusion would follow only if we assumed that authentic individuality is atomic and that autonomy requires freedom from any kind of determination, but this is precisely the view that Spinoza begins to call into question in asking us to reflect on the perspectival perplexities that we share with the worm. In fact, Spinoza's own account of individuality, as it is expounded in the *Ethics*, suggests that the viewpoint of the whole and that of the part remain partial and inadequate until they are revisioned as reciprocally determining rather than opposed. Spinoza's transformation of these perspectives aims to readjust our conceptions of the nature of our wholeness or distinctive individuality by reconsidering the boundaries of individuality through the incorporation of relationality into its very structure and nature.

How, then, are we are to understand the individual whose flourishing is the object of Spinoza's ethics? On this, as in most points of Spinoza interpretation, commentators are divided. According to one influential strand in the scholarship, which emphasizes the concept of *conatus*, or the intrinsic striving of individuals to preserve and assert themselves, Spinoza's position should be interpreted as radically individualist in orientation. This reading downplays the significance of Spinoza's metaphysical position, according to which the whole of nature should be conceived as a complex individual composed of simpler individuals, and interprets the restatement of this position in Spinoza's account of social relations as purely metaphorical. Thus, when Spinoza tells us that "if, for example, two individuals of entirely the same nature are joined to one another, they compose an individual twice as powerful as each one" and that "man, I say, can wish for nothing more helpful to the preservation of his being than that all should so agree in all things that the minds and bodies of all would compose, as it were, one mind and one body" (E, IV, Prop 18, Schol), he should be understood as saying that prudential egoism recommends cooperation with others as a means to the self-preservation of each individual.[20] On the basis of the same passages, however, an alternative interpretation has been mounted, which stresses the organicist tendencies in Spinoza's thinking and defends the claim that Spinoza envisages the expansion of the boundaries of atomic individuality and their ultimate dissolution as these individuals become parts integrated into higher-order wholes.[21]

While these standard interpretations of Spinoza seem to occupy opposite poles in the spectrum between individualism and holism, they are united by the assumption that individual identity and autonomy are threatened by the incorporation of individuals into communal bodies. It is the rejection of this assumption that forms the central component of a third kind of reading of Spinoza that aims to show how his thinking avoids this conclusion. This reading is directly relevant to feminist concerns insofar as it draws attention to the relational conception of individuality underpinning Spinoza's rejection of any account of autonomy that depends on isolating the individual, and informs his alternative account of the degree and kind of autonomy that we may seek to achieve. The starting point of this account can be found in Spinoza's discussion of mind-body relations in the *Ethics*.

It is well known that Spinoza defends a type of psychophysical parallelism. Because mind and body are modes of a single substance rather than distinct mental and material substances, there can be no causal interaction between them. Instead, their connection is explicated as a union, which is expressed in Spinoza's claim that mind is the idea or awareness of an actually existing individual body. Mind, then, is perspectival awareness of body; it is a series of ideas corresponding to the series of states of its body object (E, II, Prop 11). On Spinoza's account the states of the body that mind monitors are determined by two factors: by what the body is in itself—that is, by the maintenance of a certain ratio of motion and rest between its constituent parts—and by the influence of other bodies. As Hans Jonas explains, "The state of a body represents at each moment itself *and* those bodies of the surrounding world which affect it."[22] Spinoza closely associates these two factors. The capacity of a body to be affected by external bodies is a function of the degree of complexity of its own internal organization, which is why one of the defining features of more complex and powerful bodies is a capacity for "being acted on in many ways at once" (E, II, Prop 13, Schol). It follows that the mind's powers of perception and thought also increase in direct proportion to its body's capacity to be affected (E, II, Prop 19, Dem). Thus, the ability of a particular individual, or mind-body union, to persist and thrive is directly related to its capacity for being acted on and affected by other bodies insofar as they contribute to its survival. The human body, Spinoza tells us, "requires a great many bodies by which it is, as it were, continually regenerated" (E, II, Prop 19, Dem).

This vital interplay between our capacity to act and be acted upon, to affect and be affected, is one of the most strikingly original aspects of Spinoza's theory of the individual. For Spinoza our receptivity, or openness to what can affect us, is not the mark of our passivity in the face of the external forces of nature, but is itself a power, and a power that increases our power of acting. Jonas suggests that through this mutual dependence of passive and active power Spinoza is able to move beyond the apparent dichotomy between self-determination and determination from without. The profundity of his philosophy, Jonas suggests, follows from this insight into the complementarity of receptivity and spontaneity, a complementarity that implies that "only by being sensitive can life be active, only by being exposed can it be autonomous."[23] It is here, in this linking of our vulnerability to being affected with our capacities for agency, that we can see the potential for a productive dialogue between

Spinoza's account of individuality and feminist efforts to critically revise the traditionally conflictual interpretation of the social and autonomous self.

To recapitulate, then, an individual, for Spinoza, is an actually existing union of mind and body as well as a centre of action causally connected in a variety of ways to other individuals. Although the identity of each individual is determined in the first instance by a certain ratio of motion and rest between constituent parts, for the individual to maintain this identity—or exist—it must necessarily be connected to other bodies within a network of causal and affective relations. Spinoza's theory of *conatus* explains what it means to exist as the inherent striving of the individual to maintain identity in and through such exchanges with its environment. Thus it makes no sense for Spinoza to think of the individual in isolation from its world—what it affects and is affected by, what it seeks and avoids, what strengthens or threatens it. Just as each state of the body reflects both itself and those other bodies that affect it, so the activity of the mind reflects both its body object and its interactions with the world. This expansion of the boundaries of individuality to encompass cognitive and corporeal relations with the environment, combined with a rejection of the transcendence of the self, implies a radical rejection of atomic assumptions about selfhood. Indeed it is hard to overestimate how far Spinoza has moved from Descartes' conception of the individual as a *res cogitans*, an isolated consciousness that is separate from the body and set over against the world it apprehends.

If the Spinozist individual *is* her ongoing bodily and mental relations with the surrounding environment, it follows that not all otherness can be regarded as external to her.[24] Spinoza's relational conception of individuality involves a fundamental rethinking of concepts of interiority and exteriority that are premised on limiting the borders of the self to the spatial boundaries of the anatomical body or the self-enclosed confines of Cartesian consciousness. Interiority and exteriority are instead redefined in terms of what "agrees" or "disagrees" with the individual's identity. What is internal to the individual is that which agrees with her nature in the sense that it contributes to her self-maintenance or augments her power. On the other hand, what is external to the individual is that whose nature is contrary to her own in the sense that it opposes her striving to persevere in her being (E, III, Props 4 and 5). Thus, my relations to others who "agree" in nature with me are internal to me, whereas the virus in my body, although it is spatially inside me, must be regarded as an external cause.[25] But although Spinoza's individual is rendered permeable and dynamic by virtue of being extended to include bodily awareness of interaction, this does not destroy the possibility of internal coherence and self-identity. Rather, identity becomes a function of that particular causal and affective history of interactions that determines an individual's present capacity to affect and be affected.

So far in this discussion the affectivity of the individual has been presented only in a positive light, that is, in terms of its role in constituting our individuality and contributing to our power of acting. Yet if our vulnerability to external influence is, as Jonas argues, a condition of autonomy for Spinoza, it is *also* the source of those mental confusions and emotional disturbances that undermine the individual's striving for self-determination. What, then, does it mean for an individual to achieve autonomy? Although the word itself is drawn from a more recent philosophical lexicon, Spinoza's philosophy contains an analogue in the language of activity and passivity. We are active or act, Spinoza tells us, "when something happens, in us or outside us, of which we are the adequate cause, that is, . . . when something in us or outside us follows from our nature, which can be clearly and distinctly understood through it alone. On the other hand, I say that we are acted on when something happens in us, or something follows from our nature, of which we are only a partial cause" (E, III, D2). Spinoza's explanation of what it means to be the adequate or inadequate cause of something is complexly related to his account of the emotions or affects that move us. His definition of emotion brings together bodily transitions to greater or lesser activity and their mental equivalents, which turn out to be ideas of things that increase or diminish the body's power of acting.[26] Bodily and mental transitions to greater or lesser activity are marked by affects of joy or sadness (E, III, Prop 11, Dem). In Part III of the *Ethics* Spinoza analyzes specific emotions in terms of these primary affects of joy and sadness and considers these emotions in terms of the idea of their causes. It is this idea of the causes of our emotional states that Spinoza appeals to in order to explain the difference between passions and actions. Affects that are passions involve inadequate ideas, that is, ideas that are confused insofar as they reflect awareness of the state of my own body mixed together with awareness of external bodies impinging on it. Affects, however, cease to be passions to which we are subjected and become actions when we form an adequate idea of their causes. It is knowledge of the causes of our emotional states, rather than freedom from the affects, that is, for Spinoza, the key to active self-determination. Spinoza's version of autonomy thus involves remedying our passivity by coming to understand the causes of our emotions and actions. We become more autonomous when more of what we do and feel can be understood through our nature alone; that is, with reference to our own power, rather than the power of external causes (E, IV, Prop 59, Dem). And we become the adequate cause of what we do when we understand the sources of our appetites, motivations, and emotions and how they function in our current situation. Amelie Rorty describes this as a process in which "the mind acknowledges and absorbs as constitutive of its nature, the determinative causal line that had seemed 'external' to it."[27] To the extent that we understand something, it ceases to be "outside" us. Understanding the causal determinations of our actions, through a gradual articulation of the determinants of our ideas and affects, *is* the transition from relative passivity to increased activity. Thus, for Spinoza, freedom is a function of adequate knowledge of oneself and one's emotions. There are, however, necessary limits to our self-knowledge and activity. It is impossible, Spinoza tells us, "that a man should not be a part of Nature, and that he should be able to undergo no changes except those which can be understood through his own nature alone, and of which he is the adequate cause" (E, IV, Prop 4).

Spinoza's account of activity as a function of adequate beliefs about ourselves and our emotions contains clear parallels with more modern theories of autonomy. The notion of activity as self-causation can be linked to notions of self-determination and self-direction, and the focus on the adequacy of our ideas evokes the requirements for self-knowledge and rational reflection that are central to many accounts of autonomy.[28] These obvious parallels, however, need to be carefully qualified. If we recall that, for Spinoza, the mark of more complex and powerful individuals is a heightened capacity to be acted on and affected by other bodies, and that the mind's power to think and, therefore, to form adequate ideas, increases in proportion to its body's capacity to be acted on, then we cannot understand Spinoza's version of self-determination to imply freedom from determination. Spinoza famously rejects Descartes' version of autonomy as a function of the will's freedom from causal determination. He must do so, since he understands the details of an individual's identity to be determined by its causal history and interactions with others. Spinoza's notion of self-causation does require us to locate all the causes of our emotions within the self, but this should not be construed as a narrowing of the sphere of action to that over which the self can exert direct control. Internalizing the causes of emotions through understanding does not involve insulating the self from exposure to affection. On the contrary, the gradual effort to understand the causes of one's emotions requires attending to the complex history of one's causal and affective interactions. It can thus be said to expand the sphere of selfhood. Spinoza suggests that, like the worm in the blood, our initial perspectival self-awareness inclines us toward a microcosmic view of ourselves as narrowly enclosed and separable from the matrix of causal determinations. From this starting point, however, we may gradually widen our mental focus and, at the same time, ourselves, by including more of what we had initially perceived as "external" to us within us as adequate beliefs about causes. Thus, rather than viewing the complex tangle of relations and emotions in everyday social life as an impediment to autonomy, Spinoza sees it as the very source of our power of activity. Particular emotional reactions provide the occasion for thinking about ourselves in a certain way. If we acquire this habit of reflection we may begin to notice patterns in our emotional lives, which naturally lead us to reflect on the causes of emotions and the logic that governs their operation and, thus, ultimately leads us to a deeper understanding of the whole in which our particular individuality is realized or, in other words, the order of nature itself.

What is missing from this analysis, however, is an account of the conditions that enable us to become increasingly active. It is in his explication of these conditions that Spinoza addresses the issue of how autonomy and sociability are related. I have argued that, in his reflections on the relations between parts and wholes in his philosophy, Spinoza explains the genesis of the illusory idea of the individual as an isolated free chooser. In doing so, he draws our attention to the deleterious effects of this illusion on the individual's capacity for autonomous activity, on the one hand, and on the quality of social relations, on the other, and establishes a link between the two. Atomistic conceptions of individuality give rise to reactive postures of selfhood that contribute to antagonism and discord in interindividual relations. Such conflictual relations increase our passivity and relative powerlessness insofar as they consume our efforts to persevere in the endeavor to defend ourselves. While disagreements and discord can only arise between individuals who have something in common (E, IV, Prop 29), we become less capable of grasping these commonalities and, thus, of increasing our power and freedom, when our relations with others are discordant. In short, in cases of disagreement and conflict, which by definition involve sadness, our capacity to be affected is exercised in a way that diminishes our powers of acting and understanding.

The link established here between the quality of an individual's relationships and the capacity for autonomy follows directly from Spinoza's relational conception of individuality. Because the Spinozist individual encompasses her causal and affective relations, her own bodily and mental thriving will inevitably be influenced by the nature of those individuals with whom she interacts and by the kinds of relations she is able to establish with them. While conflictual relationships continually reduce my power, relations with others based on agreement and commonality enhance my power. Gilles Deleuze has suggested that we can understand the Spinozistic notion of agreement as a form of collaboration that preserves and respects each individual's own relations and world.[29] It is this type of collaboration, which does not suppress others, that Spinoza seems to have in mind when he tells us that there is nothing more useful to us than to join forces with congenial others so as to compose an individual twice as powerful as each one. The establishment of mutually empowering relationships based on cooperation and the combination of individual powers increases the capacity of each individual to preserve and assert itself against adverse external forces. To belong to an association of this type is to be connected to others through relations of agreement, that is, to have one's physical encounters organized in a manner that ensures that, for the most part, individuals will be affected with joy. And since joy, for Spinoza, expresses a relation of agreement between bodies, it aids the mind's power to understand what bodies have in common and so to form an adequate idea of the relations between its own and other bodies. Thus, in Spinoza's view, cooperative relationships that augment the power of all concerned are an enabling condition for the development of each individual's capacity for autonomy and rational activity.[30]

To conceive of autonomy as a capacity that individuals acquire as part of a mutually supportive collectivity is to offer what we would now describe as a causally relational account of autonomy. Most contemporary philosophical treatments of autonomy can be described as causally relational to the extent that they acknowledge the contribution made by certain kinds of social relationships to the realization of those capacities that enable us to act autonomously. Some feminists have argued, however, that it is not enough to construe social relationships as the background requirement for the development of autonomy, since this does nothing to challenge the conflation of autonomy with self-sufficiency, separation from others, and aggressive independence. To resist this confusion, feminists have suggested that we need a *constitutively* relational account of autonomy.[31] To understand autonomy as constitutively relational is to see it as a social trait or process that requires the maintenance of certain sorts of ongoing relations with others. While the kinds of normative concerns about morally responsible conduct that underpin feminist efforts to rethink the relation between autonomy and sociability are alien to Spinoza's philosophy, his treatment of autonomy does rethink this relation in a way that helps to clarify what it might mean to say that autonomy is intrinsically social.

The key to Spinoza's unique contribution to this contemporary debate lies in the manner in which his conception of relational individuality transforms our understanding of social embeddedness. We have seen that the identity of the Spinozist individual is inseparable from her relations with surrounding others, which means that she cannot be conceived as embedded in an external social context from which she might be extricated and still retain her singularity and particularity. But although Spinoza conceives of an individual's identity as a function of the history of her causal and affective relations with the world, this does not prevent him from developing an account of autonomous agency. Etienne Balibar has suggested that it is possible to overcome the apparent tension between autonomous agency and a constitutively relational conception of identity if we abandon the (individualistic) assumption that to be active, or an adequate cause, in Spinoza's sense means to be independent or to act on one's own. According to Balibar we should instead understand the process of becoming active in terms of the effort to establish certain kinds of relationships with others. In support of this reading Balibar points out that "the model of human nature" to which Spinoza refers in the preface to Part IV of the *Ethics* "excludes any individual perfection which *isolates* Man (including the 'free' and 'wise' Man). On the contrary, it is a perfection which equates the growing autonomy of the individual (greater freedom and greater singularity, or uniqueness) with closer association (or 'friendship') with other individuals."[32] Spinoza explicitly links the development of autonomy with the establishment of harmonious social relations in his claim that, if an individual "lives among such individuals as agree with his nature, his power of acting will thereby be aided and encouraged" and, thus, that it is "especially useful to men to form associations, to bind themselves by those bonds most apt to make one people of them, and absolutely, to do those things which serve to strengthen friendships" (E, IV, Appen VII and XII). It is because Spinoza's individual is constitutively rather than merely incidentally social that individual striving for self-empowerment and autonomy must be conceived as a social process, that is, as an effort to build and maintain mutual, reciprocal relationships with others that support and foster this striving for all concerned. Indeed, when Spinoza tells us that those who seek their own advantage under the guidance of reason "want nothing for themselves which they do not desire for other men" (E, IV, Prop 18, Schol), he seems to indicate, contrary to traditional assumptions, that individual striving for self-empowerment or autonomy implies and requires the empowerment and increasing autonomy of others.

Spinoza's contribution to feminist efforts to rethink autonomy derives especially from the way in which his philosophy refigures the relations between parts and wholes as reciprocally determining rather than opposed. It is this conceptual innovation, Balibar argues, that underpins the Spinozist insight that "relationships between individuals which are based on their 'common nature' build up a 'collective' . . . individual *without* suppressing their autonomy."[33] Balibar's interpretation serves to highlight the way in which Spinoza's novel conception of relational individuality serves to unsettle entrenched dichotomies between autonomy and sociability, self-sufficiency and social embeddedness, and separation and connection and, thus, enables him to avoid the pitfalls of both liberal individualism and communitarianism. It is this novel approach to individuality that also enables Spinoza to rethink the relations between autonomy and sociability in a way that lends conceptual support to recent feminist efforts to develop a constitutively relational account of autonomy.

Notes

1. See Jonathan Bennett, *A Study of Spinoza's "Ethics"* (Indianapolis: Hackett, 1984), 306, where he locates "a deep incoherence" in Spinoza's commitment to psychological egoism and to the doctrine of the transpersonal character of the individual.

2. This is the claim that Etienne Balibar makes in his essay "Spinoza: From Individuality to Transindividuality," *Mededelingen vanwege het Spinozahuis* (Delft: Eburon, 1997).

3. Diana Tietjens Meyers, "Intersectional Identity and the Authentic Self? Opposites Attract!" in *Relational Autonomy: Feminist Perspectives on Autonomy, Agency, and the Social Self*, ed. Catriona Mackenzie and Natalie Stoljar (New York: Oxford University Press, 2000), 152.

4. Jennifer Nedelsky, "Reconceiving Autonomy: Sources, Thoughts, and Possibilities," *Yale Journal of Law and Feminism* 1 (1989): 12.

5. For a comprehensive overview and critical discussion of feminist critiques of mainstream conceptions of autonomy, see Catriona Mackenzie and Natalie Stoljar, "Autonomy Refigured," in *Relational Autonomy*, ed. Mackenzie and Stoljar, 5–12.

6. Care critiques of autonomy are typically distinguished from other kinds of feminist critique by virtue of their focus on intimate dyadic relations, particularly between mother and child. I am considering them more broadly in this context as representing the critical claim that autonomy must be reconfigured so that it ceases to be defined in opposition to relations of connection and dependence.

7. Mackenzie and Stoljar, "Autonomy Refigured," 4.

8. For an analysis of the complex relationship between autonomy competencies and the social context of their formation, see Diana Tietjen Myers, *Self, Society, and Personal Choice* (New York: Columbia University Press, 1989) and "Personal Autonomy and the Paradox of Feminine Socialization," *Journal of Philosophy* 84 (1987): 619–28.

9. Nedelsky, "Reconceiving Autonomy," 12.

10. See, for example, Lorraine Code, "Second Persons," in *What Can She Know? Feminist Theory and the Construction of Knowledge* (Ithaca: Cornell University Press, 1991), 78, where she argues that descriptive accounts of human beings as capable of leading self-sufficient, isolated, and independent lives tend to lead to the prescriptive conclusion that the proper end of human endeavor is the achievement of self-sufficient individuality.

11. Mackenzie and Stoljar, "Autonomy Refigured," 17.

12. Ibid. 17.

13. See, for example, Penny Weiss, "Feminism and Communitarianism: Comparing Critiques of Liberalism," in *Feminism and Community*, ed. Penny A. Weiss and Marilyn Friedman (Philadelphia: Temple University Press, 1995); Linda Barclay, "Autonomy and the Social Self," in *Relational Autonomy*, ed. Mackenzie and Stoljar, 52–71.

14. See, for example, Marilyn Friedman, "Autonomy, Social Disruption, and Women," in *Relational Autonomy*, ed. Mackenzie and Stoljar, 35–51.

15. For a critical analysis of the differences between feminist and communitarian approaches to characterizing the social self, see Linda Barclay, "Autonomy and the Social Self," in *Relational Autonomy*, ed. Mackenzie and Stoljar, 52–71. The preceding discussion closely follows Barclay's analysis of the issues.

16. Benedict de Spinoza, "Letter 32 to Oldenburg," in *A Spinoza Reader: The "Ethics" and Other Works*, by Benedict de Spinoza, ed. and trans. Edwin Curley (Princeton: Princeton University Press, 1994), 83.

17. See William Sacksteder, "Spinoza on Part and Whole: The Worm's Eye View," in *Spinoza: New Perspectives*, ed. Robert Shahan and J. Biro (Norman: University of Oklahoma Press, 1978): 139–59.

18. Spinoza, "Letter 32 to Oldenburg," 82.

19. Sacksteder, "Spinoza on Part and Whole," 152.

20. Those who argue that Spinoza's position is methodologically individualist and that his talk of composite individuality should, therefore, be understood metaphorically include Douglas Den Uyl (see *Power, State, and Freedom: An Interpretation of Spinoza's Political Philosophy* [Assen: Van Gorcum, 1983]); Robert McShea (see "Spinoza on Power," *Inquiry* 1, no. 12 [1969]: 133–43); and Lee Rice (see "Individual and Community: Spinoza's Social Psychology," in *Spinoza: New Issues and Directions*, ed. Edwin Curley and Pierre-François Moreau [New York: E. J. Brill, 1990], 195–214).

21. Those who argue that Spinoza's philosophy belongs in the tradition of holism include Alexandre Matheron (*Individu et communauté chez Spinoza* [Paris: Minuit, 1969]) and William Sacksteder (note 17, above, and "Communal Orders in Spinoza," in *Spinoza's Political and Theological Thought*, ed. C. De Deugd [Amsterdam: North-Holland, 1984]).

22. Hans Jonas, "Spinoza and the Theory of the Organism," in *Spinoza: A Collection of Critical Essays*, ed. Marjorie Grene (Garden City, N.Y.: Anchor Books, 1973), 273.

23. Jonas, "Spinoza and the Theory of the Organism," 278.

24. Heidi Ravven discusses the flexible boundaries of the Spinozist individual in her analysis of the status accorded by Spinoza to communal bodies in his earlier and later works. See Heidi M. Ravven, "Spinoza's Individualism Reconsidered: Some Lessons from the *Short Treatise on God, Man, and His Well-Being*," in *Spinoza: Critical Assessments of Leading Philosophers*, vol. 1, ed. Genevieve Lloyd (New York: Routledge, 2001), 387–410.

25. Sacksteder, "Spinoza on Part and Whole," 156.

26. Spinoza defines *affect* as "the affections of the body by which the body's power of acting is increased or diminished, aided or restrained, and at the same time, the ideas of these affections" (E, III, D3).

27. Amelie Oksenberg Rorty, "The Two Faces of Spinoza," *Review of Metaphysics* 41 (1987): 300.

28. For an insightful discussion of the parallels between modern theories of autonomy and Spinoza's account of activity and freedom, see Douglas Den Uyl, "Autonomous Autonomy: Spinoza on Autonomy, Perfectionism, and Politics," *Social Philosophy and Policy* 20, no. 2 (2003): 30–69.

29. See Gilles Deleuze, *Spinoza: Practical Philosophy*, trans. Robert Hurley (San Francisco: City Lights, 1988), 126.

30. For a thoughtful discussion of Spinoza's understanding of the relation between freedom and community, see Susan James, "Power and Difference: Spinoza's Conception of Freedom," *Journal of Political Philosophy* 4 (1996): 206–28. James suggests that, for Spinoza, social relations based on cooperation aid individual freedom both negatively, by protecting individuals from "the kinds of relationships that threaten their power, and positively by contributing to a collective quest for understanding from which everyone benefits" (222).

31. Marilyn Friedman argues that feminist advocates of relational autonomy diverge from mainstream autonomy theorists in their calls for a constitutively or intrinsically social conception of autonomy. She claims that while mainstream theorists acknowledge that social relationships contribute to autonomy, feminists are seeking to develop an account of autonomy as inherently social in its very nature. See Marilyn Friedman, "Autonomy and Social Relationships: Rethinking the Feminist Critique," in *Feminists Rethink the Self*, ed. Diana Tietjens Meyers (Boulder, Colo.: Westview, 1997): 56–58; see also Mackenzie and Stoljar, "Autonomy Refigured," 22.

32. Balibar, "Spinoza: From Individuality to Transindividuality," 24–25.

33. Ibid., 21.

3

Spinoza on the Pathos of Idolatrous Love and the Hilarity of True Love

Amelie Rorty

In memory of Laszlo Versenyi (Hungary, 1929–Williamstown, Mass., 1988)

[In reflecting on love], I was led far beyond my individual life and time, to the point where . . . [I] became no more than an accidental focal point of something much larger; a mere vantage point for seeing and ranging over a landscape that has no clear boundaries.
—Laszlo Versenyi, *Going Home*

Differ as we do about its nature, its causes and effects, its proper objects, we all agree that love is—or can be—the beginning of wisdom. But wisdom about what? Spinoza wrote not only truthfully but wisely about love, about its travails and dangers, about its connection to knowledge and power, about individuality and the disappearance of the self. To understand what is vital and what is mortifying about the passions, to trace the movement from the bondage of passivity to the freedom of activity, we could do no better than follow his investigations. In the nature of the case, each of us necessarily understands him—as we do all else—from the partiality of our own perspectives. We shall follow Ariadne's thread, into the heart of the labyrinth, first speaking with the vulgar, telling fragmentary tales about appearances. Then we must follow the thread out again, thinking with the learned, gaining scientific understanding of what we really are; and finally we must put these two—vulgar appearance and scientific explanation—together to tell the real story, the story of reality.

Speaking with the Vulgar About Appearances: Fragmentary Images of Passivity, Idolatry, Partiality

Spinoza is, first and last, a particularist: The world is composed wholly and entirely of particular individuals, so interrelated that they form a complex individual, a unified system. To understand the pathos of love, we must therefore begin with a particular story; it will, of course, be merely a fragmentary image, only partially true, because it is, perforce, only part of the story. Nevertheless, following it where it must go will bring us to an increasingly adequate understanding of love, of the characters in our story, and of ourselves, as we love. "Ariadne loves Echo, loves him, as she thinks, for the subtlety of his interpretation of Spinoza, for his wry speech, the precision and delicacy of his courtesy, his way of looking at her with those eyes of his, and perhaps most important of all, as is the way of these things, for she knows not what." As Spinoza would see it, Ariadne's love is an elation—a sense of well-being—that she thinks Echo brings her. She feels herself more fully herself, freer to write clearly and fluently, to move gracefully because of him. ("Love is elation accompanied by the idea of an external cause," E, III, Def Aff 6.)[1] But if she thought that her University or a particular landscape were the causes of her elation—her exhilarated enhancement—she would love her University or that landscape. Although each love—indeed each moment of love—is unique, there are as many types of love as there are types of individuals. ("There are as many kinds of . . . love . . . as there are kinds of objects by which we are affected. Any affect of one individual differs from that of another in the extent that the essence of one individual differs from the essence of the other," E, III, Prop 56–57.) The elation of love is the ideational or psychological expression of a change in Ariadne's bodily thriving. Indeed every "affect is a modification of the body by which the body's power is increased or diminished, assisted or checked, together with the ideas of these modifications. If we are the adequate cause of an affect, then the affect is active; if we are not, it is passive" (E, III, D3). So in truth, Ariadne's love is her body's elation, psychologically expressed. To the extent that she thinks of this elation as externally caused, her affect is passive; to the extent that she thinks of it as a function of her own nature, her love is active.

Spinoza's *affectus*—usually translated as "affect" or "emotion"—is obviously a much broader and more encompassing notion than the contemporary class of *emotions* that is commonly contrasted to *beliefs* and *desires*. Affects include desires, wishes, a sense of health or debility: they are ideational indicants of bodily thriving or declining. A condition is passive when its cause is (regarded as) external, active when internal, to the body. So, for instance, a healing process which is a function of the body's own "internal" defensive immune system is a modification of the body, registered in the mind as an active affect; a healing process "externally" produced by medication is a modification of the body, registered in the mind as a passive affect.

So far, so good: Love is a particular sense of health, with a diagnosis of its cause. But troubles soon begin. Elation is an active contrast to a previous state; it must, in its very nature, escalate. ("Elation is . . . a passage or transition from a state of less to a state of greater perfection or vitality" [E, III, Def Aff 2].) Ariadne will try to secure Echo for herself in whatever ways she can, acting to preserve her elation and to oppose or to destroy whatever might bring dejection. ("We endeavor to bring about whatever we imagine to be conducive to elation; [and] endeavor to remove or destroy whatever we imagine to be opposed to it and conducive to dejection" [E, III, Props 26–28].) One of the ways Ariadne will attempt to secure him is to think of him a lot. When Echo is not actually around discussing Spinoza with her, she will have fantasies of their increasing intimacy, an intimacy that would still further enhance and elate her. But she will—she must—go further than fantasy: She will attempt to control Echo so that those aspects of his character that enhance her are strengthened, those that debilitate her are weakened. There is nothing special about love in this; all psychological conditions are active, relational and dynamic. Thoughts and passions alike are individuated in a field of forces. Each individual is so constituted as to attempt to perpetuate and enhance his nature, in relation to other individuals. ("Everything . . . endeavors to persist in its own being. . . . The mind endeavors as far as it can to think of those things that increase or assist the body's power of activity" [E, III, Props 6–9, Prop 12].) Indeed, the details of all an individual's activities in self-preservation, taken together, constitute its *conatus*, its essential nature. A person's thoughts and passions are the traces—the expressions and reflections—of all this activity.

Of course the satisfaction of Ariadne's desires will depend on her psychological canniness, on how well she understands Echo and herself. If Echo does not reciprocate her affections—if that way of looking at her turns out to be nearsightedness, if the intricacies of his interpretations are merely constructed to impress Ariadne in her persona as department head—her love will be short-lived, likely to be replaced by hatred for someone who has diminished her sense of herself. But would Spinoza expect their apparent happiness to continue if Echo returns her affections? The natural story of the best of such love relatively quickly leads to ambivalence, confusion, unhappiness. ("Emotional distress and unhappiness have their origin especially in excessive love towards anything subject to considerable instability, a thing which we can never completely possess. For nobody is disturbed or anxious about any thing unless he loves it, nor do wrongs, suspicions, enmities etc. arise except from love towards things which nobody can truly possess" [E, V, Prop 20, Schol].) Ariadne and Echo are complex people, with complex relations to others. She has her work, he has his; she has one set of friends, he has another. Their relations to one another are necessarily affected by the constant and subtle changes in their interactions with the rest of the world. If their friends and acquaintances endorse their mutual esteem, their love will, for a time, be reinforced. But if their common acquaintances do not respect Echo, Ariadne's love will be weakened. If, on the other hand, he is commonly thought to be too good for her, she will begin to fear—and to perceive—a change in his attentions. When his affection fluctuates, her sense of assurance falters, her grace and style crack. She will sense herself diminished and her estrangement will begin.

In loving Echo, Ariadne comes to redefine her relations to the rest of the world: Her interactions with others will be mediated, skewed by how she imagines they affect Echo and above all by how they affect Echo's relation to her. She will love what she believes enhances his love for her, hate what endangers it, become jealous of what draws his attentions away from her, envy those whom Echo envies. It is this feature of love—that it generates tangential, perspectivally fragmented relations to the world—that makes it especially blinding. The bondage of Ariadne's passive love ramifies beyond her perspectivally distorted perceptions of the complexities of Echo's qualities to similar distortions about the complex qualities of all that interacts with Echo.

For their happiness to continue, their constant changes must remain in harmony. Each must exactly register and adapt to the constant transformations in the other, and those transformations must remain mutually enhancing. Ariadne's growing reputation must somehow stand in continuous harmony with the changes that affect Echo, the reviews of his commentary on Spinoza, the adoration of his women students. As we fill in the familiar details of such stories, it becomes harder and harder to imagine the two continuing to enhance one another. How do they perceive one another's attentions to the rest of the world? Every unshared moment of delight becomes the occasion for fear, envy and jealousy. Every shared moment introduces a subtle struggle for power. But even if all goes well—and of course if it does, we have moved from a familiar story to a fairy story—things are at best precarious. Every moment of love occurs within a larger context. But since affects that are accidentally associated remain associated, the elation of love readily becomes linked with a sense of debility. ("Anything can accidentally be the cause of elation, dejection or desire" [E, III, Prop 15]. "If the mind has once been affected by two passions at the same time, when it is later affected by one it will also be affected by the other" [E, III, Prop 14].) For instance, if Ariadne tended Echo during an illness, comforted him during some disappointment, or protected him from his crippling sense of insecurity, his affection will remind him of debilities that he naturally prefers to forget. It gets harder and harder to prevent elation from sliding to ambivalence, and ambivalence from sliding to the disintegration that is associated with erratic and vacillating impulsive movements. Any love that focuses on a particular individual is idolatrous; and because idolatrous love is fetishistic and partial, it inevitably brings ambivalence and frustration.

Ariadne's natural vitality will combat disintegration; she straightway moves to preserve herself, to overcome pathology in whatever way she can. Of course she has ways to combat debility; indeed she'd have disintegrated long ago if she'd not been naturally constructed and organized in such a way as to overcome debility, to preserve her integrity. Ariadne could not be cured of envy, jealousy, fear, just by trying to stop loving Echo. After all, every chance joy and enhancement brings love with it. She must in some way go to the root of the matter of her dreadful and tiresome tendency to fall in love, always and invariably, time and again, to fall in love. Nor—however tempting that might seem—will it help her to attempt to transform her love to contempt, disdain, hate. As love is a sense of enhancement, of elation, hate is a sense of dejection, accompanied by an idea of its cause (E, III, Def App, 7). But no one can be enhanced by an affect that is itself an expression of a variety of diminution.

Ariadne can only redirect her passive love through a more powerful emotion. ("An affect or emotion cannot be checked or destroyed except by a contrary emotion which is stronger than the emotion to be checked" [E, IV, Prop 7].) It will not help Ariadne to love a more powerful person, (say) Abraham, or to acquire a more dominating passion, for (say) fame, or a passion for a more stable object, (say) Sung vases. All idolatry—any focus on a single object—brings the miseries of pathology in its wake. Love is love, with the same structure and the same consequences, even if each moment of elation is uniquely determined by the details of that moment. If she is astute, Ariadne will know that she cannot avoid the disintegration of one pathological love by finding another.

Thinking with the Learned About the Structure of Appearances: From the Bondage of Passivity to the Freedom of Activity

Let us suppose that Ariadne is psychologically canny, that she has considerable natural endowments—some of them constitutional, some acquired by the fortune of her upbringing. Central among them is a certain capacity for and energy toward clarity in reflection. She knows that idolatrous love, focused on a particular individual, necessarily involves misperception. Not that Echo wasn't what he seemed: He did have a wry turn of mind; he did have a sound understanding of Spinoza. But in fact the elation he first brought her was not just a function of *his* character: it was, rather, the expression of the fit between his traits *and* hers. Had she been the star of a hard rock music group, she'd not have been charmed by Echo's charms. Since she is canny—and this is just what it means to be canny, neither more nor less—she has a hunger for further explanations, an active passion for understanding. In fact her hunger for further explanation is another way of expressing her activity in integration, her moving from the debilities of love and its consequences. That hunger, her reflections, her drive to integrity are all different ways of describing the same thing: the active energies exercised in preserving and enhancing her existence.

Explanation-hungry as she is, Ariadne has also come to realize a number of things about herself and Echo: that she and Echo—and anyone or anything else she might love—are complex, constantly changing, compounded entities. Every aspect of their individuality is affected by their interactions with other equally historically conditioned, dynamic individuals. The details of all these interactions are themselves expressions and reflections of the details of their past history, the active traces, as it were, of many different layers of previous interactions, stretching far beyond their individual lives. Echo's interest in Spinoza expresses his grandmother's attitudes toward the world; his eyes and the look of his eyes reflect his biological inheritance. Ariadne's own penchant for fellows with a wry turn of mind derives from some of her childhood attachments, and the timbre of her voice reflects not only her constitution but also her family's passion for folksongs. Gradually, Ariadne comes to see herself and Echo in a different light. In fact, she begins to suspect—though she has as yet no way of making this suspicion anything but a vague hunch— that she and Echo just *are* the active traces of all that has happened to them, stretching far backward before their births, and far outward to distant interactive individuals. She gives up her idolatrous modes of thinking about Echo and herself as "closed and bounded entities" and instead comes to think of all individuals as complex, dynamic compounds, individuated by their history and their interactions. By changing her thoughts in this way, Ariadne's image-ideas have become reflective ideas, ideas which, besides including their direct objects, also include reflections on the relations between the idea of their direct objects and other ideas. So in thinking of Echo, Ariadne now thinks of the inter-relations between her ideas of Echo and her ideas of her brother, his grandparents, folksongs of a certain era; in thinking of herself, she now thinks of her ideas of Echo, of her grandmother, and so on.

All of these reflections give her some relief from ambivalence and its inevitably erratic behavior. Because she has traced the disparate sources of the various strands that have formed Echo, she has dispersed the intensity of her attachment. Since she now sees Echo as a mediating transmitter rather than as a Substance, her idea of the causes of her elation has correspondingly changed. The train of associated passions—fear, envy, jealousy—is deflected by this change. Her greater understanding gives her an increased sense of her own powers; and her new sense of power gives her a new source for elation. She has, for one thing, turned inadequate ideas—images—into increasingly adequate ideas. In following her own nature, in affirming the truth about its history and constitution, she has become active rather than passive. She is, in fact, active in exactly the degree to which her ideas are adequate rather than inadequate. Instead of imagining herself to be the recipient of the benefits of Echo's charms, she actively identifies herself with the system of interactive causes that have determined her. In so affirming her identity, she recognizes that what she had thought of as a passive passion, a modification produced by an external cause, actually in part also proceeds from her own nature. ("Insofar as the mind has adequate ideas, it is necessarily active; insofar as it has inadequate ideas, it is necessarily passive" [E, III, Prop 1]. "We are active when something takes place in us or externally to us of which we are the adequate cause, that is, when it follows from our nature. . . . We are passive when something takes place in us, of which we are only the partial cause" [E, III, D2]. "The more active a thing is, the more perfect it is" [E, V, Prop 40].)

It now seems as if Ariadne's original passive elation—her love of Echo—is as nothing in comparison to the active elation she has in discovering the real nature of individuals, in understanding how she and Echo came to interact as they did. ("The greater the number of causes that simultaneously concur in arousing an emotion, the greater the emotion" [E, V, Prop 8].) There is no better cure for idolatry than the analysis of its causes and objects, no better cure for the fetishism of idolatry than its dispersed and ramified redistribution. But the movement that locates the particular in its place in a pattern loses neither the particularity nor love: it transforms inadequacy into adequacy, passivity into activity.

We've talked as if Ariadne's discoveries and reflections are things *she* did in attempting to persevere, to integrate herself. In a way that is right; Ariadne's nature just is of this kind: She is psychologically canny and historically reflective. Her researches, inquiries, and reflections are, however, just as much an expression of—a determination of—her constitution and her history as are the timbre of her voice and her taste for wry minds. Her insight has—and does not have—a special status. In one sense, she neither generates nor controls it; for it, too, follows from the interactive nexus of individuals. Even her insight is nothing more (or less) than the complex and dynamic active traces of her genetic constitution and personal history. Still, if she is so fortunate as to be an active inquirer, her insight is more expressive of her nature than is the timbre of her voice or her taste for wry minds. The centrality of insight is not (alas) assured because insight lasts longer than the timbre of a voice. Treated as facts, both are timeless and unchangeable; treated as properties, both are contingent, susceptible to disease and debility. Insight does not cure or prevent senility; nor does it empower an individual mind by elevating it to transcendent objects. It is nothing more (or less) than the detailed activity of integrating ideas. It consists of painstakingly putting two and two together, and then tracing the functions of four in the system of natural numbers. There is nothing more mystical to it than that: The power of a mind is expressed in its comprehensive activity in integration.

In pursuing her liberation from the pathology of love, Ariadne is not a *homuncula* somewhere at the center of her essence, willing herself to be whole and intact, directing the strategies designed to free her from the disintegrative suffering of love. Ariadne knows better; she knows that she does not will the direction of energy. Just as Echo is not the only begetter of her elation, so too she is not the only begetter of her liberation. All these active reflections are just the fortune of her history and interactions, working in and through her. Even her realization that she necessarily is (no more and) no less than the totality of the accidents of her history and her interactions is the fortune of her history and interactions. If she has the good fortune to identify herself *with* and *as* all those dynamic interactions which have made her who she is, she will no longer think of herself as having been formed *by* them, as if she could mysteriously have been the same essential core, with a different history. Her characteristics will follow from her nature because they *are* her nature. This reflection is not a further thought; it is just the self-conscious realization of the connected significance of all the thoughts that she is.

Ariadne's conception of herself—her idea of her mind as a structure of ideas—is exactly coordinate with her conception of the boundaries that distinguish her essence from those of other individuals. It therefore exactly defines the scope of her passive affects, those she imagines to be externally caused, in contrast to her active affects, those that she thinks of as following from her nature. A person's passions are functions of her conceptions of her essential nature. It is ambiguous and misleading to say that a person bent on liberation from the pathology of passion must transform and enlarge her conception of her individuality. It suggests that there are two distinct lines of thought, one's conception of oneself on the one hand, and the range of one's affects on the other. But these are different ways of describing the same thing. To have a clearer conception of oneself just *is* to have turned and to be turning passive into active affective states, seeing them as parts of one's nature rather than as invasions. To recommend a better conception of oneself misleadingly suggests that there is a core person deciding to correct her self-image. But these processes of correction are just the various strands in the person's complex nature, expressing themselves in the many ways a complex *conatus* acts to persist in its own nature.

As we have told it so far, the story of Ariadne's increased awareness of the complex dynamic relations between herself and Echo is, in every sense of the word, a vulgar story. But in her larger understanding, Ariadne sees that there is a tale of necessity within every vulgar story. The vulgar story of love—with its trials and tribulations—is told in a very confused and as we might say, provisional language, within the realm of *imaginatio*. It is partial, fragmentary. Even Ariadne's increased self-awareness is, as the story first unfolds, a case of narrative discovery, tracing more and more of the vast expanding network of the historical and relational details that determine Echo and herself. The language of psychological canniness, even that of historical astuteness is still quite inadequate to express the deeper structures of these appearances. If Ariadne follows Spinoza's therapeutic recommendations in liberating herself from passive love, she detaches her love from her confused imagistic thought of Echo, and concentrates instead on understanding how her emotions formed an interdependent pattern. First she might think of family histories and family resemblances; then she begins to form rough generalizations about academics and men, about the relation between love and dependence, weakness and fear, envy and jealousy. ("The power of the mind over the emotions consists in . . . detaching the affect from the thought of their external cause, which we imagine confusedly; and in . . . knowing the . . . order and connection among the affects" [E, V, Prop 20, Schol].) Actively engaging in this sort of sociopsychological investigation helps Ariadne become less prey to the demons of associated passive affects. She becomes actively thoughtful. Although such rough generalizations are, to be sure, genuinely central to understanding Ariadne's condition, we—and if she is fortunate, she—can get further.

Ariadne's active elation in the power of her psychological and historical understanding can be still further enhanced by her understanding of biology and eventually of mathematical physics. Before we have a full understanding of Ariadne's love, and before we return the particularity of

Ariadne's love to her, we must stop speaking with the vulgar and leave appearances and the language of appearances behind. In truth, Ariadne and Echo are human bodies, organisms delicately and dynamically structured in such a way as to conserve and preserve their continuing complex activities in their interactions with other bodies surrounding them. Organic processes are themselves expressions of the activities of basic entities, the simple particulars (*corpora simplicissima*) of which the world is composed, no more, no less. The organization and activity of human bodies—the interactions between Ariadne, Echo, and other bodies—are functions of the dynamic interactions among the *corpora simplicissima* that compose them (E, II, Prop 13).

In truth, then, Ariadne and Echo (it is now more appropriate to ignore their individual histories and to call them A and E) are compound bodies whose properties are functions of the character of extension. Their individual minds—that is, their ideas of themselves and of one another—are ideas of the ideas of their bodies. More fully and adequately understood, the order of Ariadne's ideas—the rationale of her thoughts and affects—is the same as the order of the properties of bodies. ("The order and connection of ideas is the same as the order and connection of things.... The ... human mind is basically nothing else but the idea of an individual actually existing thing.... The object of the idea constituting the human mind is the body, a definite mode of extension, and nothing else.... The idea which constitutes ... the human mind is nothing simple, but composed of very many ideas" [E, II, Prop 7, Props 11–13, Prop 15].) What A knows of herself—in contrast to what she may imagine—is a set of ideas of the condition of a compound body (vulgarly called *hers*) which is itself a reflection of the interaction between her compound body and other sections of extension, including that compound vulgarly called Echo. What she knows of the world, she knows only through her body; her ideas are just the intellectual articulations of bodily states. Yet Spinoza's psychophysicalism is not reductive, but corelative. Relations among ideas are the articulations of the relations among parts of extension; and the relational properties of extension are the expressions—the spatial projections—of the relational structures of ideas. The properties of extension can only be characterized, can only be expressed as relations among ideas; but the relations among ideas are just the expressions of the dynamic properties of extension, nothing more and nothing less. Spinoza's insistence on the relational and dynamic character of both thought and extension preserves him from sliding into a reductivist position, either on the side of materialism or on that of idealism.

For all its graces, A's mind is nothing special. All her ideas—including her love and other affects or emotions—are articulations, expressions of the activities of her body. But that body—that relatively self-preserving organism—is, like every other extended individual, an active nexus of *corpora simplicissima* interrelated, concatenated in such a way that they preserve a particular ratio of motion and rest. Some of the central properties of A's body are properties which she has in common with all other bodies: They are properties that are as attributable to any part of her as they are to the whole of her, attributable to any part of extension as they are to the whole of extension (E, II, Prop 37). Now since the order of extension is necessarily expressed in ideas, A's mind necessarily has (is in part composed of) self-evident ideas of these common properties of extension. Her body is composed of these properties; and her ideas are ideas of the properties of her body. Since such common ideas are not fragmentary or perspectival, not qualified by their dependence on other ideas—since they are ideas of the properties of *every* body—they are adequate, necessarily and self-evidently true (E, II, Props 38–40). Like every idea, common ideas are relational, determined by their interconnection in the system of ideas. But since common ideas are universally instantiated, the ideas which determine them are identical to them. The grounds or conditions for common ideas are therefore represented within them; and since they are the bearers of their own determination, they are self-evident. Since A's power and activity is a function of the adequacy of her ideas, her power—her elation—is increased by her knowledge of the unqualifiedly necessary properties of bodies.

Every individual mind has (is partially composed of) a set of adequate ideas of extension, the common notions that express "her" body, as they do every body. To the extent that she focuses on these adequate ideas, A has a more adequate understanding of her relation to E than she has from her psychological and historical understanding, which at best forms a contingent narrative, a set of generalizations from likely stories. The common notions of mathematical physics take A beyond psychological and historical insight to *ratio*, to a necessary and deductive scientific demonstrative science of extension. All that was particular—that is, all that was merely conditional and perspectival—about Echo and herself, and all the sound but incomplete generalizations of folk psychology and history can now be supplemented by a rigorously deductive science. A now has a much more powerful idea of her own mind, because she now has placed her idea of her mind in a system of interrelated ideas: She knows *what it is to be a mind*. In focusing on these adequate ideas, in bringing them to light, she has in a sense enlarged her mind; she not only has a clear idea of how things are, but also why they are like that. She now has two quite different types of explanations of the phenomena. The first was afforded by the reflections that moved her from confused images to psychological and historical generalizations. The second is afforded by the rationally demonstrative science of extension.

In a sense A is no longer merely the passive person she was. As a mind which has realized her adequate ideas of itself, she affirms what necessarily follows from her nature. As a psychological historian, she affirmed herself as the active traces of all that made her what she is: acknowledging herself as identical with what—the world being what it is—she was caused to become. But as a mathematical physicist, A is the active expression of principles much more powerful than the relatively finite temporal incidents in the life of Ariadne and Echo, even as they might be extended to their ancestors and their communities. Her idea of herself—which was in any case nothing more than the idea of the nexus of her ideas of her body (E, II, Prop 15)—now includes an idea of herself as a systematically organized set of adequate ideas. Her idea of her mind is still exactly correlated with her idea of its "boundaries." Insofar as she is a mind composed of adequate ideas of the properties common to every part of extension, she does not conceive of anything falling outside her boundaries, her nature. Although all properties—including those that are universally instantiated—are relational, the interdependence of common properties does not make them conditional; they interact with properties that are exactly identical to them. It is for this reason that, despite their place in the nexus of ideas, adequate ideas can be self-evident. They are conditional on something identical with them.

A is active to the extent—but only to the extent—that she identifies herself as a mind composed of adequate ideas. What a powerful and integrated system of adequate ideas (and their logical consequences) she now is! The crude psychological egoism with which Ariadne began—the egoism sketched in the first, preliminary accounts of *conatus*—is by now strikingly modified, reinterpreted. The power of Ariadne's *conatus* is expressed in its actively expanding its original, narrow, and necessarily defensive conception of its boundaries. The more narrowly defined is an individual's conception of her boundaries, the more readily is she overcome by the vast number of external forces. But the more broadly she identifies herself with other free rational minds, the more actively powerful she becomes: Her nature is not then bounded by, but agrees with others (E, IV, Props 35–37). "It is of first importance to (men) to establish close relationships (with other rational men) and to bind themselves together . . . unite(d) in one body . . . to act in such a way as to strengthen friendship" (E, IV, Appen, 12).

Compared to the exhilaration of *this* rationally extended sense of her activity and action, the elation of Ariadne's original relation to Echo—even as it became extended to her activities as an inquirer into the constitution and history—was really child's play. What elation can Echo bring to A, who identifies herself with other free, rational citizens who recognize universal and timeless truths about the basic structure of Nature? After all, modestly speaking, without any trace of megalomania, she now sees that as part of an aspect of God, she cannot be enhanced or diminished by the flotsam and jetsam of *la vie quotidienne*.

We have skipped and condensed quite a bit, but in any case, we are far from through. First of all there is the extremely difficult question of just how A came to realize her adequate ideas, how she came to have a more adequate idea of herself as a mind composed of both adequate ideas and a history of confused ideas. After all, what is self-evident—even what is demonstrated as self-evident—is not always obvious. Even if A timelessly was the person she—as we confusedly say—came to be, how did the timeless story come to be just what it always was, a timeless story that seems to have *befores* and *afters* and *becauses*? Even if Ariadne's intellectual biography provides a psychohistorical answer to that question, can there be a properly scientific answer to it? It is all very well to say that A's complex condition can be explained backward historically, and outward by a nexus of interactive causes. Can it also be generated downward from adequate ideas of common properties? Having fully adequate ideas, can A demonstrate the particular set of events that caused and constituted her loving Echo? Can she have adequate ideas about such contingent, conditional matters, rather than relatively vague generalizations about the nature of love in this or that historical era? Evidently not, for it is impossible to deduce particular temporal events from ideas that are by definition common to absolutely every event. But doesn't this mean that the promise of explanation—and therefore the promise of freedom—was false, a misleading confused premise? To answer these rhetorical questions, we must move from *ratio* to *scientia intuitiva*, the highest level of knowledge that grasps the interconnections of individual essences within one unified system.

Having It All: Back to Love with Vulgarity and Learning

What happened to the confusions of the imagination, perceptions, rough generalizations, passive affects? Have they utterly disappeared? How do we preserve the particularity of appearances with which we began? What happened to individual essences and the essence of individuality? If confused ideas of the boundaries among individuals are necessary, isn't there a sense in which a timeless understanding of the order of things—of the whole of reality—must include a timeless understanding of these partial and confused appearances? And what happened to love, to the promised *hilaritas* of true love?

Ariadne has not, thank god, been transformed into a pure abstract mind, a divine geometer, not Spinoza's Ariadne, at any rate. She is, was, and will be the *particular* very finite collection of ideas reflecting a particular body. All A's mathematical knowledge of the *corpora simplicissima* is knowledge of the properties that are *common* to all bodies. Those properties—and the ideas of those properties—are still particular. What distinguishes them from other particular ideas is simply their universality and their self-evident necessity. So in having adequate ideas, in becoming actively affected, A is still Ariadne, and she still loves. For that matter she still loves Echo; but her active love is a far, far better love than she has ever loved before. It is, of course, not better in being purer or more self-sacrificing; nor scandalously, is it more perfect. Indeed on the contrary, far from being purer, it is more comprehensive in every sense of that term. Not only does she love Echo, but she loves Echo-as-a-particular-expression-of-the-vast-network-of-individuals that have affected him; through him, she loves all that has made him. Far from being self-sacrificing, her active love of Echo—now more truly, adequately understood by her—is self-expressing. In loving him, she loves herself. Nor is her truthful love more perfect, because *the idea of perfection is an inadequate idea*, formed from a fragmented, particular perspective.

It is time to unwrap Spinoza's irony. Ariadne's liberation has been described as a movement to greater perfection. That's vulgar talk. (In truth "Men are accustomed to call natural things perfect or imperfect more from prejudice than from true knowledge of those things.... Nature does nothing on account of an end.... Perfection and imperfection are only modes of thinking, that is, notions we are accustomed to feign when we compare individuals of the same species to one another.... Insofar as we attribute something to them that involves negation,—like a limit, an end or lack of power—, we call them imperfect, because they do not affect our mind as much as those we call perfect, not because something is lacking in them which is theirs" [E, IV, Pref]. "Nothing happens in nature which can be attributed to a defect in it" [E, III, Pref].) The idea of perfection is a mote in the eye of the perceiver, an idea which—like all other ideas—is a reflection of the order of things. But it is a confused and partial idea. In truth, since each thing is what it must be, nothing is, in and of itself, either less or more than it is or can be. Seen in this way, Ariadne's pathological love, necessitated as it was by the order of things, could not have been a *defect* in her.

All along Ariadne is, even with her transformation into a psycho-historian and mathematical physicist, a particular interactive finite body, a particular finite system of ideas. Now we saw that rational demonstration—the system that expresses the relations among adequate ideas—is not hospitable to such variables as *Ariadne*, let alone *Ariadne's love of Echo at a particular time*. How can the *corpora simplicissima* that compose A and E rub together to produce the explosion of a particular love? Increasing the number of *corpora* to form compounds does not increase their explanatory power, nor does increasing the complexity of the relations between their respective ratios of motion and rest. There can be no mathematical demonstration that concludes with Ariadne's love for Echo. Yet she did passively love Echo, and that passive love was interactively necessitated. ("Inadequate and confused ideas follow by the same necessity as adequate or clear ideas" [E, II, Prop 36].) Although A's rational knowledge as a mathematician gives her necessary knowledge of what she has in common with all other bodies, it cannot, in the nature of the case, provide a demonstration of the necessity of her confused, inadequate, partial, perspectival ideas. ("Whatever ideas follow in the mind from adequate ideas are also adequate" [E, II, Prop 40].) It should not be surprising that we cannot derive the dynamic, relational, historical particular from what is timeless, necessary, and invariant.

Fortunately there is, besides psycho-historical knowledge and mathematical physics, yet another knowledge—*scientia intuitiva*—which combines the other two in a single active act of understanding. *Scientia intuitiva* involves apprehending the vast system, the network of particular individuals (including of course all the properties they have in common) as a unified individual. Since there is no such thing as abstract Being as such, *scientia intuitiva* is not mystical insight into the abstract nature of Being. On the contrary, this insight preserves all particularity: reflective ideas—ideas of ideas—retain their particularity when they are systematically interconnected to form the increasingly more encompassing particular that is A's individual mind. (As, for instance, the *corpora simplicissima* of which A's body is composed retain their particularity even though they are organized to form another individual, Ariadne's body.) A cannot have an adequate idea of Echo, treated merely as a finite mode, an isolated fragment of the world; but since she can have increasingly adequate ideas of him as part of the system of ideas, and since she can treat the system of her ideas as a particular, she can have *scientia intuitiva* of the unified system of which Echo is a fragment. (Compare: While there is no *ratio* (scientific knowledge) of a particular corpuscle of hemoglobin, taken in isolation as a fragment of extension, there is scientific knowledge of hemoglobin, treated as a functional part of organic systems. Going beyond the *ratio* of discursive biochemistry, *scientia intuitiva* fuses all that is discretely encompassed by *ratio*, recognizing that it forms a unity, a particular individual.)

How does intuitive insight—psycho-historical knowledge and demonstrative rationality all wrapped into a bundle and seen as a unified, self-sustaining, self-evident whole—free us? It is, as are all ideational states, the expression of a bodily condition, one in which the body is, as it were, enlarged because "the individual body" is no longer artificially separated as a bounded, separate entity. Nevertheless, each condition of any "particular part" of extension necessarily has the properties it has, by virtue of its interconnections with all other parts. So the sense of boundary—Ariadne's experiencing herself as a bounded particular individual—is *itself* the necessary outcome, the expression of all that exists, no more and no less. Ariadne's passivity and defensiveness are, despite their being confused and conditional ideas, necessary (E, II, Prop 36). When she realizes this, she actively rather than passively preserves all the details of her individuation because she recognizes that those details, too, follow from her nature (E, V, Prop 27). Ariadne actively expresses rather than passively suffers whatever follows from the necessities of her nature; so Ariadne does not *suffer* the pathology of love, the Goyaesque furies of any passive passion. Does that mean that she will not suffer ambivalence, envy, fear, despair? Well, yes, she will not passively suffer the Goyaesque furies; but, depending on her circumstances and conditions, she may nevertheless enact some of them.

Like all Stoics, including Freud, Spinoza speaks with forked tongue about whether those who have reached the most active and comprehensive knowledge have no passive love, ambivalence, and the rest of the furies. On the one hand, those passions are, even in their experienced passivity, *necessary* natural events. On the other hand, "The truth shall make you free" is absolutely true; and there is, in principle, absolutely no barrier between any individual and truth. Affects that follow from adequate ideas are not passive, and at least some affects only follow from inadequate ideas. An individual is free and active just to that degree that she has adequate ideas. ("If we remove an agitation of the mind, or emotion, from the thought of its external cause and join it to other thoughts, then . . . the vacillations that arise from these affects will be destroyed. . . . There is no affection of the body of which we cannot form a clear and distinct conception" [E, V, Prop 2, Prop 4].) Can Ariadne turn all her inadequate ideas into fully adequate ideas? It seems not; but if she is fortunate, she can make them more adequate, and if she is even more fortunate, she can focus primarily on her adequate ideas. ("[If *scientia intuitiva*] does not absolutely remove passive affects, it at least brings it about that they constitute the smallest part of the mind" [E, V, Prop 20, Schol].)

But we have in a way been dodging the real question. Does knowledge always liberate us from suffering? What are we to make of all our wise friends whose love is passive and who suffer in loving? Here Spinoza reveals his Socratic face: Not all those who mouth knowledge genuinely have it. In the first place, *being able to discourse fluently* isn't necessarily *knowing*. Only knowledge that pervades a person's psychology and that expresses an appropriate bodily state counts as real knowledge. Knowledge is not an attitude toward propositional content: To know p is to engage in a vast number of activities of integrating p within a system of ideas, beliefs, desires. Unless an intellectual attitude really transforms the way a person thinks and acts, it does not qualify as knowledge. (Compare: Knowing a mathematical technique is not merely a matter of being able to state and defend it clearly. To qualify as knowing a technique, one must actually use it in constructions and proofs.)

In the second place, not everyone who wishes to know, not everyone who dreams of *scientia intuitiva* is in a position—a constitutional, and psychohistorical position—to have it. Whether or not a particular bit of understanding succeeds in being knowledge at any given time is—like everything else—a function of person, time, and circumstance. It is not only our own activity, but our activity in dynamic relation to what surrounds us that determines our condition. ("The force and growth of any passion . . . are not defined by the power by which we strive to persevere in existing, but by the power of an external cause compared with our own" [E, IV, Prop 5]. "It is necessary to come to know both our nature's power and its lack of power to determine what reason can do—and what it cannot do—in moderating the affects" [E, IV, Prop 17, Schol].) In any case, even our wisest friends are finite individual minds, composed of a mixture of adequate and inadequate ideas. ("The human mind does not involve an adequate knowledge of the component parts of the body . . . [or] of an external body" [E, II, Props 24–31]. "Desire which arises from knowledge of good and evil insofar as it concerns future . . . or contingent things . . . can be easily restrained by desires for things which are present" [E, IV, Props 16–17].) Starkly, not even A—that superb mathematical physicist—is, at any and every moment of her life, focused only on her adequate ideas, let alone engaged in *scientia intuitiva*. Although compared individually adequate ideas and active passions are much more powerful than inadequate ideas and their corresponding passive passions, a large number of inadequate ideas and passive passions can deflect the directions of active desires.

In the third place, we should not confuse suffering with *suffering*. When Spinoza contrasts activity with passivity, freedom with bondage, he does not identify—though he does associate—passivity and bondage with *pain*. To begin with, many passive affects are delightful. And by Spinoza's lights, however uncomfortable they may be, healthy growing pains are not *sufferings*, unless an adolescent thinks of his body as an external cause of his condition. Similarly, the hardships of difficult thought are not sufferings, unless a scholar thinks of himself as invaded or obsessed by them.

But what, you may ask, is the point of being free? Why isn't mucking along in trouble and travail, in ambivalence and uncertainty, in the pathology of idolatry, fragmentation, and fetishism good enough? Since that is what the particularity of life is, and since there is nothing but particularity, why want more? Maybe life is not directed to the hilarity of integration, but just to living. In a way, Spinoza agrees. It is not a question of striving for a better, nobler form of life. We each live according to the life force within us. Those whose constitution and circumstances make them relatively vulnerable to forces they experience as external to them will indeed suffer love and hate. Others are, by the fortune of their situation, capable of what liberation their circumstances allow. In any case, both those who are relatively passively weak and those who are relatively actively strong alike attempt to live as fully as they can. There is no teleology in the matter, no salvation, and in a way, no liberation. We are what we are no matter what. We *are* the extent and manner of our striving toward harmonic integration.

Still, be that as it must be, Spinoza thinks that liberated love is superior to bonded love: Wise lovers are not only more joyous, but more effective and beneficent than unenlightened lovers. How do the wise act on behalf of those they love? To be sure, they desire to unite with what they love. But that is, according to Spinoza, a consequence rather than the essential definition of love (E, III, Def App 6, Exp). In any case that desire does not define any particular action; it might, for instance, generate civic as well as sexual unity and harmony. Ariadne's desire to unify herself with Echo is a desire to conjoin her own welfare with his to form a single well-structured whole (E, IV, Props 35–37, Props 62–66). But passive love generates a desire to control, rather than to act on behalf of a common good. Promoting the real—rather than the partial and imagined—welfare of an extended self properly arises from a rational recognition of interdependence (E, IV, Prop 73). Since passive love is ambivalent, mingled with hate and envy, disdain, and fear, the behavior that expresses it will be erratic, each moment undermining the next. Well-formed action arises only from well-formed attitudes, from adequate ideas.

And the hilarity, the promised hilarity of true love? True love is the elation that comes of true knowledge, an intuitive grasp of the world, seen as a whole, immanent within one's ideas. Because such love is the expression of an individual's most vital activity, it carries the greatest possible self-realization. But an elation that affects the individual as a whole *is* hilarity (E, III, Prop 11, Schol). Like true knowledge, hilarity can never be excessive; when it is seen as actively following from an individual's own nature, it can never bring bondage in its wake (E, IV, Prop 42).[2]

Notes

1. I have used two translations, turning sometimes to E. M. Curley, *The Collected Works of Spinoza*, vol. 1 (Princeton: Princeton University Press, 1985) and sometimes to Samuel Shirley, *The Ethics*, ed. Seymour Feldman (Indianapolis: Hackett, 1982). But I have also substituted some translations of my own. Rather than following Shirley's *pleasure* or Curley's *joy*, I render *laetitia* as *elation* because I believe that it better captures Spinoza's view that love, like other affects, is an expression of a *change*, an increase, in the body's powers or vitality. Spinoza distinguishes two varieties of *laetitia*: *titillatio* and *hilaritas*. Titillation involves an increase of activity or power in one part of the body more than in another (the early stages of sexual excitation, for example); *hilaritas* marks an increase in vitality that affects all parts of the body equally (radiant health, for example). The corresponding distinctions for varieties of *tristitia*, which I translate as *dejection* (rendered by Shirley as *pain* and by Curley as *sadness*) are *dolor* (pain), a change which affects one part of the body more than another (a wound, for example), and *melancholia*, a change which affects all parts equally (anemia, for example). Spinoza undertakes to show that all affects arise from the three basic affects of elation, dejection, and desire (E, III, Prop 11, Schol).

2. I am grateful to Alan Hart for detailed, incisive comments, to Tom Cook and Genevieve Lloyd for many illuminating conversations. This paper was prepared for a conference on "Theoretical Perspectives on Love and Friendship" at the National Center for the Humanities. I enjoyed and benefited from Tom Hill's acute and searching discussions. Annette Baier helpfully suggested some issues that needed elaboration: Spinoza's avoidance of both reductive materialism and reductive idealism, and the problem of how the adequate ideas of common notions can be both relational and self-evident. Martha Nussbaum pressed me to give an account of the directions—and the limits—of what she sees as Spinoza's psychological egoism.

4

Spinoza and Sexuality

Alexandre Matheron

According to common opinion, Spinoza's writings about sexual love were nothing more than lamentable platitudes, narrowly inspired by the prejudices of his time and without serious philosophical foundation. That for which in the past he was congratulated is now cause for reproach or, at best, excuses.[1] Some even believe that he raised the stakes on the prevailing puritanism of his time: sexuality as such aroused in him a profound repulsion and women horrified him. If we limit ourselves to the manifest content of the texts, the second of these two assertions has no real foundation. If we invoke their latent content, to establish it with a minimum of rigor would require a study the theoretical possibility of which we do not dispute but that in fact has not yet been undertaken. The first assertion, by contrast, has all the appearance of the obvious: there seems to be nothing particularly sensational in the idea that men love women for their beauty and do not support their attachment to someone else (TP, XI, 137),[2] that the more admirers they have the more they desire them (E, III, Prop 31), that the jealousy of the male is exacerbated by the representation of the *pudenda* (shameful parts) and of the *excrementa* (excretions) of his rival (E, III, Prop 35, Schol), that sensual attachment is unstable and conflictual (E, IV, Appen XIX), that it often turns to obsession (E, IV, Prop 44, Schol), that Adam loved Eve because of their similarity of nature (E, IV, Prop 68, Schol), that he who remains indifferent to the favors of a courtesan does not offend by ingratitude (E, IV, Prop 71, Schol), that free men and women only marry among themselves and only if they want children (E, IV, Appen, XX). Now, if we add to these eight passages the two definitions of *lust* (E, III, Prop 56, Schol and E, III, Def Aff 48), and if I am not mistaken, these are the only passages that Spinoza expressly devoted to the question! Apparently, there is therefore no alternative but to draw up a report of deficiency.

However, that would be to proceed too quickly. After all, as no one would deny, Spinoza is not in the habit of writing anything lightly. We have not finished identifying in Spinoza those so-called banalities that, once reattached to their doctrinal context, take on an unexpected meaning. Why would this not be so on this point as well? Undoubtedly we will never know with complete certainty, but is it not better, all things being equal, to give credit to the author of the *Ethics*? Let us therefore suppose, by way of a methodological hypothesis, that the ten passages in question were very carefully thought through and see what their Spinozist significance can be.

In Part III of the *Ethics*, two definitions are given of *lust*, but only the second is formally presented as such: "coeundi . . . immoderatum Amorem vel Cupiditatem," ("immoderate love or desire for . . . sexual union" [E, III, Prop 56, Schol]), then "Cupiditas et Amor in commiscendis corporibus" ("desire and love of joining one body to another" [E, III, Def Aff 48]). Fundamentally there is no real opposition between them. In the explication of the second, Spinoza also employs the expression "haec coeundi cupiditas" and he then indicates that, if he no longer mentions the immoderate character of this affection, it is because it is always designated by the same word in colloquial language whether or not it is excessive (E, III, Def Aff 48, Exp). All Spinozist definitions being genetic, this one, despite its apparent triviality, must obviously be understood as implying a reference to the immediate cause of its object or, rather, since it is to do with a passion, to its two immediate causes, one internal, the other external. However, the exact determination of each poses a problem.

On the side of the subject, *lust* is both desire and love. This would have satisfied neither Saint Thomas Aquinas nor Descartes, for whom these two passions are qualitatively distinct. Undoubtedly this ambiguity could be attributed to the poverty of the usual vocabulary that has only one term to name two different things. However, is it really for Spinoza a question of two things that are truly different? Love, generally, is the joy associated with the idea of an external cause (E, III, Prop 13, Schol). Joy, for its part, consists of an increase in the power to act (E, III, Prop 11, Schol; III, Def Aff 2). The power to act, in turn, is identified with *conatus* (E, III, Prop 7, Dem), that is, with the actual essence of the individual insofar as it is determined to produce certain effects that, because of its internal noncontradiction, will maintain it in existence, other things being equal (E, III, Props 4–7). *Conatus* thus defined is desire (E, III, Prop 9, Schol; Def Aff 1 and Exp). We see, analytically, what results from this: that love is nothing other than desire itself insofar as it is favored or increased and that its increase is accompanied by the representation of an external object that fixes its particular orientation; *cupiditas quatenus*, one could say. We see it even better synthetically: to desire is to tend, with all our strength, to do all that results from our nature. When, for one reason or another, we become capable of producing more effects than before (that is precisely what it is to rejoice in ourselves), we necessarily endeavor to fully accomplish the operations that our new capacity makes possible. From this fact alone, we tend to remain in the state that authorizes these supplementary performances, like the river that digs its bed by flowing where it can, and therefore to preserve or to reactualize the cause that we assign to it and that we imagine through it (E, III, Props 12 and 13, Schol). It follows that to love is equivalent to investing our desire in what enables it to be exercised with additional strength. Colloquial language, for once, was more Spinozist than Thomist or Cartesian: there is nothing absurd or approximate in using the same term for two affects, one of which is nothing more than a mode of the other.[3]

On one condition, however. Because sadness and hatred, too, are modalities of *conatus*: they are born when it is prevented from producing its effects by an unfavorable external cause (E, III, Prop 11, Schol and Prop 13, Schol), which *conatus* then resists (E, III, Prop 6, Dem), like a river exerting pressure on a dam, and which it tends to eliminate by summoning that which excludes the existence of this unfavorable cause (E, III, Prop 13, Cor and Schol). There are sad desires as there are joyful desires. From the moment that love is assimilated to joy, to declare of a desire that it is at the same time love thus amounts to classifying it under the second of these two headings. Hobbes rather took the contrary option: he asks himself, in a passage that makes one wonder, whether what we call sexual appetite would not be simply the aversion that we feel for something whose presence inside our body is painful and from which we try to free ourselves by expelling it.[4] To which it would have been possible to respond that, if this were so, the problem would be solved by a very simple mechanical means! . . . It is true that Hobbes, a little later, clearly compares this appetite to a positive attraction; but if what he wrote earlier is to be taken seriously, it can only be a question here of a derived process: we become attached, secondarily, to the object that helps to remove what irritates us.[5] There is nothing like this in Spinoza. No doubt for him too any sad desire has joyful side effects: for example, anger is a desire that drives us to harm those we hate (E, III, Prop 40, Cor 2 and Schol) and is accompanied by the hope of succeeding, where hope consists in rejoicing in a future thing (E, III, Prop 18, Schol 2), that is to say, in loving it. However, it can never be said of this hateful impulse that it *is* love for what is opposed to its object, even if such a love results from it. Conversely, joyful desire can generate sadness and hatred indirectly when it encounters obstacles; but it *is* not, in any sense, hatred or sadness, not even *secundum quid*. By defining *lust* as "*cupiditas et amor*" (desire and love), Spinoza thus made a choice: leaving aside what often comes to contradict it from the outside, this affection is joyful through and through and from beginning to end.

It is like this from the beginning: the joy that it implies does not start with the orgasm, or love with the memory of the being who produced it for us. If it were so, the preceding desire would only consist of a discomfort the disappearance of which we would rejoice in and Hobbes would be right. It is almost an obvious Spinozist fact that sexual excitation is in reality already agreeable in itself: does it not increase our power to act, in the very simple and precise sense that it makes us capable of producing certain effects that we could not produce before its emergence? Suffering will only occur if the environment prevents us from fully actualizing this capacity. As for what occurs after, things are just as clear: no sadness *post coitum* without the intervention of external causes. How would our power to act decrease in *itself*? Quite the contrary, it finds itself increased, even if it then takes other forms by being diffused more widely. Once the effects determined by our nature have been produced, we become capable, as always, of producing the effects of these effects: capable of being affected by other bodies and of affecting them in a multitude of new ways, as well as capable of thinking more and better than before (E, IV, Prop 38 and Dem). Undoubtedly these new capacities that cause in us new desires are no longer, for a time at least, of a sexual nature, but such is the life of *conatus*. It is neither an undifferentiated impulse nor a mosaic of independent demands but a self-regulated system of operations that, because they cannot be carried out all at once and because we do, however, tend to execute them all, must follow one another according to the order defined by the laws that follow from our individual essence. The subsequent desires are the continuation of *lust* in other ways, just as *lust* was itself the prolongation of other desires. If nothing came to disturb it, the process would be cumulative and would unfold in a permanent joy. Sexuality is a necessary moment of this self-deployment of our individuality and, because joyful, is good in itself (E, IV, Prop 41).

It can admittedly lead us to excess. Sexual pleasure, in common, moreover, with the majority of pleasures (E, IV, Prop 44, Schol), is *titillatio* and not *hilaritas*: a favorable event, but one that affects one or more parts of the body more than others (E, IV, Prop 11, Schol). Since there are no watertight compartments in us, it is not that the other parts are not affected at all but simply that they are affected less. Now the strength of a passion depends on the relation that is established between that of its cause and our body part (E, IV, Prop 5). The strength of the desires that it generates is proportional to its own (E, III, Prop 37) and, in the event of conflict between several desires, the strongest prevail (E, IV, Prop 7). We can see what results from this: what causes, for example, an affection of strength 2 in part A and an affection of strength 1 in part B will generate, if it acts on us with twice as much strength, an affection of strength 4 in A and an affection of strength 2 in B; the difference then will be 2 and no longer 1, and the desire relating to A will have twice as much chance of eclipsing the desires relating to B, so long as we ourselves have not changed in the meantime. To compensate for the imbalance will require rational desires twice as powerful as in the first case, unless a modification of the environment intervenes at a given point. As a result, other things being equal, the greater the impact on our brain of an external cause, the more the desire produced by the increase in power to act localized in the privileged parts tends to prevail over those produced by the increase in power to act localized in the other parts.[6] At the limit, if no correction occurs, it can inhibit them totally. The *titillatio* then mobilizes to its exclusive profit the new capacities born of its completion. We neglect other activities that require our attention and employ all our resources to make it recur indefinitely. From this point on, everything is blocked: our body is monopolized by this affection that obstinately clings to it and ceases to develop its capacities (E, IV, Prop 43 and Dem). We turn in circles instead of evolving in spirals. In parallel, our capacity to think ceases to increase (E, IV, Prop 38, Dem). The excess thus does not come from the intensity of the pleasure taken absolutely, or from its frequency, but from the obsessional character that it takes on for our imagination. It would have only advantages and no disadvantages for the free man, in whose brain images follow in an order analogous to that of the ideas of the understanding (see E, V, Prop 10) and are constituted firmly enough not to be shaken by the play of external causes. The threshold at which pleasure risks becoming "immoderate" rises as reason develops in us, and, in the weakest, this threshold is so low that it can be crossed without there ever having been a passage to action. Comparable in his "species of madness" (E, IV, Prop 44, Schol and Appen 19) to the "*avarus*" (miser) who goes without everything in order to accumulate whatever satisfies that from which he always abstains (E, IV, Appen 29), the "*libidinosus*" is the sexual obsessive who can only think of one thing (E, IV, Prop 44, Schol), even and especially if circumstances oblige him to abstinence (E, III, Def Aff 48, Exp).

Think of what, exactly? Here arises the second problem: that of the immediate external cause, that is, of the *object* of *lust*. This problem is both simpler and more complex than the first. It is simpler because Spinoza obviously thinks that the identification of this object, in the majority of cases, at least, is straightforward. It is more complex because he really can't say for what exact reasons sexual desire comes to take this particular orientation. One explanation, of course, must be considered by him as absurd: since final causes are excluded, sexuality is no more *intended* to ensure the perpetuation of the species than eyes are made for seeing or teeth for chewing (E, I, Appen). There is procreation because there is sexuality, not sexuality in order that there be procreation, and if there are sexual beings, among other things, it is because the laws of nature are ample enough to produce all that is conceivable (E, I, Appen). This principle once posed, with the enormous ethical consequences that it implies, Spinoza need not have said anything further.

However, he does say a little more. According to the two definitions of *lust*, as we have seen, the object of this affection is the sexual relation itself, not the partner, properly speaking. There is nothing embarrassing about that: Spinoza points out that it is always a thing external to us that we love (E, III, Prop 13, Schol), but that we always love *insofar* as it affects us with a determinate form of joy and only under the aspect by which it affects us. That our pleasure then becomes associated with other aspects of this same thing changes nothing (E, III, Prop 16, Dem). Since, in addition, for significant reasons, Spinoza insists on expressing in only one phrase the distinctive features of both desire and love, and since any desire is the effort to achieve this or this act, he could hardly have proceeded differently. There remains the question of the two different denominations of this object: in the formal definition, it is the *"mixture of bodies"*; in the explanation that follows, as in the informal definition, it is more precisely *coitus*. Perhaps in Spinoza's mind the two expressions are equivalent, but perhaps also the first must be taken in its broadest meaning. In the first case, a problem would arise: love *being* pleasure, or what amounts to the same, memory of pleasure, it would have to be admitted that one cannot love sexually if one is a virgin, and that consequently one would always remain so! Saying that the culture allows our imagination to anticipate only displaces the difficulty: from whence in their turn come the cultural standards that guide us? The second interpretation, by contrast, seems more in the spirit of Spinozism. Sexual excitation, already agreeable in itself, is originally provoked by "body mixtures" consisting of all kinds of unintentional physical contact, perhaps very precocious, which we then endeavor to renew and which a series of variations and associations lead in general, through "trial and error," to the coital form, the particularly satisfactory effects of which finally stabilize our desire. As for the reasons for which those first contacts themselves increased our power to act, undoubtedly these relate to the fact that this power to act, which is measured by our capacity to affect other bodies and to be affected by them in multiple ways, only increases by being exerted in one form or another: it is by affecting and by being affected that one becomes even more capable and therein lies the pleasure.[7] Since we lack the texts, let us not go any further. Nonetheless, taking into account the unitary character of *conatus*, of which *lust* is only one modality among others, and taking into account the malleability of its investments, nothing *prohibits* Spinoza—and he is perhaps the only classical philosopher whose doctrine authorizes it—from admitting a nongenital sexuality. If the starting point is so undetermined, and if any affection whatever can be derived from object to object according to chance encounters (E, III, Prop 15), then we glimpse the infinite diversity of sexual behaviors conceivable and therefore included in the order of nature.

One of them, however, massively predominates. This is the *"amor meretricius"* that Spinoza defines as the *"libido generandi, quae ex forma oritur"* ("the lust to procreate that arises from external appearance" [see E, IV, Appen 19]), without the adjective employed here seeming to imply any particular reference to prostitution in the strict sense.[8] Thus *lust* is specified in two ways. On the one hand, it becomes *"generandi"*: we no longer simply desire the "mixture of bodies," but this mixture in its procreative form. Not that generation is our end, but at least we fix ourselves on the act that, in fact, makes it possible. On the other hand, this same lust is now born *"ex forma,"* that is from an external form, external appearance or beauty, this last translation being authorized by another passage where it is a question of *"pulchritudine"* ("beauty" [see TP, XI, 137]). Visual stimulants are thus associated with tactile stimulants, substituted for them to initiate the excitation. How is this double modification possible?

If we cast our mind back to what beauty means for Spinoza, it does not really pose a problem. Quite simply, we call beautiful those things that, when they affect our eyes, provoke movements favorable to health in the optic nerve (E, I, Appen). To be good for health is obviously to increase the power of the body to act, but in which of its parts? Here, two interpretations are equally admissible. Perhaps it is a question of an increase in the power to act *in an unspecified area of our organism:* the action of the optic nerve, by the intermediary of the brain, has effects more or less everywhere. In this case, there is no difficulty: the visual image of the person with whom we had such and such an agreeable "body mixture," or of another who happens to be beside that person (E, II Prop 15), or of another who resembles the person (E, III, Prop 16), revives in us the formerly joyful affection and causes our desire. Then projecting onto this person the state of greater perfection in which we are put by the sight of him or her, we attribute this to the person as an objective quality that properly belongs to him or her, believing thereby to discover in the person the positive pseudovalue that we baptize beauty (E, I, Appen). The judgment of beauty being subsequent to the sexual excitation, whereas the perception of external appearance precedes it, one would understand why in these conditions Spinoza wrote *"ex forma"* (from eternal causes) rather than *"ex pulchritudine"* (from beauty). However, perhaps the increase in power to act is also located *in the optical apparatus itself*. In this manner, we would feel a properly aesthetic pleasure that would give rise to the same pseudo-objectivation without inspiring in us any desire other than to continue looking. To get a better look, we approach and soon end up touching: if this contact evokes the memory of former "mixtures," the association is established between contemplative joy and sensuality (see E, III, Prop 14). In fact, both mechanisms are undoubtedly in play; from whence comes the possibility of a *fluctuatio animi* (the "vacillation of mind" [see E, III, Prop 17, Schol]): the view of one and the same being can assault our optic nerve all the while attracting us to it. Sooner or later the two contrary affects must adapt (E, V, Ax 1): either our *lust* will soon only fix itself on what brings joy to our eyes, or our eyes will become accustomed to rejoicing in anything on which they are fixed.

More obscure are the causes of its specification as *libido generandi*. It is not enough to say that society imposes it, because social norms are themselves born of the interaction of human desires. How can we conceive that the "first men" should have preferred the "first women," while abstracting from all culture in the way that one reconstructs the civil state starting from a hypothetical state of nature that undoubtedly never existed? It happens, oddly, that Spinoza himself answers the question in part, although in a passage intended to illustrate something quite different. Adam, he tells us, loved Eve because she was the being whose nature agreed the most with his and who consequently presented for him the maximum utility (E, IV, Prop 68, Schol). Supposing that this explanation applies to sexual relations, it would initially seem to suggest something completely different.[9] It is true that Adam hardly had a choice, but if he had met another man, who would have naturally resembled him by an additional feature, does Spinoza mean to say that he would have preferred him to Eve? Undoubtedly not, no more than he would want to praise the benefits of anthropophagy, applying the same principle to nutrition! And yet this principle is for him absolutely universal: the more a thing is similar to us, the more it is good for us (E, IV, Prop 31 and Cor). Once again it is a question of understanding clearly what Spinoza means here by similarity. Any being, necessarily, tends to produce effects that preserve it. A being whose nature has something in common with another therefore tends to produce, in greater or lesser number according to its degree of resemblance, effects that ensure the conservation of this common nature, that is of their nature considered under the aspect in which they resemble one another. The *conatus* of each therefore favors the other, *insofar as* they converge (E, IV, Prop 31, Dem), but such a convergence can take multiple forms according to the type of effect in question. For example, Peter and Paul agree in nature in the sense that they both desire the same thing but are opposed in the sense that each wants it for himself (E, IV, Prop 34, Schol). If Peter's nature were such that it pushed him to wish to give to Paul the exclusive possession of this thing, it would both agree with and oppose that of Paul for inverse reasons. There are resemblances that are identities just as there are those that are complementary. Two geometrical figures have something in common when their respective peripheries are exactly adjusted to one another: to this extent, if each endeavored to remain what it is, they would help each other by enclosing one another. Perhaps this is what Spinoza *also* wanted to suggest: men and women are made anatomically so that intraspecies and genital heterosexuality in general makes the "body mixtures" that they seek easier and more complete. Hence the frequency of this final choice as the outcome of "trial and error" and the possibility that the culture could intervene to indicate this in advance. Once again, we lack the texts to go any further. In any event, the explanation could be only statistical: the more or less satisfactory character of this or that solution depends in each case on an infinity of circumstances. That would in no way imply any value judgment: in the absence of any finality, to give a causal account of what is most commonly the case is not to specify normatively what must be.

One step remains but is already practically taken. In theory, the "*amor meretricius*" has as its object the beautiful bodies of the opposite sex in general. But when we love somebody, those of his or her aspects in which we rejoice are most often associated with all his or her other aspects, even if we were initially indifferent to the latter (E, III, Prop 15 and Prop 16, Dem). We arrive, then, at loving this person for what, for our perception at least, she has that is individual and that distinguishes her from all others: love "*erga faeminam*" ("toward *a* woman" [see E, III, Prop 35, Schol]) in the singular. However, this risks taking a rather dramatic turn.

For if the genetic method initially required disregarding the interhuman context of this love, it must now be reintroduced. On the one hand, the women whom we love are beings of the same species as us, with all that that implies. There are, in addition, men around us who either love or do not love these women depending on the case, but whose affects have repercussions in any event on ours. In the two preceding sentences, of course, the word "men" and the word "women" could be substituted for one another so that "we" then would be feminine: the demonstrations of the *Ethics* apply to any sex whatever. However, at the stage that we now approach (neither before nor after, it should be noted), Spinoza, in fact, assumes the point of view of men. Moreover, we can understand why: in the relations of power that obtain universally under the regime of the passions and from which no one except the wise escapes, women, for a cause that must relate to their nature but that is unclear—and that, since Spinoza expressly speaks about their possible access to the "freedom of mind" (E, IV, Appen 20), does not consist of a congenital incapacity of their reason and that undoubtedly has nothing pejorative in the eyes of a philosopher who certainly does not consider himself particularly able to subjugate others—find themselves always and everywhere in a position of inferiority (TP, XI, 136–37). Their reactions in interhuman conflicts, even though they are the same as those of men, have therefore less importance in practice. The sexual drama, essentially, *is played out between males*. From whence, precisely, its acuity.

All aspects of the question are summarized in a single sentence: *amor meretricius* (sensual love) changes easily to hatred, as, moreover, does any form of love that admits as its cause something other than the freedom of mind. Unless, "what is worse," it is a "species of madness," in which case—both translations are equally admissible—"it is maintained by discord more than by harmony," or "it is discord, more than harmony which is maintained" by it.[10] The other types of passionate love evoked by Spinoza, where it is not simply a question of friendship or of nonsexual devotion (which can also be conflictual among the ignorant), are either the *lust* that is called "perverse" because it is not *generandi* (procreative) or that which is based on something other than physical beauty of the loved being: her wealth or social standing, both of which are external causes that can bring joy and with which she can be strongly associated. Let us consider only *amor meretricius*, which Spinoza obviously takes here at its final stage, at the moment when it is already fixed on a determinate person. This passion, we are told, gives rise to an alternative, both terms of which are deplorable but the second more so than the first.

First possibility: in many cases, love easily changes to hatred. Spinoza explained this in his deduction of *jealousy*. This has completely general causes, which are likely to obscure any interhuman passionate attachment, even if it has no relation with *lust*, but when it is sexual a very particular and at first sight rather odd cause comes to aggravate it most of the time.

These general causes are well known. Insofar as we necessarily imitate the affects of those like ourselves (E, III, Prop 27), whoever they are, other things being equal we desire to give them joy in order to rejoice in the idea of ourselves as cause: such is the origin of the *ambition of glory* (E, III, Props 29, Prop 30 and Schol).[11] However, when we love anything at all we think about it more than any other thing. If this thing is a human person, we therefore want her in particular at all costs to recognize us as the cause of joy, that is, to make her love us (E, III, Prop 33 and Dem). The more we are successful, the more we are glorified (E, III, Prop 34).[12] Consequently, if we believe that she is attached to someone else, our desire for glory will be frustrated, we will be saddened, and our love will tend to change to hatred at the same time as we will detest our rival (E, III, Prop 35). Since women are human, this mechanism works for the affects that relate to them *just as* it works for those that relate to friends or benefactors.

Jealousy, however, can be more or less violent. It is particularly strong when the idea of the loved being is associated in our mind with that of a thing that we otherwise hate (E, III, Prop 35, Schol). Precisely this almost always takes place in the case of *amor erga faeminam*: the sadness produced in us by the woman whom we believe to be unfaithful is exacerbated by the representation, which we join to her, of the *pudenda* (shameful parts) and of the *excrementa* (excretions) of our rival (E, III, Prop 35, Schol), which implies that this representation by itself, before all the real or imaginary grounds that we can have to be jealous, *already* inspired in us as such an insurmountable horror. From this text and from it alone, it is often concluded that sexuality for Spinoza was the object of a deep repulsion. However, Spinoza does not claim that this dislike is rationally justified: he simply says that impassioned men feel it. Nor is this an empirical observation recorded in passing: it can be deduced, in all rigor, from the preceding propositions. In effect, once again everything follows from "the imitation of affects" but considered under another aspect. If we imagine that a being similar to us draws joy from a thing that only a single person can possess, we will do anything so that he doesn't have it (E, III, Prop 32), because we will then want for ourselves what is by hypothesis indivisible: such in its most general form is the origin of *envy* (E, III, Prop 32, Schol). This affection emerges in connection with any monopolistic good: for example, from an economic point of view, when land is private property, it divides men, since it is a singular thing the global quantity of which remains fixed. Money does not have such disastrous effects (TP, VII, 80–81), since it is a universal equivalent (E, IV, Appen 28), in principle always reproducible. Woman is like land, with the additional aggravating circumstance that no substitutable alternative is possible: physically speaking, no one can enjoy the use of her favors without at the same time prohibiting others from access to them. This is a particular case of the impossibility in which any body can find itself in fully occupied Extension: that of occupying a new position without thereby dislodging a neighboring body.[13] On this point, let us acknowledge, Spinoza's imagination is hardly Sadian! . . . From which follows the inevitable consequence that when we represent to ourselves one of our own kind in such a situation, even if his partner in no way interested us before, the idea of this pleasure from which we are excluded saddens us. One therefore understands how, in all males, the generic image of the sexual organ of all other males risks becoming unbearable: the more we are *libidinosi*, the more we hate the sexuality of others, that is to say—since the others are everyone except ourselves—sexuality in general. In Christian countries this reinforces certain historicocultural conditions: in order to prevent kings from getting control of the church, priests in the past condemned themselves to celibacy (TTP, XIX, 220).[14] Envy then pushed them to elaborate superstitious arguments in favor of all men sharing their misery (E, IV, Prop 63, Schol). This phenomenon is difficult to reverse and the marriage of pastors in reformed countries changed little. Whether or not, in spite of himself, Spinoza did or did not personally feel such an aversion, it is quite certain that he judged it unreasonable. However, since he notes the omnipresence around him of this aversion, he is driven to explain it with the theoretical means at his disposal.

Sexual love, like all love, therefore degenerates easily into jealousy, and, because of the particular character of its object, this jealousy is more violent and conflictual than all the others, but this is not yet the worst: conflicts stirred up in this way can subside, but would only do so when the hatred has undermined its own base by destroying the love from which it was born (E, III, Prop 38). Yet this is what the second possibility under consideration by Spinoza renders impossible.

The process that has just been analyzed ceases to come into play from the moment that sensual love (*amor meretricius*), becomes obsessional and takes the form of a "species of madness" (E, IV, Appen 19; see also E, IV, Prop 44, Schol). All critical sense then disappears: we systematically overestimate the loved woman (E, III, Prop 25), adorning her with all conceivable intellectual (TP, XI, 137), physical, and moral qualities; but since the overestimation never dissociates itself from pride (E, III, Prop 26 and Schol), the "virtues" that we attribute to her are above all, as if by chance, those that she must possess so that we find ourselves exalted to the maximum. We therefore believe her to be faithful in spite of everything even if the evidence of our misfortune is obvious. A compensatory feedback no longer intervenes. Does this blindness at least make us happy? No, quite the contrary; and it is again the imitation of affects that, in a third and final form, here poisons our existence. In effect, in general if we imagine that the being to which we are attached is loved by other men, we love it with all the more ardor; if, however, we believe that it inspires aversion in those who resemble us, our love is mitigated and the *fluctuatio animi* (vacillation of mind) becomes established in us (E, III, Prop 31). The woman on whom our *lust* is fixed being a monopolistic good that no one can desire without immediately being opposed to us, we understand why—according to one of the two possible translations of Spinoza's expression—the "species of madness" that it induces in our mind draws its nourishment from discord rather than harmony:[15] the competition maintains our obsession, whereas this would subside if no one took part in it and if everyone left us in peace.[16] However, such an attenuation would be felt by us as painful because love, being a joyful affection, necessarily tends to maintain itself. We thus deploy all our effort to make others love what we love ourselves (E, III, Prop 31, Cor): paradoxically, the *ambition of domination*, the political and religious effects (intolerance, fight for power) of which Spinoza especially studied, also plays out with regard to sexual taste. This is why our madness—according to the other possible translation of the same expression—feeds the discord much more than the harmony:[17] it maintains it in order to be better nourished by it. In our foolhardiness, we wish to have as many rivals as possible and nothing delights us as much as being universally envied—even if, as it goes without saying, nothing, moreover, frightens us quite as much. From whence the inextricable contradiction: if the others refuse to adopt our tastes, we make ourselves unbearable in their eyes by striving to constrain them to do so;[18] if they allow themselves to be persuaded, the result is the same, since they then become our enemies.

As a result, we want and do not want the same thing: singing the praises of the loved being, we nevertheless fear to be believed (E, IV, Prop 37, Schol 1). This time, consequently, there is no longer any solution, not even provisional. If the second possibility is even more dramatic than the first it is because, as soon as its obsessional character deprives it of any regulating mechanism, sensual love (*amor meretricius*) renders the conflicts between human males inescapable and inexpiable.

Sexual passion can thus have two disadvantages absolutely related to one another: on the individual level, it risks blocking our power to act and our power to think; on the interhuman level, it is inseparable from a climate of competition hardly compatible with harmony. However, this double excess does not at all result from the fact of it being sexual but from it being a passion, in other words, alienated. The worst alienation is obviously that by which our *lust*, under the action of external causes the mechanism of which escapes us, fixes itself in a purely exclusive way upon a particular being for whom we sacrifice all and from whom we require that they also sacrifice all. It is then that our field of consciousness is the most restricted at the same time that the conflicts in which we engage are the most fierce. Our dependence would be less narrow if we no longer alienated ourselves in a singular individual but in persons of the opposite sex in general: the more numerous the causes to which we relate an affection, the less they prevent us from thinking and the less each of them renders us passive (E, V, Prop 9). Similarly, it could be said that the existence of substitutable alternatives would attenuate somewhat the violence of the rivalries. Would an even greater generalization be further progress? Perhaps, although Spinoza evidently says nothing about this. In any event, this is not yet authentic freedom: alienation remains alienation, even if its object becomes broader; libertines, too, are often sexual obsessives.[19] Sexual emancipation only occurs among those in whose minds adequate ideas predominate.

In effect, under the regime of the passions only palliatives are conceivable. What is essential, of course, is to preserve civil peace by reducing to a minimum the causes of discord. On this point there is only one sound method, the one that is also appropriate for the regulation of access to public office and ownership of land. Since it is men who in any event make the law, they will "democratically" divide the women on the basis of equality in order to attenuate envy. However, contrary to what happens in the case of land, which can be nationalized if in addition avarice (*avaritia*) fixes itself on money (TP, VII, 80), the generally very individualized character of *lust* makes necessary the private ownership of sexual goods: each one will thus have his wife, as each Hebrew had a field identical to that of his neighbor (TTP, XVII, 198–99). Politically speaking, Christ was right to condemn adultery and to declare at the same time that those who covet the women of others have already committed it in their heart (TTP, V, 60): as far as possible, the social norms must be interiorized. However, within this framework a margin of tolerance is admissible. The stoning to death of unfaithful women is only effective in an institutional system analogous to that of Mosaic theocracy, which would subject the population to a "training in strict obedience" (TTP, XVII, 199). If such a system is not wanted, then it will be necessary to authorize whatever cannot be prevented, including debauchery (TTP, XX, 230–34); taken separately, prohibitive measures can only exasperate the appetites (TP, V, 131). Undoubtedly this liberalism would be exercised above all to the benefit of the stronger sex; women known as "loose [*legère*]," even if they give themselves freely and even if it is they who pay, would only ever be *meretrices*;[20] from which comes the adjective that, without particular reference to money, qualifies the love that "weak [*legère*]" men have for them. But at least flexible monogamy is what is best adapted to the civilized countries for which Spinozist constitutions are conceived. This sums up the whole of Spinoza's sexual politics.

What remain is his sexual ethics. From this point of view, how will men and women behave under the rule of reason? Men *and women*, because nothing prevents us thinking that the latter can reach true freedom and because Spinoza *posits* that they can.[21] Here, things are completely clear. The sexual act, like the action of striking taken in itself, is "a virtue, which is conceived from the structure of the human body" (see E, IV, Prop 59, Schol). Reason thus takes responsibility for it, as it does with regard to all that was positive in what we do under the influence of our passions (E, IV, Prop 59). Nothing is more banal or finally more repressive, it will be said, than to declare that the sexual life is good on the condition that it is regulated by reason: who has not proclaimed this and with well-known practical consequences? Spinoza in no way continues this tradition. According to him, free men and women set themselves the fundamental goal of knowledge (E, IV, Prop 26) and the diffusion of truth (E, IV, Prop 37). To this double end, they search at the same time for what ensures the parallel development of their physical and mental capacities (E, IV, Props 38–39) and what supports harmony (E, IV, Prop

40). All the non-unstable joys (E, IV, Props 41–43) are in this category: why would what Spinoza says of food, drink, perfumes, games, and the theater (E, IV, Prop 45, Schol) not also apply to sexuality, unless there were some incomprehensible exception the existence of which it would only be necessary to admit were it expressly mentioned? Moreover, in the case of sexuality, would this not apply without taboo of any kind, since procreation is not its end? This equally excludes, it should be said in passing, the obligation to devote ourselves to it at all costs at the risk of appearing ridiculous! It is for each of us to judge to what extent and in what way it is good to make use of sexuality. The only condition, we have seen, is that it become neither obsessional nor conflictual, but we have seen also that it is less likely to become so the more reason develops: from a certain threshold all danger would be eliminated. Understand, and do what you will: here as elsewhere, this is the sole norm.

It is on this basis and this basis alone that the question of marriage arises. This has nothing in common with, for example, the Thomist problematic: it is not a question of wondering whether one has the right to have sexual relations, or of responding that the latter are legitimate under such and such readily predictable conditions. It is implicitly understood that, in any event, free men and free women will have sexual relations if they judge it good to do so and in the form that agrees with them the most. The only problem is to know if they will have these within the framework of the matrimonial institution. This is an institution of substantive law that exists only because there are those who are ignorant. If all were reasonable, Church and State would disappear (TTP, V, 63), along with juridical property, including that in women. Moreover, it is difficult to see who could then preside over the ceremony! But since the institution is there, does it conform to reason to yield to it? Yes, responds Spinoza, but only if both of the two following conditions are fulfilled together: if, on the one hand, the *"cupiditas miscendi corpora"* (desire for physical union) does not come from beauty alone but also from the joy that we feel at the idea of having children (*ex Amore liberos procreandi*) and educating them wisely, and if, on the other hand, the reciprocal love of the man and the woman (*utriusque, viri scilicet et faeminae, Amor*) does not have beauty alone as its cause but above all the freedom of mind (E, IV, Appen 20). There is nothing "puritan" in this. The so-called motivation "of convenience" (wealth, social ambition, obedience to the father, and so on) is absolutely excluded. The twice-mentioned motivation of beauty goes without saying but is insufficient. A free man will never marry a foolish woman, or a free woman an imbecile: it would be absurd to legally commit ourselves to spend our whole life with a person whom we would have not even the hope of one day bringing to authentic rationality. If we nevertheless want to have temporary sexual relations with her and if she agrees, we should have them outside marriage. We would, on the one hand, have no interest in having the church or the state officially intervene in our relations with a truly free person with whom we would not wish to have children or who would not wish to do so with us, a situation that, in truth, is not very likely in the case of two beings whose greatest joy would be to educate others (E, IV, Appen 9), although one can conceive of particular counterindications, and, if only from reading the Bible, Spinoza must be aware of the existence of at least one means of contraception that his antifinalism prohibits him from condemning. If, on the other hand, we want children without having found a free person, it will be necessary to proceed like Descartes! When the two conditions are met, the common freedom of mind of the couple removes any disadvantage from marriage and, for obvious social reasons, the needs of educating children makes it useful. Without any exclusivism, however, since free man and free woman as such are incapable by definition of any jealousy and they do not have any rational reason to refrain from parallel experiences—or if they have had none, any rational reason to feel compelled to seek them out. Doctrinally, Spinoza cannot have thought otherwise.

However, under current conditions our chances of meeting an authentically free partner, or one capable of becoming so under our care, are slight. We will then arrange ourselves as best we can, without fear or shame, or provocation either, but without ever losing sight of the fundamental requirement to which we subordinate the totality of our existence: to understand and to make others understand. As in any calculation, this implies the acceptance of the lesser evil (E, IV, Prop 65). It goes without saying that the free man will never resort to constraint of any kind whatever. Nor will he ever make untrue promises in order to better seduce: all *dolus malus* (deception) is prohibited by reason (E, IV, Prop 72). Never, however, will he impose superfluous obligation: if he has committed the imprudence of accepting the favors of a *meretrix* (there are degrees in rationality! [see E, IV, Prop 70]), at least he will not consider himself bound to express his gratitude by yielding to her desires when she no longer pleases him (E, IV, Prop 71, Schol); of course, this also goes for the free woman who solicits an admirer.[22] Above all, since reason prescribes that he preserve civil peace (E, IV, Prop 73), the free man will respect the established laws. In the countries where these are very strict, this excludes all relations with married women or underage girls. In the same way, externally at least, he will conform to the established mores in order not to compromise his assigned task by unnecessary scandal (E, IV, Appen 15): from this point of view as well, one should be "Greek among the Greeks."[23] This is not something that any longer poses a problem in Holland! When the external situation is unfavorable, it does risk giving rise to many awkward restrictions, which however it will be necessary to fully support if these were calculated to be the least-bad solutions. Undoubtedly this is what happened to Spinoza himself. If he endured sexual misery, at least he lived it with discretion as an inevitable disadvantage because of circumstances of fact, without seeking to theoretically valorize it or impose it on others.

Translated by Simon Duffy and Paul Patton

Notes

1. See, for example, the very curious work by J. Segond, *Vie de Spinoza* (Paris: Perrin, 1933).
2. The translation of the *Tractatus Politicus* (TP) used in this translation of Matheron's original article is *Political Treatise*, trans. S. Shirley (Indianapolis: Hackett, 2000). *Editor's note*: Although Matheron's original paper refers to the Gebhardt edition (in Latin) of Spinoza's collected works, I have substituted references to the best translations that are readily available in English (at the present time). However, the interpretative nature of Matheron's notes 10, 16, and 17 require reference to the Gebhardt edition: Benedictus de Spinoza, *Opera*, vols. 1–4, ed. Carl Gebhardt (Heidelberg: C. Winter, Auftrag des Heidelberger Akadamie des Wissenschaften, 1924). I have supplied an English translation for the Latin words and phrases (in parentheses).
3. *Editor's note*: In the original published version of this chapter, Matheron used the French equivalent of "feeling" rather than "affect." In personal correspondence Alexandre Matheron wrote: "If I had rewritten this article today, in place of 'feelings' I would write 'affects,' and in place of 'imitation of feelings,' 'imitation of affects.' (In France in 1977, the translation of *affectus* by 'affect' was not yet universally accepted)." I have adopted the use of "affect" (rather than feeling) throughout this chapter, both because it reflects Matheron's preference and because this volume uses Curley's translation of Spinoza's *Ethics* (unless otherwise specified), which translates the Latin, "*affectus*," as "affect."
4. T. Hobbes, *Leviathan*, ed. Richard Tuck (Cambridge: Cambridge University Press, 1991), chap. 6, 40.
5. Ibid., 41–42.
6. It is at the level of the brain, through the mechanism of the formation of images, that the relation between the external cause and our body is established. See E, II, Prop 17, Cor and Dem, and the commentary that M. Guéroult gives of it in *Spinoza*, vol. 2 (Paris, 1975), 201–9.

7. See E, II, Prop 14; III, Prop 11; IV, Prop 38 and Dem; and Prop 41, Dem.

8. *Editor's note*: Strictly speaking, "*amor meretricius*" translates as "love of a courtesan." However, Curley, whose translation of the *Ethics* we follow here, argues that a more appropriate translation is "sensual love." See *The Collected Works of Spinoza*, vol. 1, ed. and trans. Edwin M. Curley (Princeton: Princeton University Press, 1985), 591n40, where Curley refers to the article by Matheron here translated in support of doing so.

9. Of course, above all, Spinoza wants to say that Eve was useful to Adam insofar as she was a rational being like him. But we do not "know" one another, in the biblical sense, by reason alone.

10. *Editor's note*: Matheron here quotes in Latin (from the Gebhardt edition) E, IV, Appen 19—"*tum magis discordia, quam concordia fovetur*"—in order to make an interpretive point. Matheron's footnote reads: "In his manuscripts, Spinoza did not put the accent on the final 'a' of the singular ablative of the first declension, as Gebhardt moreover indicates in his critical commentary (vol. II, p. 388). Gebhardt, in following the editor of the *Opera Posthuma* and opting for the ablative rather than for the nominative, therefore made a choice to which only he is committed."

11. *Editor's note*: Curley translates what Matheron here terms the "ambition of glory" as the "love of esteem" or "self-esteem."

12. *Editor's note*: Readers of Curley's translation will see that E, III, Prop 34 refers to "exulting" in "being esteemed" rather than being "glorified." See note 11, above.

13. See Descartes' *Principles of Philosophy*, in John Cottingham, Robert Stoothoff, and Dugald Murdoch, eds., *The Philosophical Writings of Descartes*, 3 vols. (Cambridge: Cambridge University Press, 1985–91), vol. 2, 225–26.

14. The translation of the *Tractatus Theologico-Politicus* (TTP) used in this translation of Matheron's original article is *Theological-Political Treatise* (trans. S. Shirley), 2nd ed. (Indianapolis: Hackett, 2001). See editor's note, note 2, above.

15. See note 10, above.

16. E, III, Prop 31, Cor (Ovid citation). If we opt for the ablative, we are referred to the end of the Corollary, not to the Scholium. Gebhardt is therefore illogical when he corrects the *Opera Posthuma* on this point by replacing "Cor" with "Schol."

17. See note 10, above.

18. E, III, Prop 31, Schol. Only the choice of the nominative makes possible the reference to this scholium (see note 16, above).

19. The passage on sexual obsession (E, IV, Prop 44, Schol) is just as applicable to them as to lovers.

20. See E, IV, Prop 71, Schol: it is indeed the *meretrix* who tries to buy the favors of a man.

21. See E, IV, Appen, 20: the man and the woman love one another reciprocally for *their respective freedom of mind*.

22. Claire van den Enden, we are told, married for a string of pearls. Does Spinoza transpose the situation by inverting the sexes, thereby defending himself against an old resentment that would nevertheless betray the employment of the word *meretrix* to designate the one he now puts in the position of buyer? It is impossible to build anything at all on so little evidence.

23. Like Saint Paul, but obviously in a completely different domain! See TTP, III, 44.

5

Reason, Sexuality, and the Self in Spinoza

David West

Spinoza provides a distinctive and intriguing alternative to the West's dominant philosophical and theological understandings of sexuality. He clearly points the way beyond, even if he does not entirely evade, the two main metaphysical and moral "constellations" of reason, sexuality, and the self that have dominated western thought. The West's philosophy, theology and sexual morality have been distorted for more than two millennia by *either* an idealist conception of reason and the self with usually ascetic implications *or* a typically hedonist view of rationality as an instrument of the self's psychological and bodily satisfactions.[1]

The *idealist* constellation is authoritatively expressed by Plato but assumes its most pervasive, persistent, and arguably detrimental form within Christianity. Augustine, Aquinas, and other Church fathers melded philosophical idealism and scripture into a resilient orthodoxy that survives surprisingly intact until today. At the heart of what Nietzsche terms "ascetic idealism" is a notion of transcendent reason and the self variously associated with the eternal intellectual realm of Platonic Forms, with God and immortal souls or, in derived secular forms, with either pure reason or the supposedly necessary goals of nature and society. The association of this constellation with a dualistic view of human beings as an uneasy combination of soul and body, angelic and bestial, readily translates into an ascetic devaluation of the body and its "merely" physical or sensual sexual pleasures.

Ascetic idealism has long been challenged by a second, *hedonist* constellation of rationality, sexuality, and self. This constellation is represented most clearly by Benthamite utilitarianism, but related conceptions have a long history within western thought, including the ancient Epicureanism of Epicurus, Lucretius and their followers, "sexual realism" and cynicism from Ovid's love poetry to the Renaissance, the early-modern materialism and empiricism of Bacon and Hobbes as well as the more explicit materialism and atheism of eighteenth-century Enlightenment thinkers like Hume, La Mettrie, de Sade, and Bentham. At the heart of this alternative constellation is a less elevated notion of rationality as the merely calculating, instrumental servant of our psychological and bodily inclinations. Sex and other bodily pleasures can be accepted as intrinsically harmless or even valuable, although ascetic principles may still be justified on extrinsic grounds.

Although Spinoza does not address the issue of sexuality in great or explicit detail, his philosophy presents a substantial alternative to both ascetic and hedonist constellations. In the first place, without abandoning the terrain of religious discourse altogether, he expunges it of those "superstitious" elements and interpretations that have supported the Judeo-Christian tradition's narrow and rigid sexual morality. His vision of "God or Nature" offers no foothold for spiteful or self-sacrificial religious asceticism. But Spinoza's particular fascination results, further, from the ethical implications of the rigorous metaphysical monism that informs his religious-secular cosmology. Spinoza's monist metaphysics is systematically resistant to the western tradition's habitual reductions of self and sexual experience to *either* mind and reason *or* the body and its desires. The result is a highly original, if not unproblematic, perspective on reason, self, and sexuality, which illuminates the deficiencies of both ascetic-idealist and hedonist paradigms.

The Metaphysics of Freedom

Spinoza's novel ethical perspective is a direct consequence of his metaphysical monism, which undermines both philosophical mind-body dualism and conventional Judeo-Christian theology. For Spinoza, there is emphatically only *one* indivisible and infinite "substance," which he ambiguously and, in the religiously charged context of seventeenth-century Europe, provocatively dubs "God or Nature" (*Deus sive Natura*). "God or Nature" is understood both in active-creative and passive-substantive terms as *natura naturans* (or "nature naturing") and *natura naturata* ("nature natured"). The former is, in effect, the single substance in its manifestation as God the Creator, the latter as Nature or God's Creation. Spinoza's distinctive formulation emphasizes the fact that creator and created are one and indivisible.[2] At the same time, the single substance has an infinite number of "attributes," though it is known to us through only two of these as both a *mental* world of mind and thought and as a *physical* or *material* world of bodies extended in space.

Evidently, Spinoza's philosophy directly attacks the dualism implicated in the two constellations of reason and sexuality considered above. His implicit challenge to Judeo-Christian cosmology, on the other hand, is initially disguised by the deliberate ambivalence of his metaphysical terms, which certainly allow a religious interpretation. Everything is God and God is everything, so there can be no doubt—indeed Spinoza frequently asserts—that God exists. Spinoza has been understood, accordingly, as an essentially religious thinker.[3] But as with other early modern figures, the interpretation of Spinoza's apparent belief in God is not straightforward. This uncertainty is compounded by his hermeneutically sophisticated attitude to religious discourse. Spinoza recognizes that rational truths useful to the philosopher may be too difficult and so useless for the common "multitude," who must be subjected to less-than-rational religious inducements and civil penalties if they are even to approximate to the path of reason (TTP, V, 63–65).[4]

Whether or not his thought should ultimately be regarded as theist or atheist, Spinoza is dismissive of the personal and interventionist Creator-

God of the Old Testament. He laments the fact that "men commonly suppose that all natural things act, as men do, on account of an end; indeed, they maintain as certain that God himself directs all things to some certain end, for they say that God has made all things for man, and man that he might worship God" (E, I, Appen). There is no place for such anthropocentric purpose or teleology within Spinoza's all-encompassing conception of the one Substance, "God or Nature." God is just Nature conceived under a different attribute. God is not some being or agency *outside* or *beyond* Nature, who might willfully interfere in, and impose some purpose upon the natural course of events.

So despite his ostensibly religious discourse, Spinoza is without question a long way from the Judaism and Christianity of his time. Indeed, his philosophy has been interpreted instead as a form of pantheism—the view that God is everywhere and in everything—though it is more accurately described as "panentheism," which implies that everything *depends on* or *subsists in* God. In any case, for Spinoza's conventionally superstitious contemporaries, this philosophy looked very much like atheism. A God who is everywhere might as well be nowhere, particularly if God is not allowed to intervene providentially in the preordained course of events in order to reward good deeds and to punish evil ones. Even his more sympathetic followers and successors saw Spinoza as an early and particularly forthright advocate of materialism.[5]

Spinoza's position is nevertheless significantly different from that espoused by mainstream materialists and hedonists, because his "materialism" always coexists in a fruitful if uneasy tension with elements of philosophical idealism and rationalism. Spinoza is, of course, notorious for his "geometrical" or deductive method of exposition, which is more reminiscent of rationalism. More fundamentally, he explicitly rejects the empiricist model of knowledge usually associated with materialism. Although he refutes the dualism of his immediate philosophical predecessor, René Descartes (1596–1650), Spinoza retains the latter's rationalist conviction that the truth about all things both human and natural can be logically deduced from "clear and distinct" ideas. It is these rationalist principles that rule out any reductively materialist and hedonist account of morality as no more than the maximal satisfaction of our inclinations. Like Nietzsche, Spinoza sees humanity as a part of nature that must nevertheless not be *reduced* to nature: human beings must strive to transcend nature in order to attain their genuine freedom within it.[6]

The distinctiveness of Spinoza's position is made clear in comparison to the more straightforwardly empiricist, materialist, and hedonist philosophy of his near contemporary, Thomas Hobbes (1588–1679). In fact, the two philosophers have much in common, not least their strikingly similar political philosophies (TP, II, 38).[7] More importantly, Spinoza shares Hobbes's individualist moral ontology, which dispenses with any notion of generic human essence. Both philosophers deem the essence of every individual thing, whether animate or inanimate, animal or human, to be just its individual will or *conatus*: "Each thing, as far as it can by its own power, strives to persevere in its being" (E, III, Prop 6). Hobbes refers in parallel terms to the "general inclination of all mankind, a perpetual and restless desire of power after power, that ceaseth only in death."[8] The essence and supreme good for each individual are unique.

The moral individualism shared by Spinoza and Hobbes denies rationalist claims to identify a *universal* essence and standard of human flourishing. So, for example, it rules out Aristotle's definition of the "supreme good" (or *summum bonum*) for *all* human beings as the life of philosophical contemplation. Discredited too are any attempts inspired by such universal standards to *impose* the same norms of behavior on everyone. We have already encountered one common corollary of moral universalism, namely the insistence that there can be only one natural and healthy form of sexuality. By contrast, because for Spinoza human actions, like events in the natural world, are simply expressions of an individual's will or *conatus*, there is no reason why sexual acts must always serve the goal of procreation. They can be understood instead as just idiosyncratic expressions of an individual's striving for perfection.

In *contrast* to Hobbes, however, Spinoza's residual rationalism nevertheless leads him to regard rationality as far more than a mere instrument for the satisfaction of our impulses and inclinations.[9] Rationality is seen instead as the indispensable means for the fullest development of our individuality and so, in Spinoza's distinctive sense, for our freedom as well. Though he shares with Hobbes the belief that all our actions are causally determined, Spinoza is not satisfied with Hobbes's reconciliation of free will and necessity by means of a merely *negative* conception of freedom. According to that conception, whatever the causes of our actions, we are free as long as no person or agency forces us to act in some way. Beyond this absence of coercion, Spinoza's *positive* conception of freedom requires that the causes of our actions are genuinely our own or are, as it were, "internal" to us. Only in that case are we truly free, or "active" rather than "passive" in our actions and emotions (or "affects"):

"Actions," or "affects . . . that are related to us insofar as we act," must be contrasted with "passions," or occasions when we are passive or unfree in relation to our affections (E, III, Prop 58).[10]

The "internality" of the causes of our actions seems, at first sight, to bear no obvious relationship to either rationality or our freedom. But in fact, the criterion of internality is simultaneously a criterion of understanding or rationality. It is only emotions or affections that are genuinely "internal" to us (or really our own) that we can hope to understand in the strong sense implied by Spinoza's residual rationalism. As Stuart Hampshire helpfully explains, "I can only have adequate knowledge of the causes of those of my 'affections' which are not the effects of external causes," and only those affections can be deemed to be active.[11] So actions that are "internally caused" and those that can be "adequately conceived" are the same. Passive affections, on the other hand, inevitably resist the efforts of the understanding, because their causes are external to the individual. Ruled by passive affections, the self acts from reasons that are not its own, acts less than rationally and so is less than free. The self acts freely only when its reasons are truly its own.

Of course, an individual human being is only a small part of nature, which can never be completely independent of external influences. Only the one eternal substance "God or Nature" is, because it includes everything, necessarily determined only by things internal to itself and so absolutely free, despite being bound by its own necessary laws. Spinoza nevertheless believes that the *extent* of the individual's dependence on external causes is subject to the exertions of his or her understanding. Rationality or the "improvement of the understanding" is not merely a *symptom*, it is also a *means* of increasing our freedom from bondage: "An affect which is a passion ceases to be a passion as soon as we form a clear and distinct idea of it. . . . The more an affect is known to us, then, the more it is in our power, and the less the Mind is acted on by it" (E, V, Prop 3 and Cor). Each of us "has—in part, at least, if not absolutely—the power to understand himself and his affects, and consequently, the power to bring it about that he is less acted on by them" (E, V, Prop 4, Schol).

The ethical implications of Spinoza's moral ontology depend further on the fact that the freedom of individual *conatus* is necessarily constrained by consideration for other people. For someone living according to reason, it is evidently useful to live in an organized political society, which secures and enhances the power—and hence, freedom—of otherwise isolated and weak individuals: "To man, then, there is nothing more useful than man. Man, I say, can wish for nothing more helpful to the preservation of his being that that all should so agree in all things that the Minds and Bodies of all would compose, as it were, one Mind and one Body; that all should strive together, as far as they can, to preserve their being; and that all, together, should seek for themselves the common advantage of all" (E, IV, Prop 18, Schol). This need for society is the basis of morality and law, which regulate the relations between citizens. If people were completely rational, they would simply obey the rules of morality for the sake of the many advantages that accrue to them as members of an organized society: "From this it follows that men who are governed by reason—i.e., men who, from the guidance of reason, seek their own advantage—want nothing for themselves that they do not desire for other men. Hence, they are just, honest, and honorable" (E, IV Prop 18, Schol). Because most people are *not* rational, however, they must be restrained by the coercive laws of the state.

The common striving of a rational community of individuals does *not* depend, however, on the moral universalism of those brands of rationalism hostile to individual difference, but only on the political unity of the state. It is only in this sense that "The greatest good of those who seek virtue is common to all, and can be enjoyed by all equally" (E, IV, Prop 36 and Schol). So whereas for the ascetic-idealist tradition of reason the notion of a rational "essence of man" implies universal and potentially oppressive norms of human behavior, within the overall assumptions of Spinoza's individualist moral ontology there is no reason to suppose that the need to live together in society means that all must live in the same way. Our need for society means only that there must be certain morally and socially defined limits to the expression of individual *conatus*. Otherwise, each individual is free to realize its own essence in its own way.

The Ethics of Pleasure, Sexuality, and Love

Spinoza's distinctive ethics of pleasure, sexuality, and love follow from both his more positive metaphysical doctrines and his critical demolition of superstition. For the latter, whether or not he should ultimately be regarded as a religious thinker, Spinoza's unorthodox interpretation of scripture is undoubtedly at odds with Judeo-Christian theology and sexual morality. In his *Theologico-Political Treatise*, Spinoza claims that we can make sense of the contradictions and inconsistencies of scripture, only if we understand the utterances of the prophets not as the direct and infallible pronouncements of the deity but as reflections of their own limited characters and times. So we should expect to find only very general principles of piety and morality rather than any specific moral prescriptions, let alone eternal theological and philosophical truths. In these terms, the exhaustive laws of ritual purity enunciated by Moses and other Old Testament prophets should not be treated as eternal moral prescriptions but only as temporary rules reflecting the secular needs of the ancient Hebrew nation (TTP, III, 38–9).

It follows that the Judeo-Christian tradition's stubborn, if inconsistent, reliance on the minutiae of the Mosaic sexual code is without foundation. The condemnation of homosexuality so starkly evinced by Leviticus (20:13) has as little relevance for contemporary sexual morality as other similarly harsh but more rarely adduced injunctions. The chapter of Leviticus that castigates homosexual acts in a single uncompromising verse also condemns to death any Israelite who curses his father or mother, commits adultery or bestiality, sleeps with his mother or daughter-in-law and anyone "that hath a familiar spirit, or that is a wizard." Surely, rather than attempting to fashion our contemporary morality from such ancient and eccentric sources, we should limit our attention to the perennial but more abstract moral truths still to be found in scripture.

The prejudice that nature, and therefore humanity, must have some God-given purpose is, of course, the other linchpin of Christian sexual morality, which regards procreation as the only proper *telos* or goal of sexual activity. Any ambiguity in Plato's late (and perhaps hypocritical) condemnation of homosexuality in *The Laws* as unnatural or "contrary to nature" is eliminated by later Christian theology. With the help of a scattering of obscure and sometimes dubious scriptural authorities—chiefly the stories of Sodom and Gomorrah and the sin of Onan, the Mosaic code and the divine injunction to "go forth and multiply"—theologians such as Augustine and Aquinas forged an enduring orthodoxy condemning all nonprocreative sexual acts.[12] But according to Spinoza's antiteleological cosmology, human beings and their sexual acts can, like nature, have no such preordained goal. So a sexual morality that sanctions only reproductive sexual acts is founded on an illusion. Corresponding views of the patriarchal family as the divinely decreed means for the rearing of children are similarly undermined.

Spinoza's endorsement of pleasure takes a more enthusiastic form in the later *Ethics* where, amidst more austerely metaphysical axioms and propositions, we find a remarkably forthright attack on "superstition." It is worth quoting at some length:

> No deity, nor anyone else, unless he is envious, takes pleasure in my lack of power and my misfortune; nor does he ascribe to virtue our tears, sighs, fear, and other things of that kind, which are signs of a weak mind. On the contrary, the greater the Joy with which we are affected, the greater the perfection to which we pass, i.e., the more we must participate in the divine nature. To use things, therefore, and take pleasure in them as far as possible—not, of course, to the point where we are disgusted with them, for there is no pleasure in that—this is the part of a wise man.
>
> It is the part of a wise man, I say, to refresh and restore himself in moderation with pleasant food and drink, with scents, with the beauty of green plants, with decoration, music, sports, the theater, and other things of this kind, which anyone can use without injury to another. For the human Body is composed of a great many parts of different natures, which constantly require new and varied nourishment, so that the whole Body may be equally capable of all the things which can follow from its nature, and hence, so that the Mind also may be equally capable of understanding many things. (E, IV, Prop 45, Schol)

The radical implication—radical, at least, from the predominantly ascetic perspective of western philosophy and theology—is that even *physical* pleasure can be taken as a sign of our proximity to the "divine nature." Hostility to pleasure, on the other hand, is a destructive imposition of priests and false religion: "Superstition . . . seems to maintain that the good is what brings Sadness, and the evil, what brings Joy." In fact, the "morality" of superstition and fear is really neither rational nor moral, for "he who is led by Fear, and does the good only to avoid the evil, is not governed by reason" (E, IV, Appen XXXI).

More than just a corollary of his hostility to superstitious religion, however, Spinoza's defense of pleasure follows directly from his monist metaphysics and positive conception of freedom. Philosophical hedonism, albeit qualified, is apparent from Spinoza's earliest writings. In his first published work, the *Treatise on the Emendation of the Intellect*, Spinoza describes his motivation for turning to philosophical reflection as liberation from greed, ambition, and obsessive hedonism. His suspicions of hedonism would not be out of place in the broader philosophical tradition:

> For as far as sensual pleasure is concerned, the mind is so caught up in it, as if at peace in a [true] good, that it is quite prevented from thinking of anything else. But after the enjoyment of sensual pleasure is past, the greatest sadness follows. If this does not completely engross, still it thoroughly confuses and dulls the mind. (TdIE, 4)

But significantly, he never proposes to dispense with sensual pleasures altogether. It is sufficient that they are kept within their proper limits as means to the fulfillment of one's other needs and concerns:

> I saw that the acquisition of money, sensual pleasure, and esteem are only obstacles so long as they are sought for their own sakes, and not as means to other things. But if they are sought as means, then they will have a limit, and will not be obstacles at all. On the contrary, they will be of great use in attaining the end on account of which they are sought, as we shall show in its place. (TdIE, 11)

Amongst his provisional rules of living at this stage is thus the cautiously hedonist—in fact, characteristically Epicurean—principle, "To enjoy pleasures just so far as suffices for safeguarding our health" (TdIE, 17).

Spinoza's developed position provides a more substantial basis for his distinctive version of philosophical hedonism. The denial of dualism undermines mainstream philosophical rationalism and asceticism by ruling out any categorically superior status for rational or mental pleasures and the corresponding demotion of the merely bodily and sexual. The experience of joy or pleasure of any kind is, for Spinoza, simply the mental state accompanying the individual's transition to a state of greater perfection. In fact, joy and sadness are *defined* as the mental signs of increasing or diminishing perfection: "By *Joy*, therefore, I shall understand in what follows that *passion by which the Mind passes to a greater perfection*. And by *Sadness*, that *passion by which it passes to a lesser perfection*" (E, III, Prop 11, Schol).

Monism allows the transition to a state of greater perfection to be understood not as the progressive ascendancy of reason over merely physical impulses—as it is for ascetic idealism—but as a process whose physical and mental aspects are of equal intrinsic value. As Moira Gatens puts it, "Spinoza's monistic view of human being dictates that what increases the power of action of the body also increases the power of the mind. Hence bodily pleasures are as important for the well-being of the individual as is the cultivation of reason."[13] In Spinoza's words, "The idea of any thing that increases or diminishes, aids or restrains, our Body's power of acting, increases or diminishes, aids or restrains, our Mind's power of thinking" (E, III, Prop 11). Other things being equal, *all* pleasures are good, *all* pains intrinsically bad.

Spinoza's rehabilitation of physical pleasure also applies to sex. We can only assume, in Gatens's words, that "The sexual relation, in so far as it give rise to joyful feelings, is good."[14] Spinoza's philosophy undermines the idealist tradition's habitual demotion of "base" (because bodily) sexual *desire* for the sake of an idealized, purely spiritual *love*. As Alexandre Matheron's close and illuminating analysis has shown, the ontological unity of body and mind translates into the moral equivalence of love and desire, which are equally valuable expressions of an underlying "endeavor to persist in our own being." Spinoza defines love as "joy associated with the idea of an external cause" and, as we have seen, joy is defined as "an increase in the power to act." But the power to act is just the same thing as *conatus*, and "*conatus* so defined is the same as desire." Accordingly—and in contrast to Hobbes's seemingly hydraulic understanding of sexual desire as a simple wish for relief ("exoneration")—sexual desire and pleasure are, as much as love, intrinsically and positively joyful manifestations of increasing perfection.[15]

Spinoza's identification of love and sexual desire might seem reminiscent of Plato's conception of *eros* in the *Symposium*, which similarly treats both drives as the manifestations of a single force. But Spinoza's denial of any overriding purpose in nature is inconsistent with Plato's idealist vision of *eros* as forever striving towards higher and more spiritual goals. According to the Priestess Diotima—whose views are related towards the end of the dialogue by Socrates and seemingly represent both his own and Plato's views—*eros* fulfils its proper purpose only when it is able to ascend from particular beautiful things, such as young men, to more abstract and universal ideals of beauty and goodness. It is, of course, the idealism of this Platonic vision that provides one of the main inspirations for later western and Christian sexual asceticism.[16] Contrastingly, by avoiding Plato's teleological idealism, Spinoza retains the possibility of a positive evaluation of sex.

Accordingly, Spinoza's principles are compatible with (even though he never explicitly discusses) a variety of sexual acts and relationships beyond the pale of the heterosexual norm.[17] Certainly, as we have seen, his basic assumptions rule out the normative or prescriptive application of concepts of "nature," "natural" and "unnatural" that has been fundamental to the West's long hostility to homosexuality and other nonreproductive sexual practices. As a result, the definition of sexuality is substantially transformed, as Freud's account of sexuality would later make clear.[18] Reproduction cannot be the *essential* sexual "aim," so sex need not be confined to, or even centered on the genital regions and activities of bodies. The choice of sexual "object" is similarly broadened beyond potentially fertile heterosexual couplings to what Jeremy Bentham tactfully termed "improlific" connections. Even autoeroticism can be recognized as an instance of sexuality without normative or conceptual embarrassment. Different individuals—whether homosexual, heterosexual, or bisexual, alone or in any combination—are free to approach perfection through the enjoyment of their diversely erotic pleasures and preoccupations.

As with any other area of life, of course, an individual's sexual activity must also be compatible with his or her membership of a political community. In fact, Spinoza's views regarding the state's regulation of sexual behavior are, where actually stated, quite conventional. It is not surprising that he says nothing explicitly in defense of sexual nonconformity. The state must, it seems, decide what kinds of sexual relationship and activity are compatible with the stability and security of society. His strong views on freedom of thought and religious belief, though certainly more liberal than those of Hobbes, do not translate into support for dissident *behavior* (TTP, XX, 224). He has no reason to oppose, but neither does he show any sign of advocating, the kinds of "experiments of living" contemplated—albeit only in very abstract terms and some two centuries later—by John Stuart Mill.[19]

Further ethical strictures follow from Spinoza's distinctive account of freedom, because under certain circumstances love and sexual desire may be potential sources of bondage. When desire is partial and obsessive, it is liable to threaten the rational and free activity of an integral self. Physical pleasure (*titillatio*) that is confined to a particular part of the body distracts the individual from concern with its overall well-being.

Although "all things that bring Joy are good," human striving has a tendency to excess: "since Joy is generally related particularly to one part of the body, most affects of Joy are excessive (unless reason and alertness are present). Hence, the Desires generated by them are also excessive" (E, IV, Appen, 30). Lust, in particular, is a persistent source of passive emotions and bondage, because it is a one-sided physical desire rendering the individual dependent on the whims of another and readily giving rise to jealousy and hatred: "A purely sensual love, moreover, i.e., a lust to procreate that arises from external appearance, and absolutely, all love that has a cause other than freedom of mind, easily passes into hate—unless (which is worse) it is a species of madness" (E, IV, Appen, 19).

The problematic tendencies of lustful *titillatio* seem, at first sight, to cast doubt on the value of *exclusively* sexual relationships, which are usually thought to focus on particular parts of the body in such potentially distracting ways. But liberated from the narrowly genital sexuality of the dominant tradition, there is no reason to suppose that a sexual interaction should not attend to the whole of another person's body and, indeed, mind as well. This intriguing possibility is elucidated by Simone de Beauvoir. If men and women can escape the damaging distortions of the "battle of the sexes," sexual relations may transcend the dualism of mind and body, so that "Under a concrete and carnal form there is mutual recognition of the ego and of the other in the keenest awareness of the other and of the ego."[20] Sex in this guise would have no intrinsic tendency to distract the individual from concern with its overall well-being. It is only the dominant tradition's dualist and teleological conception of sexuality that drives such a deep wedge between (merely physical) sex and (potentially spiritual) love, so that sex, understood as little more than genital coupling, can have nothing in common with "true" love.

Spinoza's radical understanding of sex also leads him to diverge from the misogyny of the western tradition's ideal of love which, at least before Romanticism, tends to be understood as a relationship that is more likely to exist between *men*.[21] Aristotle's influential understanding of love (*philia*) as a spiritual association unsullied by considerations of mere usefulness or transient pleasure was fatefully distorted by the patriarchal outlook of ancient Greece. Only relationships between men were thought capable of transcending the utilitarian and hedonist considerations predominating in marriage for the sake of a more lasting and purified bond.[22] The homophobia of late medieval Christianity stripped Aristotelian *philia* of any vestige of homosexuality, leaving the seemingly innocuous ideal of "friendship" (rather than "love") between men as an idealized counterpoint to the unavoidable necessities of marriage and procreation, family and inheritance.[23]

It is hardly surprising, of course, that Spinoza's seventeenth-century sexual-political vision does not entirely escape from the patriarchal limits of his time. His unfinished *Political Treatise* ends disappointingly with a paragraph justifying the political subjection of women as a consequence of their natural weakness (TP, XI, 136–37). Women occasionally figure in the *Ethics* in the role of "prostitutes" or "courtesans" (objects, that is, of *amor meretricius*), who may threaten the individual's rational composure through the distracting enticements of lust. But Spinoza's views of marriage are more radical. Beyond its conventional function as the proper social context for the upbringing of children, marriage offers the possibility of a loving relationship based on "freedom of mind" rather than merely "external appearance" (E, IV, Appen, 20).

Spinoza is able to apply something like Aristotle's ideal of genuine love or friendship to heterosexual love, because for him both love and sexual desire are equally valuable expressions, under the alternative attributes of mind and body, of the same underlying will or *conatus*. Love does not have to be understood in the terms of Platonic idealism as the higher but always uncertain destination of an originally base sexual infatuation. Spinoza's more expansive account allows for—indeed seems to require—the continued coexistence of love and sexual desire. So sexual desire and love can be understood as mutually reinforcing rather than mutually exclusive alternatives.

At the same time, Spinoza's antiteleological ontology promises to liberate love from the *compulsory* asymmetry of gender that was later enshrined in Romantic conceptions of love. For Romanticism, *only* heterosexual unions can fulfill the highest possible ideal of love, because they alone promise to fuse the complementary qualities of men and women into a uniquely valuable whole. According to Friedrich Schlegel, for example, love combines the focused activity, strength, and reason of man with the childlike spontaneity, emotional warmth, and harmonious balance of woman.[24] For Roger Scruton's more recent and purportedly "metaphysical" account, it is the *absence* of such gender complementarities that confirms the inferior status of same-sex unions.[25] In contrast, Spinoza's philosophy is compatible with the equal value of homosexual and heterosexual love, because he does not resort to such stereotypical assumptions. Complex individuals may conjugate according to their diverse and unpredictably shared and contrasting qualities, their complementary and mutually reinforcing needs, capacities, and will.

At the root of Spinoza's freedom from sexist assumptions is his radical conception of biological sex. If sex is no longer understood as essentially reproductive activity, then men and women need not be defined first and foremost according to their complementary roles in sexual reproduction. So there is no reason why we should not contemplate the actual multiplicity of "intersexual" variations and gradations between the bipolar extremes of "male" and "female," no reason why everyone must be forcibly assigned to one or other of these alternatives. By implication, too, sex and sexual orientation should not be the primary basis for defining and classifying human relationships. The opposition between homosexual and heterosexual sex and love represents (even with the supplementary category of bisexuality) just one of many possible classificatory schemes. Spinoza is able to recognize without essentializing the actual differences and multiple possible relationships amongst individuals.[26]

By the same token, the Spinozist conception of sex offers an alternative to the distinction between sex and gender that has become almost canonical within recent feminist thought. The opposition between sex and gender gained particular ascendancy with the rise of "second-wave" feminism from the nineteen-sixties and seventies. It served, above all, to drive a wedge between, on the one side, supposedly unchangeable, biological differences of male and female "sex" and, on the other, socially constructed or imposed and presumably changeable differences between masculine and feminine "genders." The programmatic implication was that the elimination of gender differences could bring about the social and political equality of men and women, despite remaining, and presumably inevitable, differences of sex.[27]

However, as Gatens has argued, Spinoza's philosophy both undermines the sex/gender dichotomy and offers an alternative way of conceiving sex differences. Spinoza's antidualism implies that gender and sex, like minds and bodies, should be regarded as indivisible attributes of one underlying reality. Minds and social identities are not free-floating constructions only loosely associated with their bodies. But abolition of the sex/gender distinction need not condemn women and men to an unchanging essentialism of sex roles either. That would follow only for a conventional view of biological sex, which conceives bodies in the limited terms of a binary biological opposition between male and female. In fact, bodies, just like minds, can be conceived as varied and changeable. Indeed, because bodies just *are* minds under a different attribute, they are not the passive and inert bearers of malleable and active minds. Bodies can change themselves, bodies are active too. So even without a distinction between sexed bodies and gendered minds, we can understand how women, whose bodies under patriarchal conditions have been trained for passivity and subjection, can nevertheless refashion themselves in order to escape their subordinate condition. Women's (and men's) bodies and minds can be conceived or "imagined" and so *lived* differently as well.[28]

But does Spinoza liberate himself (albeit incompletely) from the dominant tradition's asceticism and sexism only to recommend something close to the ideal of intellectual contemplation (or *theoria*) advocated by Aristotle? Spinoza is certainly uncompromising in his advocacy of reason. As he states, in words that could almost be taken from the *Nicomachean Ethics*: "No life . . . is rational without understanding, and things are good only insofar as they aid man to enjoy the life of the Mind, which is defined by understanding" and "those that prevent man from being able to perfect his reason and enjoy the rational life, those only we say are evil" (E, IV, Appen, 5). But if we avoid reading Spinoza in the dualist terms of Cartesianism, it is clear that the "perfecting of reason" cannot be conceived without the parallel, indeed *identical*, process of perfecting the body. Like many of his ostensibly religious statements, Spinoza's encomia on reason reproduce the *language* of the philosophical tradition, but to very different effect.

It is more difficult to avoid the conclusion that Spinoza's philosophy ultimately threatens to devalue the particular, personal attachments that are inseparable from conventional ideas of love. For Spinoza, rational contemplation of the universe "from the perspective of eternity" (*sub specie aeternitatis*), which he deems essential for the individual's freedom from the bondage of passive emotions, issues in a Stoic acceptance of the order of nature and the world. Faced with our own limited powers, we should learn to bear adversity calmly: "For insofar as we understand, we can want nothing except what is necessary, nor absolutely be satisfied with anything except what is true" (E, IV, Appen, 32). But from this perspective, it seems that our particular relationships and commitments must fade to insignificance as well.

A possible rescue of interpersonal love from the detached abstraction of the "perspective of eternity" depends on the interpretation of Spinoza's third, highest, and most obscure category of knowledge. According to Amelie Oksenberg Rorty, *scientia intuitiva*, or what Spinoza sometimes describes as the "intellectual love of God," transforms without abolishing our more local and contingent relationships. Our "intuitive knowledge" of the world "involves apprehending the vast system, the network of particular individuals (including of course all the properties they have in common) as a unified individual" and so combines the particularity of mere imagination (the first level of knowledge) with the universal truths of *ratio* or reason (the second level).[29] As Spinoza more cryptically remarks, "The more we understand singular things, the more we understand God" (E, V, Prop 24). On Rorty's interpretation, the "adequate ideas" of reason diminish our individuation but not our individuality. Individuals may become more alike (and so less individuated) as they come to share more and more of the adequate ideas of reason, but their *individuality*—or in other words their ability to realize their own individual *conatus*—is enhanced rather than diminished as a result.[30]

It may still seem difficult to resist the conclusion that Spinoza's philosophy diminishes, at least to some extent, the localized pleasures and attachments of interpersonal love. Although the complex individual that is "God or Nature" does, in theory, include every individual thing in all of its infinite particularity, Spinoza's project of liberation nevertheless urges us to focus as much as possible on the perspective of eternity and so implies a less than absolute attention to more local involvements. Our difficulties in this regard may, however, simply reflect our unconsciously Romantic and post-Romantic sensibilities, which share the tendency to exaggerate the distance between love and reason. Spinoza invokes the alternative insight that love and sex may rather be *enriched* by the contemplation of realms beyond their enchanted but potentially limiting domain.

Notes

I am grateful to Moira Gatens for detailed and incisive comments on an earlier draft of this chapter.

1. For a more detailed account of these constellations, see D. West, *Reason and Sexuality in Western Thought* (New York: Polity Press, 2005), chaps. 1–3.

2. Benedict de Spinoza, *The Ethics*, in *The Collected Works of Spinoza*, vol. 1, trans. Edwin Curley (Princeton: Princeton University Press, 1985), Parts I–II. On Spinoza's metaphysics, see, for example, Stuart Hampshire, *Spinoza* (London: Penguin, 1951); Alan Donagan, *Spinoza* (New York: Harvester Wheatsheaf, 1988); and Genevieve Lloyd, *Spinoza and the Ethics* (London: Routledge, 1996).

3. On Spinoza's relationship to religion, see Richard Mason, *The God of Spinoza: A Philosophical Study* (Cambridge: Cambridge University Press, 1997) and A. C. Fox, *Faith and Philosophy: Spinoza on Religion* (Nedlands: University of Western Australia Press, 1990).

4. Cf. Christopher Norris, *Spinoza and the Origins of Modern Critical Theory* (Oxford: Basil Blackwell, 1991).

5. Spinoza can be regarded as a major source of what Jonathan Israel calls the "radical Enlightenment": see Jonathan I. Israel, *Radical Enlightenment: Philosophy and the Making of Modernity, 1650–1750* (Oxford: Oxford University Press, 2001), part V, chap. 37, 707–9.

6. Both are, in Paul Tillich's phrase, "ecstatic naturalists." See Richard Schacht, "The Spinoza-Nietzsche Problem," in *Desire and Affect: Spinoza as Psychologist*, ed. Yirmiyahu Yovel (New York: Little Room Press, 1999), 211–12.

7. On the direct influence of Hobbes on Spinoza, see, for example, Margaret Gullan-Whur, *Within Reason: A Life of Spinoza* (London: Pimlico, 2000), 289–91 and passim.

8. Thomas Hobbes, *Leviathan, or the Matter, Forme and Power of a Commonwealth Ecclesiasticall and Civil*, ed. Michael Oakeshott (Oxford: Basil Blackwell, 1955), part I, chap. 11, 64.

9. On Hobbes's conception of reason, see *Leviathan*, I, 5.

10. On Spinoza's concept of freedom and its relationship to Hobbes, see my "Spinoza on Positive Freedom," *Political Studies* 41 (1993): 284–96. On the related issue of whether the principle of *conatus* should be seen as a covertly teleological principle, see Schacht, 225–6.

11. Hampshire, *Spinoza*, 136–37.

12. See West, *Reason and Sexuality in Western Thought*, esp. chap. 1, §§1, 3 and 4 on Plato, Augustine, and Aquinas.

13. Moira Gatens, *Imaginary Bodies* (London: Routledge, 1996), chap. 9, 132.

14. Ibid.

15. See the translation of Alexandre Matheron's "Spinoza et la sexualité" in Chapter 4 of this volume.

16. See West, *Reason and Sexuality in Western Thought*, chap. 1, §1.

17. Cf. Matheron, Chapter 4 in this volume.

18. Sigmund Freud, "Three Essays on Sexuality," in *On Sexuality: Three Essays on the Theory of Sexuality and Other Works* (Harmondsworth: Penguin, 1977), Essay I, 45ff.

19. John Stuart Mill, "On Liberty," in *Utilitarianism, On Liberty, and Considerations on Representative Government*, ed. H. B. Acton (London: Dent, 1972), chap. 3, 114ff.

20. Simone de Beauvoir, *The Second Sex*, 421–22 and see Debra B. Bergoffen, *The Philosophy of Simone de Beauvoir*.

21. On friendship between women, see L. Faderman, *Surpassing the Love of Men: Romantic Friendship and Love Between Women from the Renaissance to the Present* (New York: Morrow, 1981).

22. For Aristotle's view, see *Nicomachean Ethics*, Part VI (§§1155ª1–1172ª18).

23. Ironically, the nominal celibacy of this ideal of friendship also made it a suitable alibi for covertly homosexual liaisons.

24. F. Schlegel, "Philosophy of Language," in *The Philosophy of Life, and Philosophy of Language, in a Course of Lectures*, trans. A. J. W. Morrison (New York: AMS Press, 1973), 361ff and cf. West, *Reason and Sexuality in Western Thought*, chap. 3, §3.

25. Roger Scruton, *Sexual Desire: A Philosophical Investigation* (London: Weidenfeld and Nicolson, 1986), chap. 10, 305ff.

26. See Gatens, *Imaginary Bodies*, chap. 5, esp. 73.

27. Feminist futurists such as Shulamith Firestone even envisaged an eventual technological solution for women's biological condition. See Gatens, *Imaginary Bodies*, chap. 1, esp. 5–7 and Shulamith Firestone, *The Dialectic of Sex: The Case for Feminist Revolution* (New York: Morrow, 1970), chap. 10.

28. Gatens, *Imaginary Bodies*, chap. 1, passim and chap. 4, esp. 55ff.

29. Amelie Oksenberg Rorty, "Spinoza on the Pathos of Idolatrous Love and the Hilarity of True Love," reprinted as Chapter 3 in this volume.

30. Amelie Rorty, "The Two Faces of Spinoza," in *Spinoza: Critical Assessments*, vol. 2, *The Ethics*, ed. Genevieve Lloyd (London: Routledge, 2001), 279–92.

6
What Spinoza Can Teach Us About Embodying and Naturalizing Ethics

Heidi Morrison Ravven

I present here a précis of the project I have been developing over the past few years on embodying and naturalizing philosophical ethics by critiquing and rethinking standard ethics through a Spinozist lens. I propose that standard modern Western philosophical ethics even now, in the early twenty-first century, is theologically driven and I introduce an overview of the line of research I am undertaking to expose standard philosophical ethics as originating in, and as still beholden to, a number of dogmatic Christian theological theses mandated in the thirteenth century. I suggest that the way philosophers think about ethics may also reflect a Christian anthropology of identity formation. So I challenge the claim of modern philosophical ethics to universality and reframe it, instead, as an expression of an unacknowledged Christian cultural provincialism. I argue that standard philosophical approaches to ethics harbor underlying Christian presuppositions that deracinate mind from body, nature from spirit, will from desire, the individual from its history, and the self from others. An indictment of modern moral thinking as unable to emerge fully from its Christian origins has been taken up at times and by some as a commonplace ever since Nietzsche attacked Christian values in contrast with classical ones. It was reintroduced into the debate by Elizabeth Anscombe in 1958 as an attack on Kantian deontology as presupposing and requiring a divine lawgiver,[1] a claim that was built upon by Anscombe and echoed by Philippa Foot[2] as an important component of the argument to return to an Aristotelian-inspired virtue theory. Perhaps most recently the Christian theological hold upon contemporary moral philosophy has been argued by Owen Flanagan in his book-length indictment of the Christian (and especially Catholic) version of the separable soul as the major contemporary obstacle to a realistic and sensible moral psychology.[3] My work argues a different but related point: I contend that the precise problem is the ongoing and barely challenged hold of the Augustinian notion of the free will upon our standard conceptions of the human. Instead of making a general claim about the essential nature of Christianity as basis for the indictment I trace the formation of the concept of free will and then the arguments about free will from Augustine on in the history of the mainstream (Latin) Christian theological tradition. My work brings together current scholarly investigation on how it responded to challenges; when it became hardened on the matter and why; and how it still plagues not only theology but, in a disguised secularized version, also philosophy and our standard and pervasive Western commonplaces about ethics even today. I offer a review of the current research on the theological considerations and doctrines from which that notion arose and of the several historical moments of dogmatic intervention that made it standard and even compulsory. My work builds on the general insightful glimmering of these philosophers to raise the more historical question: if we look at Christian theological notions of the human ethical capacity in a more historically precise way, what do we discover about Western cultural anthropology?

I maintain that a comparison with Spinoza's approach to ethics, one that I argue derives from a different (but parallel) philosophical, theological, and cultural milieu, both enables these underlying fatal problems of standard ethical reflection to become visible to us. It also offers some resources for their resolution. The philosophy of Spinoza provides us a far deeper critique than most standard feminist ones, for they remain within the orbit of the Christian dogmatic and anthropological presuppositions brought together in the notion of the free will as it was transformed in modernity in the standard Cartesian and Kantian approaches to philosophy generally and to ethics in particular.[4]

Spinoza was able to envision ethics in a thoroughgoing, different key—one that has recently been described as "outside the structures of dualism, transcendence, and representation"—because he was heir to an alternative and rival philosophical-theological tradition, namely, the Judeo-Islamic.[5] So I propose that in looking to Spinoza we also embrace a revival of central tenets and practices of the Arabic Judeo-Islamic medieval philosophical tradition, a tradition that was eclipsed by the hegemony of church doctrine in the thirteenth century, as I shall argue below.[6] The critique and the alternative approach to ethics that a turn to Spinoza opens up for us resonate with familiar contemporary feminist concerns: with the search for an embodied and situated kind of thinking, a nonreductive materialist perspective that can overcome dualisms. It is one that takes into account the indelible marking of every person by history, social location, and natural endowment but that, at the same time, does not reify or essentialize a particular perspective but can open us up to ever wider viewpoints and broader understandings.[7] We will be able to enrich our resources for the resolution of a number of problems feminists have identified in standard philosophy to include not only Spinoza but also the religiophilosophical tradition from which he sprang and to which he gave modern expression. We find in Spinoza a way to overcome standard philosophical ethics' basic underlying otherworldly, detached, and reified Christian Platonism—the tradition and presuppositions that undergird its modern Cartesian and Kantian expressions—with an embodied and located radical Aristotelian naturalism, a naturalism described by Julie Klein as "a materialist, nominalist, and strongly non-hierarchical immanentized Aristotelianism."[8] The latter was the shared project of nearly all the great medieval Islamic and Jewish philosophers in their shared golden age. It is a past that, I propose here, is both usable and even points to a truer way of seeing the human person. And it is a tradition that was marginalized and even suppressed—outlawed and vilified—by the dominant Christian theological authorities and that I propose continues to be so by their unknowing modern and contemporary heirs.[9] The revival of, and a contemporary rethinking inspired by, the common glorious Judeo-Islamic past could engage contemporary Jewish and Muslim philosophers, scholars of Spinoza, and feminist philosophers in a joint endeavor to transform philosophical ethics. I hope that what I introduce here might spark projects of this kind.

Free will or its lack is a central point of contention between Spinozist ethics and the Cartesian-Kantianism that pervades modern and contemporary philosophical discussions of ethics. Upon examination we find that standard philosophical ethics in both its Analytic and Continental versions maintains and secularizes, and thereby disguises and bolsters, a miraculous view of the human person that, I suggest, is inherent in the voluntarist notion of free will. The latter encompasses a number of related claims that paint a quite specific philosophical anthropological picture. The noted philosopher Christine Korsgaard articulates well the centrality of conscious choice as the sine qua non of contemporary approaches to ethics in the introduction to her *Creating the Kingdom of Ends*.[10] Although Korsgaard is a noted interpreter of Kant, her presuppositions are widely accepted across rival camps:

> Our practically rational nature ... brings with it both the capacity and the necessity of *choosing* our actions. *Choice is our plight, our inescapable fate, as rational beings*. The project of critical moral philosophy is to determine what resources we can find in reason for solving the problem which reason itself has set for us. Since we are looking for laws for the employment of *our powers of choice and action, we do not, in this investigation, regard ourselves as natural, causally determined beings—as the objects of scientific understanding. We regard ourselves as free, as the authors of our actions*. This is not because there is any reason to deny that we are natural, causally determined beings, but because for the purpose at hand [namely, ethics], that conception of ourselves is *irrelevant*.[11]

So it is upon the reasons for the embrace by all contemporary and modern philosophical schools of philosophy of the freedom of the will that I focus here. Free will presupposes a human person who, as it were, intervenes from "above" into nature and history on the analogy of the way that God intervenes miraculously in biblical creation and history. The doctrine entails a human person who is not *of nature and history* but instead has powers to transcend the natural and historical and social character of human life. It sets as the human ideal an absolute mastery over the self and the world. A few recent scholars have recognized that free will is a "mystery," but none, as far as I know, has recognized its religious origins and character and traced its origins to Christian doctrine or biblical understandings of the divine. The doctrine of the freedom of the will is problematic because it both misdescribes the human person and also has negative personal, social, and public policy consequences. Assigning to the individual complete responsibility for his or her triumphs or failures aggrandizes the privileged and blames the poor and needy for their situation. It suggests that all solutions are individual rather than primarily social and systemic.

The doctrinal mandate of radical voluntarism harks back to the church Condemnations of 1277 of Judeo-Arabic Aristotelian naturalism, whose general rejection was under the banner and rallying cry of Free Will.[12] It was at this point that the free will went from informality and lack of precise definition to the subject of heated debate, high nuance, clarification, and crystallization. The adoption was now compulsory, although the spectrum within that adoption was fairly broad. That we can choose our actions ex nihilo or de novo (the latter is the philosophical view that we *originate our actions* whether they are chosen from alternatives or not), the voluntarist thesis in some form, is an idea dependent on a deep Christian anthropology because a person is *converted* to Christianity thus making Christianity normatively *an identity one adopts or chooses* rather than one that one is born into.[13] Thereby Christian identity is defined as rejecting the natural facts of birth and context and replaced by a choice articulated in the language of *born again* and *converted to*. Christianity is normatively an identity that involves an embrace of change from a prior to a subsequent state.[14] To wit, it is the rite of baptism that initiates and defines the Christian, and baptism represents the *choosing of Christianity* even and especially symbolically and not literally, since most Christians are baptized in infancy. Baptism as the mode of Christian identification is precisely a *symbol of conversion*, for that was (and remains) its function in the Judaism from which the custom was borrowed. For Jews, only those converted to Judaism are *immersed*, but *all Christians are immersed*, that is, all Christians take on Christianity symbolically from some prior (unsaved) state. Being born again implies an antinaturalism insofar as one symbolically rejects an identity emergent from one's natural and historical contexts but, instead, chooses one. It is this deep anthropology that,

I believe, gets replayed and transformed in dogmatic theology and haunts philosophical ethics even today.

Harry Austryn Wolfson, the great historian of medieval Jewish, Islamic, and Christian philosophical theology, recognized that the freedom of the will as defined by the Western philosophical tradition was, in fact, a theological doctrine assigning a miraculous status and capacity to the human mind and personality.[15] Wolfson maintained that the entire Western medieval philosophical-theological tradition was defined by its embrace of a miraculous notion of the will whose original adoption was an attempt to reconcile Greek philosophical and Hebrew biblical traditions. According to Wolfson, all three Western religious traditions effected this compromise, a compromise initiated, in his view, by the Hellenistic Jewish philosopher Philo in the first century and dismantled by the Jewish philosopher Spinoza in the seventeenth. But he was at the same time at pains to find one Jewish philosopher who actually fit the bill![16] Wolfson regarded Spinoza's philosophy as a deconstruction of the reconciliation of Greek and Hebrew traditions into their original components. (Charles Taylor similarly sees Spinoza as a revival of a form of Greek philosophical paganism.)[17]

The several decades of scholarship since his death on all three philosophical traditions have exposed that Wolfson erred in claiming that all three Western religious-philosophical traditions embraced the reconciliation of Greek and Jewish thought in a miraculous doctrine of the freedom of the will. For it is now clear and generally accepted that the Islamic and Jewish medieval philosophers maintained an Aristotelian and Stoic naturalist view of human action rather than a miraculous one.[18] And Spinoza, rather than deconstructing the ubiquitous medieval reconciliation of Greek naturalism and Hebrew miracle, instead, modernized Judeo-Arabic naturalism by updating its Aristotelian-Stoic determinist basis in the light of early modern breakthroughs in science. For Spinoza all causes are in webs of relation and systems nested within systems, the social and natural being continuous and the human deeply embedded within the larger webs, both contributing to them and expressive of them.[19] The person is not divided and modular, having a discrete ruling part but potentially smoothly integrated and the mind and body flexible and at best ever learning and developing and reintegrating new experiences and memories. It was medieval Christian philosophical theology alone that embraced the miraculous freedom of the will, the autonomy of the self to enable its self-origination or self-invention with the aim of assigning to the person full praise or blame, complete responsibility for the effects of one's actions.[20] In modernity the doctrine was reinterpreted in secular guise and recontextualized within a modern scientific and philosophical framework, principally by Descartes and Kant. The freedom of the will implies that the human person is taken out of the causal system and is not subject to normal scientific causal explanation or sociohistorical description. Spinoza insists, instead, that there is one system of natural causality ("Nature is always the same")[21]—described actually in two, but potentially infinite, ways, all of which, according to the *Ethics* (E, II, Prop 7), grasp the same system or series of causes—and that the mind is as natural as the body and within the causal domain, which is infinite and leaves nothing outside it.[22] Spinoza clarifies his claim that the order of ideas and the connection of things is one and the same when he insists that, rather than being a claim of parallel ontological domains, as we might be tempted to wrongly conclude from a superficial reading,

> thinking substance and extended substance are one and the same substance, comprehended now under this attribute, now under that. ... And so, whether we conceive Nature under the attribute of Extension or under the attribute of Thought or under any other attribute, *we find one and the same order, or one and the same connection of causes*—that is the same things follow one another.... As long as things are considered as modes of thought, we must explicate the order of the whole of Nature, or the connection of causes, through Thought alone; and in so far as things are considered as modes of Extension, again the order of the whole of Nature must be explicated through the attribute of Extension only. The same applies to other attributes. (E, II, Prop 7, Schol; my emphasis)

Hence the very definition of truth and adequacy is that thought must grasp and express the same reality (and causal system) that extension manifests. Hence there cannot be a valid claim of the contingency, and hence room for the "free" (self's) overriding of the causality of the mind that would be compatible with a claim of the determinism of the material, for the same determinist causality is being expressed in two explanatory systems. Spinoza even claims that imaginative thinking, thinking that does not adequately grasp the reality of things, although it may regard itself as contingent, is in fact as necessarily determined as any other kind of thinking.[23] Nor could one legitimately claim, according to Spinoza, that human action must be bracketed as outside the causal system when we speak of ethics. In fact, Spinoza inveighs against just this notion in his famous preface to Part III of the *Ethics* when he indicts Descartes and others like him who "conceive man in nature as a kingdom within a kingdom." This natural causal infinitude, encompassing the mental as well as the corporeal, is the basis for the claim that no free will, which is to say, no separate causal origination, is possible. This is exactly the position that the claim of free will denies in its placing of human agency as capable of originative (and hence responsible) action in analogy to a divine will above, and intervening in, nature. But Spinoza denies that kind of will, the free will above nature, even to God! (See E, I, Prop 29 and E, I, Prop 32 and Cor 2.) While the Augustinian notion of the direct intervention of God into the human soul to bolster the will as free through Grace (a freedom that had, according to Augustine, been lost with the Fall of Adam but could be regained through the embrace of Christian faith made possible to the believer) was, it seems, eliminated as too theological and miraculous for inclusion in the modern philosophical understanding of ethical action, the underlying conception of the human person as itself capable of a God-like independence from nature and history was retained and disguised.

The miraculous character of the free will haunts standard philosophical ethics to this day because, I believe, its original Christian theological presuppositions have not been exposed and acknowledged and therefore brought to conscious awareness so that they can be reexamined and reevaluated. For it is the medieval Christian tradition of philosophical theology that triumphed and became the basis of modern philosophical ethics rather than Judeo-Islamic naturalism and the Spinozist modernization of it. In fact, the latter was roundly rejected by not only medieval Christianity in the thirteenth century but also again at the inception of modern philosophical ethics. Philosophy thus reasserted in the early twentieth century, first through G. E. Moore, the (miraculous) power of the human person to wrest the self from nature, history, context, community, relationships, and natural endowments as the sine qua non of ethics; and that view remains the standard foundation of philosophical ethics today.[24] Descartes characterized it as the "indifference" of the will (that is, to all its natural endowments and historical location) and in the early twentieth century the challenge to this conception of the person as self-originating was attributed to Spinoza and anathematized. Mainstream philosophy, unbeknownst to itself, is still fighting ancient theological battles with Islam and Judaism and also still engaged in a battle to repudiate Greek naturalism.[25]

In his 1905 book, *Fives Types of Ethical Theory*, C. D. Broad, following up on a suggestion of G. E. Moore, presented Spinoza's ethics as outside the limits of all legitimate ethical theory because of its foundational determinism and naturalism. For Spinoza had committed what Moore regarded as the "naturalistic fallacy," a fallacy that in and of itself was said to undermine the possibility of making ethical claims or judgments. Spinoza's ethics thus was held to vitiate ethics rather than to explain it. Upon the outcasting of Spinoza, the entire edifice of modern ethical theory stands. Spinoza still occupies the outside, the dangerous and prohibited beyond whose boundary must not be approached, let alone breached. Most of the secondary literature on Spinoza's ethical theory by his philosophical partisans tries to defend Spinoza from the charge of having committed the naturalistic fallacy.[26] It argues that Spinoza's modern excommunication from philosophy is unfounded and should be rescinded and makes the further case that his philosophical ethics should be reconsidered as within the boundaries set by Broad.

I propose that the modern philosophical "ban" on Spinoza has, ironically, had far more serious consequences than the rabbinic excommunication of Spinoza in the seventeenth century, for it is a reprise of the church's 1277 condemnation of central theses of Aristotelian and Stoic radical naturalism, precisely the kind of naturalism exemplified by Maimonides and Gersonides, Crescas, Alfarabi, Averroes, and others and taken over by Spinoza.[27] The 1277 ban not only prohibited Catholic scholars from holding naturalist determinist positions about the will (maintained by Maimonides and nearly all medieval Jewish and Islamic philosophers and later elaborated by Spinoza) but also mandated in their stead a number of voluntarist dogmas advocating a radical version of the freedom of the will. Thus it is the conservative Catholic theological response to the thirteenth-century influx into Christendom of Judeo-Arabic philosophical naturalism in translation under the rubric of "Averroism," which is replayed in Moore's and Broad's casting out of the determinist naturalism of Spinoza but this time without any conscious awareness of the underlying Christian theological presuppositions driving the move. Thus Spinoza, ironically, was cast out of the modern ethical canon for holding what amount to non-Christian views. As a result, standard philosophical ethics today remains unconscious of its dependence upon an underlying Christian philosophical anthropology to which it is unquestioningly committed.

The litmus of the rejection of Spinoza becomes not a sideline but, in fact, central to the self-definition of the entire tradition and practice of philosophical ethics, as Moore and Broad intuited but failed to grasp why. For they were reinstating (renaming, secularizing, modernizing, and universalizing) a canonical practice of Christian ethical reflection as it originally crystallized and was defined against just the Judeo-Arabic naturalism and determinism that Spinoza, for his part, reclaimed, secularized, and modernized. Thus the modern practice of philosophical ethics with its various lines of development in the nineteenth and twentieth centuries retains its character as emerging from Descartes and Kant as modernizers of the medieval Christian theological anthropology of the freedom of the will whose impetus was a rejection of precisely the radical naturalist wing of the religiophilosophical tradition exemplified and modernized by Spinoza, an insight glimpsed through a glass darkly by Moore and Broad.

When and why the standard modern discourses of philosophical ethics went wrong has been of concern to philosophers since Anscombe raised the question in her 1958 essay and especially since Alasdair MacIntyre, in *After Virtue* (1981), proposed an answer that is still hotly debated.[28] According to MacIntyre, modern Western society has lost the rich and homogeneous cultural settings that make ethical life possible and discussions about the good life intelligible. MacIntyre proposed a turn away from a modernity that he considers too deracinated and fragmented to support a moral inquiry that could result in a degree of consensus, and he suggested a turn toward a revival of premodern (or, perhaps, merely romanticized) societal forms or, in their absence, the withdrawal into subgroups where a shared life pointing to some ethical consensus is possible. Contra MacIntyre and Taylor and others who hold that the deracinated atomic person is the hallmark of modernity's philosophical break with its theological past, my critique exposes the problem with contemporary ethics as exactly the opposite, an insufficient understanding of the ongoing hold and use of the religious past in the standard conversations. While MacIntyre's insight that modern philosophical ethics has lost a sense of its own originating context, its history and narrative, turns out to be in a sense correct (pace MacIntyre), I argue that philosophy's Christian narrative and history have been suppressed in modernity, rather than transcended in a broad universalism, as philosophers claim. While

MacIntyre claimed that philosophical ethics was dysfunctional because its attempt at universalism rendered it no longer able to grasp the homogenous cultural setting that originally made sense of it and justified its claims, I propose that in order to maintain the myth of its own universalism, philosophical ethics has suppressed and continues to suppress its Christian presumptions and origins. Thus it is not that it is not Christian enough that haunts ethics but that it is too provincially Christian! Moreover, that Anscombe, MacIntyre, and others do not consider the sciences and the social sciences to be delved into in complex and nuanced ways as rich sources for the investigation of what human flourishing might consist in or include is ongoing witness to even their insufficient emergence from the Augustinian past. For the exclusion of the human from the natural order still haunts their presuppositions.[29] The human ideal must be found outside the natural, and the natural cashes out as the reductively material—a problem (and one that is a profound error from a Spinozist perspective) that still haunts all kinds of philosophical thinking.

Far from not being homogeneous enough to support an ethics, philosophical ethics is in fact too homogeneous, too culturally narrow. It is problematic in both its narrowness and its need to disguise from itself and from others its origins in order to claim universal applicability. But its deeper problem is that it is simply wrong. The doctrine of the free will is a mistaken account of the human person and one that entails unsavory consequences: a tendency to triumphalism, to blame the victim and aggrandize the victor; a failure to see moral actions as necessary consequences of natural and social systems and therefore to focus on punishment as vengeance and coercion rather than on wider understandings that could recommend more indirect ways to effect social and personal change; the rejection of compassion, empathy, while not of pity. It has a tendency to devolve into individual arrogance and self-righteousness and into sociopolitical imperialism. Other religiocultural viewpoints on ethics need to be looked at as potential resources for a cultural corrective. Muslim and Jewish, along with feminist, philosophers could work together to rethink ethics from the shared medieval philosophical tradition and, in the case of feminist philosophers, from our feminist concerns.

Although the freedom of the will, and the claim that such freedom is necessary to make ethical life possible, are still widely accepted across all philosophical practices and traditions, there are just now beginning to be some signs of discomfort with it and of a plausible alternative. As Joseph

Keim Campbell, Michael O'Rourke, and David Shier put it in the introductory essay to their compilation of essays, *Freedom and Determinism*, a volume that gives an overview of the state of the field: "Until recently, all parties in the freedom and determinism debate . . . first, . . . held that the kind of freedom required for moral responsibility was *free will*. Second, it was accepted that free will requires that persons have *alternatives* to at least some of their actions."[30] So even today "few philosophers accept determinism" and "the majority of contemporary philosophers agree that some kind of freedom—*moral freedom*—is required for moral responsibility."[31] Philosophical positions have been divided along these lines:

> *Compatibilists* believe that determinism is consistent with the *free will thesis*—the view that at least some persons have free will—whereas *incompatibilists* believe that it is not. *Soft determinists* are compatibilists who accept both determinism and the free will thesis, whereas *hard determinists* are incompatibilists who endorse determinism but deny the free will thesis. Finally, *libertarians* are incompatibilists who deny determinism and endorse the free will thesis.[32]

The two respectable philosophical positions have been until recently either voluntarist incompatibilism or compatibilism, that is to say, either that there is a break or indeterminacy in nature that enables the human will to be free or, instead, that nature is causally determined but free will is still compatible with that causal determinism. The uncertainty principle in quantum mechanics has been taken by many philosophers to bolster a causal indeterminism that could be used as evidence in support of free will and undermine causal determinism as the normative scientific position. The position thereby embraced has been called "hard indeterminism."[33] The latter seemed to be the final nail in the coffin of viewing scientific naturalism as forcing upon philosophers a hard determinism. One could embrace free will in ethics and still view oneself as having a modern scientific worldview, even regard oneself as having a more contemporary scientific worldview than a seemingly old-fashioned, pre–quantum theory causal determinist would. But for Spinoza compatibilism would be both incoherent and deeply inconsistent with his basic understanding of nature. For Spinoza maintains that the mind is the idea of the body (E, II, Props 12 and 13 Dem), which is to say that the mind minds the body, or put another way, the mind imagines or conceives only the body and its relations (E, II, Prop 16 and Cor 1), and the memories thereof. Hence, for Spinoza to hold a doctrine of compatibilism (of the compatibility of an actual natural determinism but an equally valid mental free will) would be completely and utterly incoherent and go against his most committed beliefs about the nature of the intimate relation, in fact, identity between mind and body (see also E, II, Prop 19 and Dem and E, II, Prop 23 and 26). The claim of compatibilism could amount to only an inadequate idea for Spinoza insofar as it would amount to an idea whose content did not adequately grasp the content of the body and its infinite relations (in God), which is the standard of adequacy and truth (E, II, Prop 32, Dem). Spinoza's claim that "an idea that excludes the existence of our body cannot be in our mind, but is contrary to it" (E, III, Prop 10) suggests the incoherence of a claim that amounts to directly denying the body as a source of the data from which the understanding of the world and the self are to be gathered!

Things have changed or are now changing for us today in a Spinozist direction. Quite recently some few philosophers have been reclaiming hard determinism in the name of the most up-to-date contemporary science.[34] That position is, of course, Spinoza's (as well as that of Jewish and Arabic medieval philosophy) and Spinoza regarded the understanding and recognition of its truth as the sine qua non not only of a sophisticated scientific worldview but also of a true and mature ethical point of view, a nonmoralistic ethics. This is the perspective not of quantum physics but of a more relevant science of how our minds work, namely, the perspective of neuroscience. The standard way that philosophy approaches ethics separates actions from thoughts and understandings, and desires from choices. The way that the person is conceived is as divided into discrete divisions—into parts, faculties, and modules—rather than as networks that integrate and relate different layers and capacities of a self.[35] But the focus of neuroscience upon integrated networks pushes us in a Spinozist direction. And neuroscience is also deterministic and materialist but not reductively materialist (just as Spinoza's understanding of the identity of mind and body is nonreductionist) and with that perspective, especially that of the neuroscience of the emotions, Spinoza is in full agreement and anticipated many of its conclusions and also worked out many of the implications for a revision of ethics without praise and blame but with a complex multifaceted account of how and why we act the way we do, why we lay claim to our actions as our own and feel responsibility for them despite our determinism, and how we can intervene in social systems to promote cooperation and also in our understanding of the necessary causes of our beliefs and emotions to initiate changes in our own feelings and actions.[36] To come to grasp the full range of the social, natural, and personal causes of our desires and actions and those of others, rather than to see ourselves and others in isolation as uniquely originative of ourselves and hence completely and utterly responsible and worthy of complete praise or blame, was, according to Spinoza, the mark of the mature ethical point of view. He regarded the most widely contextual view of the self and of others as not only the truest but also the most humane and least self-serving because of its moral attitude of acceptance and compassion. While eschewing a judgmental and self-righteous posture, Spinoza's ethics at the same time provides an astute awareness of the irrationality and self-serving and often vicious character of much human motivation and action. He devoted two treatises to outlining recommendations for developing appropriate social, political, and religio-ideological mechanisms for limiting and channeling the worst human tendencies and for isolating wrongdoers. Although nonpunitive, Spinoza's ethics is neither naive nor relativistic.

My project, described briefly here, is to expose some of the underlying reasons why Western philosophers have been so reluctant to part with what amounts to a magical account of the human person as different from and above nature or the rest of nature, why it feels culturally right to us, and why philosophers revert to it at the slightest opportunity.[37] And then my intention is to develop in Spinozist, Judeo-Islamic, and feminist fashion what ethics would look like from a position within nature, situation, and history. As Spinoza proposed, our aim should be to understand rather than to praise or to blame and to use that understanding toward the furthering of social harmony and individual joy.

Notes

An earlier version of this chapter was delivered as an address at the conference "Gendered Intersections: Feminist Scholarship in Islamic and Judaic Studies," at Dartmouth College, August 7–10, 2005. This project has been undertaken with the generous support of the Ford Foundation. I thank, in particular, Constance A. Buchanan, senior program officer, for initiating the project and for her ongoing encouragement, support, and critique.

1. Elizabeth Anscombe, "Modern Moral Philosophy," reprinted in *Ethics, Religion, and Politics* (Minneapolis: University of Minnesota Press, 1981). Ruth Anna Putnam, in a review essay, "Reciprocity and Virtue Ethics" *Ethics* 98, no. 2 (1988): 379–89, gives a succinct account of the origins

of the current movement to reintroduce an Aristotelian form of moral theorizing into philosophy. J. B. Schneewind, in "The Misfortunes of Virtue" *Ethics* 101, no. 1 (1990): 42–63, offers a counterattack in defense of Kant against both the new Aristotelians and against Humean naturalism.

2. See, for example, Philippa Foot's influential "Morality as a System of Hypothetical Imperatives," *Philosophical Review* 81, no. 3 (1972): 305–16 where she calls the Kantian ought "magic force" "relying on an illusion" (315).

3. Owen Flanagan, *The Problem of the Soul: Two Visions of Mind and How To Reconcile Them* (New York: Basic Books, 2002).

4. See my essay "Spinoza's Ethics of the Liberation of Desire," in *Women and Gender in Jewish Philosophy*, ed. Hava Tirosh-Samuelson (Bloomington: Indiana University Press, 2004), 78–105.

5. Julie R. Klein, "Spinoza's Debt to Gersonides," *Graduate Faculty Philosophy Journal* 24, no. 1 (2003): 38. Idit Dobbs-Weinstein, in "Thinking Desire in Gersonides and Spinoza," in *Women and Gender in Jewish Philosophy*, ed. Tirosh-Samuelson, 51–77, has made a related argument about the eclipse of the Judeo-Islamic Arabic tradition of philosophy by the Christian tradition and also called for a revival of the former for both generally philosophical and feminist reasons.

6. See especially Bonnie Kent, *Virtues of the Will: The Transformation of Ethics in the Late Thirteenth Century* (Washington, D.C.: Catholic University of America Press, 1995).

7. For a related approach to the feminist uses of the Judeo-Islamic Spinozist tradition, see Dobbs-Weinstein, "Thinking Desire," which focuses more on epistemology and ontology, whereas my focus here is on ethics and moral psychology. Kwame Anthony Appiah's recent coinage of "rooted cosmopolitanism," to describe his approach to the ethics of identity (*Ethics of Identity* [Princeton: Princeton University Press, 2005]) also, I believe, aptly describes Spinoza's thrust, which is the one I am recommending here to feminists.

8. Muhsin S. Mahdi, in *Alfarabi and the Foundations of Islamic Political Philosophy* (Chicago: University of Chicago Press, 2001), 2–3 and elsewhere, describes how Alfarabi, although educated in Christian Neoplatonism and by Nestorian teachers, deliberately turned his back on that tradition and embraced an Aristotelian naturalism in its stead as well as a Platonism not read through the Neoplatonic hierarchical emanationist and transcendent tradition as his true philosophical position (while retaining some Neoplatonic doctrines as a rhetoric with which to address the masses). Thereafter Aristotelian naturalism became normative in all subsequent Islamic medieval, and then Jewish, medieval Arabic philosophy.

The quotation is from Julie R. Klein, "Aristotle and Descartes in Spinoza's Approach to Matter and Body," unpublished manuscript, 4. Klein suggests that Spinoza's radically naturalist version of Aristotelianism, which he inherited from the Judeo-Arabic philosophical tradition, included the following positions: (1) the intrinsic causal power of nature; (2) the complete rejection of a hierarchical cosmos; the Aristotelian relation of potency and act (*dynamis* and *energeia*) is absorbed into two ways of regarding, two aspects of one thing, the actual providing the definition of the potential; (3) "the identity" in Spinoza "of actuality and productivity" with the corollary that "logical relations are actual relations"; there is no becoming but simultaneity between God and modes for this is not a temporal relation; (4) for Spinoza as for Aristotle "causation is non-linear and causes and effects are intrinsically connected"; hence Spinoza's "immanence"; and (5) Spinoza's "face of the universe" is analogous to or a modernization of Aristotle's eternal circular motion of the universe, which produces constant coming to be and passing away. In opting for this view of nature, Spinoza thereby rejects these Cartesian positions on nature: (1) Descartes' elimination of activity from nature, which must then be supplied by a transcendent God and (2) Cartesian reduction of extension to geometry; and Descartes' introduction of (Platonic) innate ideas into the mind to explain the possibility of knowledge, that is, ideas that are part of the transcendent arena but placed in our mind and that are explanatory of the material world.

9. Idit Dobbs-Weinstein suggests that the Judeo-Islamic Arabic philosophic tradition has been "occluded." The claim of suppression was introduced by Dobbs-Weinstein and elaborated by Julie

Klein. I contribute to that discussion by elaborating some of the Christian historical context, by specifying Spinoza's unique role as anathema in modern philosophical discussions of ethics, and by introducing the doctrine of the freedom of the will as the central point of contention.

10. Christine M. Korsgaard, *Creating the Kingdom of Ends* (New York: Cambridge University Press, 1995). I am grateful to Professor John McCumber of the University of California, Los Angeles, for pointing out this passage to me.

11. Ibid., xi. The emphasis on the second sentence of this passage is mine; all other italics are original.

12. Bonnie Kent makes this argument at great length in *Virtues of the Will*, arguing against both those who see free will as originating with Augustine (one standard view) or as a modern innovation beginning with Duns Scotus (another standard view).

13. See, for example, Joseph Keim Campbell, Michael O'Rourke, and David Shier, eds., *Freedom and Determinism* (Cambridge: MIT Press, 2004), 6.

14. That Christian identity involves a change or transformation is true whether one understands that change as personal conversion of belief (the standard view) or as a socioethnic transformation as Denise Kimber Buell has recently redescribed it in *Why This Race: Ethnic Reasoning in Early Christianity* (New York: Columbia University Press, 2005). Buell refers to it as "the acquired nature of [Christian] identity" (163). Buell also points to the Roman imperial background and analogy to the Christian foreground: as Roman rule expands outward to a wide range of ethnonational groups, particularly local elites come to transform their identity and come to identification (religio-ethno-racial-national) with Rome by the introduction of imperial religious practices.

That other contemporary religious groups in addition to Christians also had conversionary anthropologies and rituals (as Nancy Shumate has shown in *Crisis and Conversion in Apuleius' Metamorphoses* [Ann Arbor: University of Michigan Press, 1996]) does not belie my claim that it is through Christian doctrinal articulation that the anthropology of identity that I am pointing out comes to theoretical expression and normativity in philosophical ethics. I thank Constance Buchanan of the Ford Foundation and Karen King of Harvard University for pointing me to Denise Buell's fascinating rethinking of the early Christian dynamics of identity formation. And I thank Bernadette Brooten of Brandeis University for widening my perspective on conversion by pointing me to Nancy Shumate's fascinating study of a conversion narrative to the cult of Isis.

15. See, for example, Harry Austryn Wolfson, "Spinoza and the Religion of the Past," in *Religious Philosophy: A Group of Essays* (Cambridge: Belknap Press of Harvard University Press, 1961), chap. 10.

16. I am grateful to Zeev Harvey for calling my attention to this point.

17. Charles Taylor, *Sources of the Self: The Making of Modernity* (Cambridge: Harvard University Press, 1989), 313.

18. I thank Zeev Harvey of the Hebrew University in Jerusalem for pointing this out to me. See Aviezer Ravitzky, "The Paradoxical Concept of Free Will in Mattathias Ha-Yizhary," in *Joseph Baruch Sermoneta Memorial Volume*, ed. Aviezer Ravitzky, Jerusalem Studies in Jewish Thought 14 (Jerusalem: Faculty of Humanities, Hebrew University of Jerusalem), 239–58. Gersonides is often cited as a possible exception to the absence of free will in Jewish philosophy. But his position does not fit the criterion that I am raising. Although he attributes some form of contingency to particulars, only automatic natural processes are operative in the world and in the mind. There is no suggestion in his philosophic thought that non-natural causality has a role to play in the human or divine. Hence there can be no voluntarism, in the strict sense. (See Levi Ben Gershom [Gersonides], *The Wars of the Lord* [New York: Jewish Publication Society, 1999], book 3, chaps. 4, 5.) Jesse Mashbaum has shown (in his edition of Gersonides' *Supercommentary* on Averroes's *Epitome of the [Aristotle's] "De Anima"*) that in psychology Gersonides follows Averroes faithfully. See Steven Harvey's essay "Islamic Philosophy and Jewish Philosophy," in *The Cambridge Companion to Arabic Philosophy*, ed. Peter Adamson and Richard C. Taylor (Cambridge: Press Syndicate of the University of Cambridge,

2005), 348–69, especially 362 and 368n50. Deborah L. Black has argued the point for Islamic falsafa in "Psychology, Soul, and Intellect," in *The Cambridge Companion to Arabic Philosophy*, ed. Adamson and Taylor, 308–26. Black has also reiterated the point in private communication.

19. See my "Spinoza's Systems Theory of Ethics," in *Cognitive, Emotive, and Ethical Aspects of Decision Making in Humans and in Artificial Intelligence*, vol. 3, ed. Iva Smith and Wendell Wallach (Windsor, Ont., Canada: International Institute for Advanced Studies in Systems Research and Cybernetics, 2004). See also my earlier "Notes on Spinoza's Critique of Aristotle's Ethics: From Teleology to Process Theory," *Philosophy and Theology* 4, no. 1 (1989): 3–32.

20. Most early and medieval Christian discussions of free will occur in the context of the question of assigning moral responsibility for a person's actions. (Origen's discussion of free will in the context of conversion to Christianity seems to be an exception to this general pattern. See Buell, *Why This Race*, 123–26). Augustine's treatment of the issue in his early *De Libero Arbitrio*, for example, takes this form, although he has a complex theory that reconciles free will and divine grace. For the latter, see especially Harry Austryn Wolfson, "St. Augustine and the Pelagian Controversy," in *Religious Philosophy*, chap. 6. See also James Wetzel's "Will and Interiority in Augustine: Travels in an Unlikely Place," *Augustinian Studies* 33, no. 2 (2002): 139–60. I thank Jim Wetzel, at Villanova University, for several helpful discussions of free will in Augustine and generally in Christianity and for pointing me to Bonnie Kent's *Virtues of the Will*.

21. A frequent refrain of Spinoza; see e.g., E, III, Pref. Please note that in this chapter all quotations are from Samuel Shirley's translation *Ethics, Treatise on the Emendation of the Intellect, and Selected Letters* (Indianapolis: Hackett, 1992).

22. See E, II, Prop 48 and Schol. Mark especially the scholium where Spinoza elaborates his denial of free will to claim that "in the same way it is proved that in the mind there is no absolute faculty of understanding, desiring, loving, etc."

23. See E, II, Prop 36. Just before this proposition, in the scholium to Prop 35, Spinoza had denied free will, ridiculing those who held such a view: "Men are deceived in thinking themselves free, a belief that consists only in this, that they are conscious of their actions and ignorant of the causes by which they are determined. Therefore the idea of their freedom is simply the ignorance of the cause of their actions. As to their saying that human actions depend on the will, these are mere words without any corresponding idea. For none of them knows what the will is and how it moves the body, and those who boast otherwise and make up stories of dwelling-places and habitations of the soul provoke either ridicule or disgust." This is surely a jab at Descartes' notion of the pineal gland!

24. G. E. Moore, *Principia Ethica* (Cambridge: At the University Press, 1903). See my "Spinoza's Individualism Reconsidered: Some Lessons from the *Short Treatise on God, Man, and His Well-Being*," *Iyyun: Jerusalem Philosophical Quarterly*, no. 47 (July 1998): 265–92 (reprinted in Yirmiyahu Yovel and Gideon Segal, eds., *Spinoza* [Aldershot: Ashgate, 2000] and in Genevieve Lloyd, ed., *Routledge Critical Assessments of Leading Philosophers: Spinoza*, vol. 1 [New York: Routledge, 2001]), where I write: "The attempt within Anglo-American philosophy to characterize and situate Spinoza's ethical theory begins with G. E. Moore's passing references in *Principia Ethica* (1903), e.g., 113, to Spinoza's *Ethics* as a paradigmatic example of what Moore characterizes as committing the Naturalistic Fallacy in ethical theorizing. Moore maintains that '[t]o hold that from any proposition asserting, "Reality is of this nature" we can infer, or obtain confirmation for, any proposition asserting "This is good in itself" is to commit the naturalistic fallacy,' Moore, p. 114" (267–68n10).

25. Julie Klein points out that it is the Judeo-Islamic naturalist reading of Aristotle that has been ignored and perhaps even denied by mainstream philosophy, which continues to read Aristotle through the Latin tradition. Klein, "Spinoza's Debt," 38.

26. As I argued in "Spinoza's Individualism Reconsidered," note 10: "Broad set off a debate about Spinoza's (meta-) ethics which is still continuing among some Anglo-American philosophers ninety years after Moore published his book. Edwin Curley, for example, redefines an ethical naturalist as

'someone who thinks that there is some property common and peculiar to all good things and who thinks this common property may be identified with some empirical property which they have,' Curley, 'Spinoza's Moral Philosophy'" (in Marjorie Grene, ed., *Spinoza: A Collection of Critical Essays*, [New York: Anchor Books, 1973], 362) and that definition has become the focus of recent debate regarding Spinoza's ethics. Whether or not, and if so in what sense, Spinoza ought to be considered an ethical naturalist has been a major concern of the majority of English-language scholars who have addressed the issue of the nature and success of Spinoza's ethical theory. These have included C. D. Broad, as mentioned above, and David Bidney, in his lengthy study of Spinoza, *The Psychology and Ethics of Spinoza: A Study in the History and Logic of Ideas* (1940), especially chap. 15, "On Spinoza and Contemporary Value Theory." Bidney's study addresses Spinoza's place in the history of psychology as well as in the history of ethics. Moreover, Bidney also sets Spinoza in dialogue with a variety of both modern and recent (pre–World War II) ethical theorists—including Kant, Nietzsche, and Dewey, as well as G. E. Moore and, more recently, Edwin Curley (1973); William Frankena, "Spinoza's 'New Morality': Notes on Book IV," in *Spinoza: Essays in Interpretation*, ed. Eugene Freeman and Maurice Mandelbaum (LaSalle, Ill.: Open Court, 1975), 85–100; Paul Eisenberg, "Is Spinoza an Ethical Naturalist?" (1977), in *Speculum Spinozanum 1677–1977*, ed. Siegfried Hessing, 145–64; Robert McShea, "Spinoza: Human Nature and History" (1971), reprinted in *Spinoza: Essays in Interpretation*, ed. Mandelbaum and Freeman, 101–16; McShea, "Spinoza in the History of Ethical Theory," *Philosophical Forum* (Boston) 8 (Fall 1976): 59–67; McShea, "Spinoza's Human Nature Ethical Theory," in *Proceedings of the First Italian International Congress on Spinoza* (1982), ed. Emilia Giancotti, *Bibliopolis* (1985), 281–90; Herman de Dijn, "Naturalism, Freedom, and Ethics in Spinoza," *Studia Leibnitiana*, Band XXII/2 (1990); and Frank Lucash, "Spinoza's Two Theories of Morality," *Iyyun* 40 (January 1991).

27. Like Idit Dobbs-Weinstein in "Gersonides' Radically Modern Understanding of the Agent Intellect," in *Meeting of the Minds*, ed. Stephen F. Brown, Rencontres de Philosophie Medievale 7 (Turnhout: Brepols, 1998), 191–213 and Klein in "Spinoza's Debt" and "Gersonides's Approach to Emanation and Transcendence: Evidence from the Theory of Intellection," I read Gersonides as a radical naturalist, although, as Klein also points out in "Spinoza's Debt" (23), there are conservative aspects to his thought and passages that suggest more conservative readings. Gersonides' more conservative positions would seems to include some version of divine creation and also of voluntarism, as S. Klein-Braslavy argues in her article "Gersonides on Determinism, Possibility, Choice, and Foreknowledge," *Daat* (in Hebrew), 22 (1989): 5–53. Zeev Harvey suggests that Gersonides' tendency to voluntarism may reflect his Christian context despite his clear radical Aristotelian naturalism and the obvious influence upon him of Averroes, upon whose *Epitome of Aristotle's "De Anima"* he wrote a *Supercommentary*. Aviezer Ravitsky, by contrast, holds that the only Jewish medieval philosopher to hold a clear and full-blown voluntarist position as Wolfson describes it is (the obscure) Mattathias Ha-Yizhary, in his article, in Hebrew, "The Paradoxical Concept of Free Will in Mattathias Ha-Yizhary," *Mehkere Yerushalayim be-mahashevet Yisra'el* 14 (1988): 239–58.

28. Alasdair MacIntyre, *After Virtue* (Notre Dame: University of Notre Dame Press, 1981).

29. John Rist, in his study of the philosophical ideas of Augustine and both their emergence and difference from the classical philosophical tradition, writes as follows of a crucial Augustinian innovation: "By 'natural order' Augustine now means only the order which we find in the physical world. As *The Literal Commentary on Genesis* will put it (8. 9.17), the operations of human (and angelic) wills are no longer included within the realm of 'nature.' Thus, briefly, 'eternal law' has come to have two areas of application: one in nature (excluding human and angelic agency), *the other in the will*. For the purposes of a study of human law and human institutions we need only be concerned with the relation of the eternal law to the will" (John M. Rist, *Augustine* [Cambridge: Cambridge University Press, 1994], 214 –15; my emphasis).

30. Joseph Keim Campbell, Michael O'Rourke, and David Shier, "Freedom and Determinism: A Framework," in Campbell, Rourke, and Shier, *Freedom and Determinism*, 3.

31. Ibid., 6.
32. Ibid., 4.
33. Ibid., 6.
34. In addition to the essay advocating hard determinism in the Campbell volume, it has come to my notice very recently that a number of philosophers and scientists are embracing determinism and have founded a society to promote and disseminate information on that position to others. They have founded the Center for Naturalism and also have a Web site (www.naturalism.org) and an e-mail discussion group.

35. See my "Spinoza's Anticipation of Contemporary Affective Neuroscience," in the interdisciplinary science and philosophy journal *Consciousness and Emotion*, ed. Ralph Ellis and Natika Newton, 4, no. 2 (2003): 255–88; "Was Spinoza Right About Ethics? A Look at Recent Discoveries in the Neurobiology of the Emotions," in "Spinoza on Mind and Body," ed. Lee C. Rice and Thomas J. Cook, special issue, *Studia Spinozana* (Wurzburg) 14 (1998); and "Spinoza and the Education of Desire," *Neuro-Psychoanalysis* 5, no. 2 (2003): 218–29. My review essay is part of an extended exchange between neuroscientists and philosophers: the neuroscientists Jaak Panksepp, Douglas Watt, and Antonio Damasio and myself on Antonio Damasio's recent book, *Looking for Spinoza: Joy, Sorrow, and the Feeling Brain*. Antonio Damasio's response to my review essay appears just after it, as does his response to the review essay of Panksepp and Watt.

36. The Center for Naturalism also identifies a transformation in our standard ideas about praise and blame and generally about punishment as retribution as a main implication of the embrace of determinist naturalism. Whereas for Kantians and standard philosophical ethics of all kinds, it is the kind of responsibility made possible by the embrace of a notion of our own origination of our actions (even within constraints) that makes ethics possible (as the early quote from Korsgaard testifies), for Spinoza and determinist naturalists, on the contrary, it is the embrace of the opposite position that marks a mature ethical point of view.

37. See Campbell, O'Rourke, and Shier, *Freedom and Determinism*, 310.

7

Adam and the Serpent

Everyman and the Imagination

Paola Grassi

"Spinoza's references to the story of 'the first man' may be read as more than a critical account of Genesis and Adam's 'fall'; it may be read as an account of the condition of 'everyman.' Adam's story is an allegory of the human condition—a condition which is necessarily defined by illusions."[1] Spinoza's references to the story and to the *name* of the first man constitute more than an exercise in biblical exegesis. As the quotation above suggests, the few references in his *Opera* to the subject of Adam and original sin may be understood as "an exercise in theologico-political, or indeed social, criticism that in broad outline has universal significance."[2]

In keeping with this volume's theme of re-reading the Spinozistic canon, in this chapter I will consider the narration of the original fall as an expression of a *continuum* that connects the main elements of Spinoza's philosophical system: the ontological, the gnoseological, and the ethical. Whenever Spinoza broaches the topic of the fall and the question of sin—whether perforce, as in his correspondence with Blijenbergh, or as a requirement of his theologicopolitical project, or as a logical step in the construction of the *Ethics*—Spinoza's *work on the name of Adam* goes beyond hermeneutics to become something else: a paradigm of a theory of knowledge.[3] The originary drama of the fall of the first man becomes an expression of the emancipation of the *human* by means of knowledge. And it is through the notion of emancipation that Spinoza's reading of original sin may be seen as heretical, as a *heretical allegory*.

The "orthodoxy" to which Spinoza runs counter is that of the theologians he addresses in the *Tractatus Politicus* (TP, II, 39–40). They are the "defenders of the faith" perfectly represented by the nameless correspondent from Dordrecht: they claim that the cause of "weakness in human nature is the vice or sin whose origin was the fall of our first parent" (TP, II, 40). In contrast, Spinoza's account of original sin focuses on the idea that the first man, having no power over the proper use of reason, was an everyman—a victim of the *noxious effects of the imagination*, that is, of the "emotional" or "affective" life; and this condition is natural, not sinful. Insofar as Spinoza's definition of sin (*peccatum*) is generated in contrast to the orthodox interpretation of original sin, it entails a broad criticism of the notion of vice (*vitium*). This is a new perspective that also critiques the concept of "the vice of imagining" (*vitium imaginandi*), a concept that forms the basis of the demonization of the imagination in the modern era.

The Spinozistic notion of *virtus imaginandi* (the virtue of imagining) both signals and involves a clear and significant rethinking of the role of the imagination as a cognitive tool with positive and productive connotations, and Spinoza proceeds by a two-pronged attack. On the one hand, the faculty of the soul as an organ of the human body—in the Cartesian lexicon the *vis imaginativa* (the drive to imagine)—becomes for Spinoza a *vis imaginandi* (the drive to use the imagination), a dynamic power of the mind. On the other hand, in the framework of an anthropology that sees emotional expressions as properties of human nature, the "function of the imagination" is seen as a virtue.

In the present chapter I explore the hypothesis that Spinoza's rehabilitation of the imagination is the result of a virtual dialogue with—among others—the Jewish tradition. Spinoza's perspective on man as an imaginative creature seems to be the result of a mediation with what has been defined as "Spinoza's *Jewishness*."[4] Medieval Jewish iconological interpretations of the biblical text heavily underlined the negative meaning of the "faculty of the imagination." The allegorical icon of the *vis imaginativa* (the drive to imagine) was the serpent, which was closely identified with the domain of the fantastic: the consonantic Hebrew sequence "*nhs*" stands for both the reptile and the practice of magic and enchantment.

Maimonides himself writes that "the act of imagination *is not* the act of the intellect, but rather its contrary,"[5] and thus foreshadows a distinction that will become one of Spinoza's principal systematic oppositions: "The philosophers say that when you call a thing *impossible*, it is because it cannot be imagined, and when you call a thing *possible*, it is because it can be imagined. Thus what is possible according to you is possible only from the point of view of the imagination and not from that of the intellect."[6] Maimonides' interpretation of the encounter of the first man with the world of the imaginary—the serpent—necessarily involves a dismissal of the faculty of reason. In addition, human weakness and man's inability to remain in the world of reason is represented by the woman—Eve. The allure of the imagination brings with it adherence to the imaginary. In other words, the fall of the first man and woman, signifying the beginning of human history, was the result not of some vague disobedience but rather of the fact that they chose to imagine—and mistook the products of the imagination for products of the intellect: they gave in to their imaginative nature, mistaking the act of composing images for the act of producing ideas.

Spinoza's demythologizing approach focuses on this allegorical perspective: his reflection critiques and goes beyond the Maimonedean interpretation, yet retains something of it. In a sort of alchemical process, the serpent or the seduction of imagery comes to be understood as a *fictional aptitude* (*praecipitantia fingendi*), and the weakness and inability of man and woman to choose rationality is expressed by what is repeatedly called human foolishness (*humana imbecillitas*)—both seen as expressions of human nature. So the question is this: how is the myth of the fall transformed into a paradigm of a theory of knowledge related to the ontological and the ethical dimensions?

Spinoza's emblematic reference to the fall is key in relation to his positive evaluation of affectivity: it is seen as a natural expression of human activity that runs counter to a conception of the absolute power of the mind—a conception that renders unacceptable the notion that the mind is unable to control its own activity. As protagonist of the fall, Adam is for Spinoza a symbol of the potential for human development rather than a symbol of corruption—an example of virtue rather than vice. Spinoza's *Adamus* is a "paradigm of human life" (*exemplar humanae vitae*), and the episode of the first man is not an allegory of the fall into corruption that leads to earthly death, but rather a sort of alternative allegory of the fall of man into the Self that leads to earthly life—a life of emancipation, transformation, and relationships. If we take into account Spinoza's thought as a whole, we can argue that he reinterprets the traditional view of the fall. Rather than defining Adam's weakness as a vice, Spinoza defines it as an inability to understand external causes. For Spinoza this is the seduction of imagery, inasmuch as these causes have their origins in the imagination: they are somehow internalized by the *Adamus*. The *vis imaginativa* (the drive to imagine) thus becomes a *vis imaginandi* (the drive to use the imagination), the principal dynamic element in the process of the *ethics*, or self-determination. The process of working through affect, a process engaged by the act of imagining, is a way of getting into the *adamah*, or the essence of man himself, his earthly dimension—an essence that realizes itself during life on earth rather than after death. The *locus* of Spinoza's *Opera* where this transformation of the myth of the fall into a gnoseological paradigm occurs is, emblematically, at the core of the *Ethics*. This is where the reader is led immediately from a discussion of the affective effects of imagination to a discussion of the well-known proposition that "a free man thinks of nothing less than of death, and his wisdom is a meditation on life, not on death" (E, IV, Prop 67).

For Spinoza it is false to hypothesize that if man were born free, as long as he remained free he would form no conception of good and evil. He argues that a free man is someone who is led solely by reason, and that anyone born free and remaining free would have only adequate ideas. He challenges the hypothesis by example, citing the history of the first man:

> This and the other things I have now demonstrated seem to have been indicated by Moses in that story of the first man. For in it the only power of God conceived is that by which he created man, that is, the power by which he consulted only man's advantage. And so we are told that God prohibited a free man from

eating of the tree of knowledge of good and evil, and that as soon as he should eat of it, he would immediately *fear death, rather than desiring to live* (vivendi cupiditas); and then, that, the man having found a wife (uxor), who *agreed completely with his nature* (quae cum sua natura prorsus conveniebat), he knew that there could be nothing in Nature more useful to him than she was; but that after he believed the lower animals to be like himself, he immediately began *to imitate their affects*, and to lose his freedom; and that afterwards this freedom was recovered by the patriarchs, guided by the Spirit of Christ; that is, by *the idea of God*, on which alone it depends that man should be free, and desire for other men the good he desires for himself (bonum, & suum esse conservare ex fundamento proprium utile cupiditas). (E, IV, Prop 68, Schol; emphasis added)

The deferral of desire and the recognition of self in the other are essentially what determine the conversion or reorientation of animal energy and constitute that "naming of things" of which man is incapable after the fall—victim as he is of the principle of contradiction. This energy can be destructive when it feeds off us, or salvific and a source of joy when it feeds us from its dynamic.

Desire enslaves the unconscious individual man. Suffering is the result of a disordered projection onto objects in the external world, that is, of submission to the power of causality: these, symbolically, are the seductions of the serpent. The breach between internal and external is overcome by the realization that true desire is the desire for God. The significance of "likeness" derives from the fact that the desire for God is both the expression and fulfillment of man made in God's likeness. And this likeness becomes apparent to Spinoza's Adam when he recognizes his likeness to an other: Eve. In other words the development of intuitive knowledge seems constituted as a recovery of original likeness, *demah*, a likeness that had been transformed into *dimyon* (that is, a derived, or only apparent, likeness) caused by human foolishness (*humana imbecillitas*), but that had remained latent within the internal *adamah*.[7]

In the twelfth chapter of the *Tractatus Theologico-Politicus* Spinoza affirms that "God's eternal Word and covenant and true religion are divinely inscribed in men's hearts, that is, in men's minds—and that this is the true handwriting of God which he has sealed with his own seal, this seal being the idea of himself, with the image of his own divinity, as it were" (TTP, XII, 145). Religion was handed down to the ancient Hebrews in the form of a written law, because in that era they were as if in a childish state. But then the prophets foresaw a future era when God would write his law "in the recesses of their hearts."

Genesis (1:26) says that the voice of God said, "Let us make man in our image, after our likeness," and Rashi glosses thus: "In our image—modelled on us. After our likeness—with the power to understand and discern." The medieval commentator explains the verse by affirming that "in our image," or literally "with our image," means "let us make man using the form that has been prepared to create him, let us make man with a seal, like a medal made by means of a die or cast"; "in our image, after our likeness" means, let us make man capable of "thinking and understanding."[8] Spinoza enters into dialogue with this constellation of texts—whether directly or indirectly is unimportant. He seems to be affirming implicitly that the fall, or more precisely the error, of Adam was to give over his own nature to the animal world: from Spinoza's point of view, then, man's real sin (*peccatum*) consists in not adhering to his own natural ontological condition as a being-of-desire. This desire flows from man's tendency to assimilate to himself beings and things which are external to and different from him. Such a desire is unnatural simply because it is not understood: once understood it is converted into natural desire, *conatus* oriented towards preservation of the self and adherence to the divine Self. However, once he recognized himself in Eve, a being much of his own nature, Adam recognized that nothing in the world could be more in his likeness.

It is only when man acts in conformity with his own nature—a nature he recognizes in his closest likeness—that he can experience the true joy of existence: "Self esteem is a joy born of the fact that a man considers himself and his own power of acting" (E, III, Def Aff XXV). Self-esteem, or—better—self-satisfaction (*acquiescentia in se ipso*) is the esteem derived from a tranquil contemplation of one's own interiority, a self-consciousness that results from the proper orientation of *conatus*. It is no longer merely a changeable interiority, a subjectivity dependent on the external world: it is adherence to the Self by an individual emancipated from external causes, where the "self" (*ipse*) signifies primarily a being that cannot be provoked by a cause external to human nature.

The geometrical deduction of the *Ethics* can be interpreted as a progressive immersion of the subject—imagining, remembering, knowing, acting—in the rich life-giving soil of affectivity: full immersion, illuminated by reason, in the shadowy backstage that constitutes the subject and on which he builds his own individuality. We traverse this at times painful dimension to arrive at the joy of discovery, or rather rediscovery, of the eternal latent in the human being and expressed in Spinoza's notion of self-esteem (*acquiescentia in se ipso*).

The theory of the imagination that Spinoza deduces geometrically in the second part of the *Ethics*—a geometrical deduction of the mechanisms that produce images—lays the logical foundations for a true "science of the imaginary": a science of the outcomes of the mechanisms of the imaginary in action, which develops into a geometrical deduction of the affects in Part III of the *Ethics*. This can also be interpreted—though it is perhaps a dangerous extrapolation from the geometric structure—as an existential journey of self-determination. A scientific understanding of the products of the imaginary can also be experienced by the subject phenomenologically, as a progressive penetration of the latent (*quid latens*) darkest, lavalike dimension, of affectivity.

The formulation of a theory of the imagination by means of genetic criteria is Spinoza's response, among other things, to a specific need to understand which is implied in his own text. Implicitly contained in the concluding section of the appendix to Part I of the *Ethics* is the need to understand the constitution of the imagination, which is not even suggested—let alone explained—by the primitive notions we form of things and their causes. Spinoza affirms that the notions most men use to explain the nature of things are really only ways of imagining, and instead of pointing to the nature of things, they point to the constitution of the imagination itself. The need to understand, to *really* explain (rather than merely point to) the constitutive properties of the imagination—by adhering, that is, to the authentic nature (*rei natura*) of each object—is an implicit but nonetheless strong hermeneutic topos that influences directly, in the geometric articulation, the mechanisms of image formation.

This topos runs throughout Spinoza's whole analysis of the imagination; it is linked from the beginning to the project of political demystification and intersects with it in the context of the interpretation of politics by means of a geometric cluster of references. In short, it can be stated thus: most men judge things according to the structure of their brains; rather than understanding them they imagine them—or, in other words, they mistake imaginary affects for reality. A concrete understanding of the structure of the imagination is situated at the origins of a process of understanding reality that is presented, in Spinoza's terms, as adherence to reality rather than to the imaginary. It involves the comprehension of the authentic nature of each thing, rather than mistaking it for an imaginary affect. The imaginative understanding of things is a nonunderstanding of reality, in great part a consequence of the natural inclination to imagine, rather than to understand, defined by Spinoza in the *Treatise on the Emendation of the Intellect* as "*praecipitantia fingendi*" (an aptitude for forming fictions). Taking up Spinoza's hint, we can extend this notion to that of *praecipitantia imaginandi*: human beings believe they understand the nature of things but their judgments express merely the nature of their own bodies.

The specific limit of the imagination is implicit in the fact that images—the ideas that we form from the affections of external bodies—point to the constitution of our own body rather than to the nature of external bodies. This is a limit that, precisely as a limit, signals the need that it be exceeded—and, we might add, that it be interpreted—the need, that is, for a *real* understanding of how images are produced. It is this that enables an understanding of the self—the need for which is the result of the need to "see" the other for what it is in reality. In the biblical story it is Eve, the being in the whole of nature most like Adam, who exculpates him, rescues him from any negative judgment—since it is she who brings about his self-recognition as an "imaginative being." In other words, it is imagined rather than understood otherness that is at the root of discord between men. This articulation of the problem of the other as a problem of the imagination situates the contrast between imaginary and real in the specifically political realm, as is borne out by Spinoza's epigram in the preface to the *Tractatus Theologico-Politicus:* "Men generally know not their own selves" (TTP, Pref, 1).

Translated by Tim Fitzpatrick

Notes

A more extensive treatment of the ideas in this chapter may be found in Paola Grassi's book-length study on Spinoza and the imagination, *L'interpretazione dell'immaginario: Uno studio in Spinoza* (Pisa: Edizioni Ets, 2002).

1. Moira Gatens and Genevieve Lloyd, *Collective Imaginings: Spinoza Past and Present* (London: Routledge, 1999) 95.
2. Ibid., 95.
3. For the correspondence with Blijenbergh, see Letters 18–24, 27, in *The Collected Works of*

Spinoza, ed. and trans. Edwin Curley, vol. 1 (Princeton: Princeton University Press, 1985), 354–92, 394–95.

4. Genevieve Brykman, *La judéité de Spinoza* (Paris: Vrin, 1972), 12.

5. Moses Maimonides, *The Guide of the Perplexed*, ed. and trans. Shlomo Pines (Chicago: University of Chicago Press, 1963), 206.

6. Ibid, 210.

7. *Adamah* is Hebrew for ground or earth, the original material out of which Adam was formed. *Demah*, also a Hebrew word, meaning "original likeness," is transformed by imagination into a derived likeness (*dimyon*). Intuitive knowledge is the means through which Adam (*adamah*) recovers his true nature (*demah*).

8. "Rashi" is the way scholars refer to the important French medieval biblical commentator Rabbi Shlomo Yitzchaki (1040–1105). Rashi quoted in J. Askénazi, "La parole éternelle de l'Ecriture selon Spinoza," *Les Nouveaux Cahiers* 6 (1971): 15–39; see 23.

8

The Envelope

A Reading of Spinoza's *Ethics*, "Of God"

Luce Irigaray

Definitions

"*By cause of itself, I understand that, whose essence involves existence; or that, whose nature cannot be conceived unless existing*" (Baruch Spinoza, *Ethics*, 355).[1]

This definition of God could be translated as: *that which is its own place for itself*, that which turns itself inside out and thus constitutes a dwelling (for) itself. Unique and necessary. Solitary. But in itself. Sufficient. Needing no other in its reception of "space-time." Men may, perhaps, contemplate or seek to contemplate God in his place; men do not give God his place.

Which also means: that which by nature can be conceived only as existing, or: *that which provides its own envelope* by turning its essence outward, must necessarily exist. That which provides its own space-time *necessarily* exists.

Hence:
— We do not exist *necessarily* because we do not provide ourselves with our own envelopes.
— Man would thus exist more necessarily than woman because he gets his envelope from her.

Twice over:
— in or through his *necessary fetal existence*,
— in his role as *lover*. Which is contingent? Except for happiness? And becoming necessary again for procreation.

That is, he is enveloped as fetus, as lover, as father.

But
— man *receives* that envelope. By nature, it is true! And the reversal can operate just as well. Man does not provide himself with his own envelope, unless it is his nature to be conceived in woman. By essence, to be conceived in woman.
— woman would theoretically be the envelope (which she provides). But she would have no essence or existence, given that she is the potential for essence and existence: *the available place*. She would be cause for herself—and in a less contingent manner than man—if she enveloped herself, or reenveloped herself, in the envelope that she is able to "provide." The envelope that is part of her "attributes" and "affections" but which she cannot use as self cause. If she enveloped herself with what she provides, she could not but necessarily be conceived of as existing. Which, to an extent, is what happens: women's suffering arises also from the fact that man does not conceive that women do not exist. Men have such a great need that women should exist. If men are to be permitted to believe or imagine themselves as self-cause, they need to think that the envelope "belongs" to them. (Particularly following "the end of God" or "the death of God," insofar as God can be determined by an era of history in any way but through the limits to its thinking.) For men to establish this belonging—without the guarantee provided by God—it is imperative that that which provides the envelope should necessarily exist. *Therefore* the maternal-feminine exists necessarily as the cause of the self-cause of man. But not for herself. She has to

exist but as an a priori condition (as Kant might say) for the space-time of the masculine subject. A cause that is never unveiled for fear that its identity might split apart and plummet down. She does not have to exist as woman because, as woman, her envelope is always *slightly open* (if man today thinks of himself as God, woman becomes, according to Meister Eckhart, an adverb or a quality of the word of God).

"That thing is called finite in its own kind [in suo genere] which can be limited by another thing of the same nature. For example, a body is called finite, because we always conceive another which is greater. So a thought is limited by another thought; but a body is not limited by a thought, nor a thought by a body" (355).

From which it would follow that:
—God is infinite and unlimited because nothing of the same nature exists;
—man is finite and limited
  both by men of the *same nature*
  and by that which is *greater*, therefore
—by the/his mother, even if he doesn't think so,
—by the/his woman, even if he doesn't think so, due to the extension of the place-envelope;
—and by *God*: but he may be so ignorant that he does not want to know that universe and thought are always greater than he is at any given moment. Does God, then, limit man by the creation and self-sufficiency of thought?

Within sexual difference, there would, it seems, be at once *finiteness and limit*, as a result of the meeting of two *bodies*, and two thoughts, and also infiniteness and unlimitedness if "God" intervenes.

If there are not *two* bodies and *two* thoughts, according to Spinoza, an evil infinite may occur: with the thought of the one limiting the body of the other and vice versa. There is no longer finiteness, or limits, or access to the infinite. At best, is matter made into form by the act? Which would virtually happen once, then once more, plus one, plus one, plus one. . . . A multiplicity of feminine formations that have access neither to the finite nor to the infinite.

If man and woman are both body and thought, they provide each other with finiteness, limit, and the possibility of access to the divine through the development of envelopes. Greater and greater envelopes, vaster and vaster horizons, but above all envelopes that are qualitatively more and more necessary and different. But always *overflowing*: with the female one becoming a cause of the other by providing him with self-cause. The setup must always be open for this to occur. It must also afford a *qualitative* difference. Essence must never be completely realized in existence—as Spinoza might say? Perhaps, for men, the movement is made in reverse? Men would not unfold their essence into existence but by virtue of existence would, perhaps, successfully constitute an essence.

Within sexual difference, therefore, *finiteness*, *limit*, and *progression* are needed: and this requires two bodies, two thoughts, a relation between the two and the conception of a wider perspective.

Clearly, for Spinoza, a body is not limited by a thought or a thought by a body. The two remain "parallel" and never intersect. The question of sexual difference, a question to be thought out particularly after and with the "death of God" and the period of the ontic-ontological difference, requires a reconsideration of the split between body and thought. The whole historic or historial analysis of philosophy shows that being has yet to be referred to in terms of body or flesh (as Heidegger notes in "Logos," his seminar on Heraclitus.)[2] Thought and body have remained separate. And this leads, on the social and cultural level, to important empirical and transcendental effects: with *discourse* and *thought* being the privileges of a *male* producer. And that remains the "norm." Even today, bodily tasks remain the obligation or the duty of a female subject. The break between the two produces rootless and insane thinking as well as bodies (women and children) that are heavy and slightly "moronic" because they lack language.

Does the act of love then mean that thinking about the body receives an infusion of flesh? Clearly, to take may be to give. And this is already a way out of parallelism. The two sexes would penetrate each other by means of theft or a rape, a more or less mechanical encounter whose goal would be to produce a child. To produce a body? Or just body? As long as our thinking is unable to limit the body, or vice versa, no sex act is possible. Nor any thought, any imaginary or symbolic of the flesh. The empirical and the transcendental have split apart (just like the roles fulfilled by man and woman?) and the body falls on one side, language on the other.

"By substance, I understand that which is in itself and is conceived through itself; in other words, that, the conception of which does not need the conception of another thing from which it must be formed" (355).

Here Spinoza is talking about God. Only God is in himself, conceived by himself; needing the concept of no other thing in order to be formed. Only God generates his existence out of his essence; which means also that he engenders himself in the form of concepts without having need of concepts different from himself in order to be formed.

God alone is *in self, by self* (*en soi, par soi*), in an autodetermination that is linked to the in-itself (*en-soi*). Does *in self by self* amount to a definition of place that develops itself? Does *in self conceived by self* mean: capable of providing and limiting its place? Never to be determined and limited by anything but self. Itself autoaffecting itself, potentially, as in the middle-passive, but never passively affected by anything else. Not knowing passivity. Never power (*puissance*), body-extension, available to suffer the action of an other than self.

That said, if this definition can be applied to God alone, the definition is defined, and God is defined, by man and not by God himself. Therefore God determines himself conceptually out of man. He does not proffer his own conception, except through the mouth of man. Obviously, in certain traditions and at certain periods, God designates himself: in words, in the texts of the law, through incarnation in different modes. But, in most cases, it is man who names in the form of conceptions, and who situates God in that space as far as the generation of conception goes.

It also seems that *Man* conceives himself without anyone else, except God, forming his conception. But the relation of man to God, of God to man, often seems circular: man defines God who in turn determines man.

This would not be the case for *woman*, who would correspond to no conception. Who, as the Greeks saw it, lacks fixed form and idea, and lacks above all a conception that she provides for herself. As matter, or extension for the concept, she would have no conception at her disposal, would be unable to conceive herself or conceive the other, and, theoretically, she would need to pass through man in order to have a relation, for herself, to man, to the world, and to God. If indeed she is capable of any of this.

Axioms

"*Everything which is, is either in itself or in another*" (355).
Being is determined by the place that envelops it:

—either the envelope is the essence of the existing thing or of existence (see "Of God," Definitions, I). That which is, is *in self*.

—or else that which is, is *in something other*, depends on the existence of something other: is not cause of self.

That which is, is determined by that in which it is contained—by that which envelops it, envelops its existence.

"That which cannot be conceived through another must be conceived through itself" (355).

Refer to the commentary on the Definitions, III. Definition of substance.

Not to be *in* self means being in something other. This is still the problem of place, of the need to receive place (unless one is God), as a result of the passage from middle-passive to passive, from auto-affection to hetero-affection, from auto-determination, auto-engendering, to determination, creation, even procreation by someone other. From the necessary circularity and conceptional self-sufficiency of God to the difference of that which can be conceived *by*, or even *in*, something other.

"From a given determinate cause an effect necessarily follows; and, on the other hand, if no determinate cause be given, it is impossible that an effect can follow" (355).

Everything takes place in a chain of causalities, in a genealogical sequence of *there is*'s. There has to be a cause that is already given, already existing, if there is to be an effect, a necessary effect. But does the cause that is already given result from an essence that is not given as such? Not in the words of Spinoza? Where God and nature are coessentials?

What relation is there between the given cause and the revealed cause? The *data*, the *there is*, the problem of the neuter case, and the fact God will be referred to in the neuter as *indeterminatum, non datum*.

But, to return to my hypothesis, if the feminine does not manifest itself as cause, it can engender no effects. And yet the maternal-feminine is also *cause of causes*. Does that mean that it too is an *indeterminatum* in its way? Insofar as it always lies behind the *data*. Behind that which is already determined in the chain of causalities. Or else: the chain of causalities on the female side remains unrevealed. Still to be revealed. The maternal-feminine would unfold, offer, manifest itself in the form of data that are not determined, not given *as such*. No effects would thereby ensure. And all this would remain possible for lack of any thought about the body and the flesh. For lack of a reciprocal determination of the one by the other, as opposed to the parallelism that prevents the maternal-feminine from being inscribed in duration as causes and effects. This in fact leaves the masculine *lost* in the chain of causalities as far as the male body, the male flesh, is concerned, as well as their relations to conception, the cause of self, except by means of the absolute causality that is God.

As for the feminine, this absence of inscription of its causes and effects in the chain of causalities leads, for example, to Aristotle's notion that woman is engendered as if by *accident*. A genetic aberration. An illness. A monstrosity. Or again, the notion that the child is engendered from the male seed alone. The female seed would not be necessary. It is not a cause and, if anything, *impedes* the possibility of generation. (See this strange quotation, among many others, from Aristotle, who was, nevertheless, a doctor: "Here is an indication that the female does not discharge semen of the same kind as the male, and that the offspring is not formed from a mixture of two semens, as some allege. Very often the female conceives although she has derived no pleasure from the act of coitus; and, on the contrary side, when the female derives as much pleasure as the male, and they both keep the same pace, the female does not bear—unless there is a proper amount of menstrual fluid [as it is called] present.")[3]

The female, it seems, is pure disposable "matter." Pure receptacle that does not stay still. Not even a place, then? Always belonging to a threatening primitive chaos. That even God should never approach. For fear he may suffer its obscure effects? Could the female be effect(s) without cause? Necessary cause. Raised as an issue only as the *accidental* cause of man? A genetic mistake. Or a divine whim? With God giving birth to the woman out of the body of the man.

"The knowledge [cognitio] *of an effect depends upon and involves knowledge of the cause*" (355).

Does knowledge of an effect envelop knowledge of the cause by a retroactive process? Which, however, by enveloping, hides the knowledge, veils it, and perhaps gives birth to it by a roundabout or return route to generation?

When knowledge of the effect envelops that of the cause, this can evoke the maternal-feminine, even in its most physical effects of generation as it doubles back on the "masculine" and its thought, and overwhelms it. Because it is not thought of as a cause, does the maternal-feminine mask cause? Overwhelm it with a veil (that of the illusion of flesh? Or the veil of Maya?). Hide it? We shall need to decipher, work through, interpret the knowledge of *effects* in order to achieve knowledge of *causes*. Is this a reverse knowledge? Why is it that the *data* are not already thought of as effects? Why is *cause* already *caused*? Because it comes from God? With cause already being effect, but of God. We can agree that there should be no effects without cause, but cause is already a given effect, or even an effect of an effect. To the genealogy of causes corresponds a hierarchy of effects. Two parallel chains which do not always cross and yet mutually determine each other, in particular as they roll and unroll reciprocally. That which is self-cause is an envelope for itself, which develops into existence(s), but is enveloped by our knowledge of its effects. As it reveals its existence to us, we envelop-veil it with the knowledge of its effects, on the basis of which we seek knowledge of its cause(s).

Does knowledge of the effect envelop knowledge of the cause? The effect overwhelms the cause from the point of view of knowledge. A double movement in "theology," moving up and down. Essence envelops existence if there is *cause of self*, knowledge of the effect envelops that of the cause if there is no cause of self. If I start with the creatures, I move up the chain of effects (until, perhaps, I reach an uncreated cause whose knowledge, or ultimate cause, escapes us?); if I start with God, I move down the chain of causes, on the basis of a *causa sui*.

There are no effects without an already given cause. And this is linked to the question of *miracles* for Spinoza. There might be effects without *data*: inexplicable, "miraculous" effects. Before deciding for a "miracle," Spinoza notes our inability to perceive the extension of the chain of causalities and, in particular, our inability to analyze the relation of contingency to necessity. A belief in "miracle" or in "chance" is often a result of weakness or narrowness in the field of conception.[4]

"Those things which have nothing mutually in common with one another cannot through one another be mutually understood, that is to say, the conception of the one does not involve the conception of the other" (355).

Conception means taking hold of, perceiving, and conceiving an available matter or power. Conception is more active than perception; or, more exactly, conception designates the active pole of the mind, and perception designates the passive pole. Whence the fact that, traditionally, the feminine, insofar as it has access to mind, remains in perception, while the conception is the privilege of the masculine.

I am often asked this question: if sexual difference exists, what path can there still be between man and woman? Which amounts to saying that in the past relations between men and women were not determined by sex. In Spinoza's terms, this is to assume that woman cannot conceive. Or else that man can't? (but that cannot be so, since Spinoza is conceiving his system . . .).

If sexual difference exists, does that mean that man and woman hold nothing in common? There is at the very least the child as an effect, as we know. In our thinking, clearly, the child is still thought of as an effect of man's, of the male seed, even if biology has established that this is not so. Our thinking still thinks of the ovum as passive, of the female body as passivity, of woman as remaining in the domain of perception, or even at times of the perceived.

What would man and woman have in common? Both conception and perception. *Both*. And without any hierarchy between the two. Both would have the capacity to perceive and conceive. *To suffer and to be active*. To suffer the self and to understand the self. To receive the self and to envelop the self. Becoming more open because of the freedom of each, male and female. Since freedom and necessity are correlated. With each giving the other necessity and freedom. In self, for self, and for the other.

If I exist, that would mean that I correspond to a necessity. Therefore that I should be free. For this to become so, the concept of the masculine would have to cease to envelop that of the feminine, since the feminine has no necessity if it is uniquely an effect of and for the masculine.

Between man and woman, whatever the differences may be and despite the fact that the concept of the one, male or female, cannot envelop that of the other, certain bridges can be built, through two approaches:

—that of generation,
—that of God.

But, historically, in Genesis, the feminine has no conception. She is figured as being born from man's envelope, with God as midwife. Whereas woman envelops man before his birth. Could it be that God is he who intervenes so that there should be a *reciprocal limitation* of envelopes for both? Which is why it is necessary to go through the question of God every time the sexual act comes under consideration.

The openings in the envelopes between men and women should always be mediated by God. Faithless to God, man lays down the law for woman, imprisons her in his conception(s), or at least in accordance with his conceptions instead of covering her only for God, while awaiting God. Woman, who enveloped man before birth, until he could live outside her, finds herself encircled by a language, by places that she cannot conceive of, and from which she cannot escape.

It's nothing new for man to want to be both man and woman: he has always had pretensions of turning the envelope inside out. But by willing to be master of everything, he becomes the slave both of discourse and of mother nature.

Notes

Editor's note: This piece is reprinted from Luce Irigaray, *An Ethics of Sexual Difference*, translated from the original French by Carolyn Burke and Gillian C. Gill (Ithaca: Cornell University Press, 1993). Given that the text is translated, it seems necessary to retain the quotations from Spinoza in the English text used by the translators. The propositions discussed are few and all come from the first few pages of the *Ethics*. The reader will not find it difficult to match them up with the translation favored in this volume: *The Collected Works of Spinoza*, vol. 1, ed. and trans. Edwin M. Curley (Princeton: Princeton University Press, 1985).

1. Page references following quotations are to Baruch (Benedict de) Spinoza, *Ethics*, Part I, "Of God," trans. W. H. White, Rev. A. H. Stirling, in *Great Books of the Western World*, vol. 31, *Descartes, Spinoza* (Chicago: Encyclopaedia Britannica, 1952), 355–72.

2. Martin Heidegger, "Logos (Heraclitus, Fragment B 50)," in *Early Greek Thinking: The Dawn of Western Philosophy*, trans. David F. Krell and Frank A. Capuzzi (New York: Harper and Row, 1975), 59–78.

3. *Aristotle: Generation of Animals*, trans. A. L. Peck (Cambridge: Harvard University Press, 1963), 97–98.

4. See, for example, E I, P33S1 (367): "But a thing cannot be called contingent unless with reference to a deficiency in our knowledge."

9

Re-reading Irigaray's Spinoza

Sarah Donovan

Contemporary feminist theory has routinely turned to the history of philosophy for the dual purposes of critiquing it and using it as a resource. While not among the most frequently referred-to historical figures, seventeenth-century philosopher Benedict de Spinoza has been interpreted for both purposes. In *An Ethics of Sexual Difference*, Luce Irigaray is primarily critical of Spinoza.[1] Rather than engage Spinoza in a sustained play of critique and mime, as she does in other texts with thinkers such as Freud, Lacan, and Heidegger, she criticizes Spinoza without fully engaging with his work. In this chapter I provide a reading of Spinoza that is different from Irigaray's and demonstrates productive aspects of his view that she does not discuss. I suggest that, in spite of Irigaray's categorization of Spinoza within the philosophical tradition of devaluing the body in favor of the mind, a different reading of Spinoza demonstrates that the projects of Irigaray and Spinoza share some concerns. Both seek to overcome dualism; to elevate the status of the body and emotions; and to rethink Western, Judeo-Christian ideas about God. I then point to one manner in which contemporary feminist philosophers are returning to the philosophy of Spinoza, and I suggest how this might be useful to Irigaray's discussion of politics.

Irigaray's Critique of Spinoza

As indicated throughout *Speculum of the Other Woman*, Irigaray believes that the history of philosophy since Plato is founded upon the division of the mind and the body and upon the association of the former with the masculine and the latter with the feminine.[2] The outcome of this division is that men are subjects within Western culture, and, following Simone de Beauvoir's famous analysis in *The Second Sex*, women are "the other."[3] As the other, women are the unacknowledged support of masculine subjectivity. To place Irigaray's well-known criticism of Western culture into the psychoanalytic terms that she often employs, women are associated with the imaginary, repressed, and unconscious element of society. The symbolic order, or conscious and linguistic order, is masculine and it dominates the social and political order. As Irigaray says in *An Ethics of Sexual Difference*, "Man had been the subject of discourse, whether in theory, morality, or politics."[4] The symbolic order represents in language the male imaginary that is projected onto the world. However, the symbolic order is sustained by the repressed feminine. According to Irigaray, women support the creation of and maintain the symbolic order, but are not acknowledged or rewarded for their efforts with positive social or political representations of their subjectivity.

Irigaray's philosophical project in *An Ethics of Sexual Difference* is both to re-read the philosophers in order to highlight the exclusion of the feminine, and to characterize genuine ethical relationships between the sexes. She accomplishes this task through her well-known, and much debated, method of mimesis and strategic essentialism.[5] Irigaray criticizes Spinoza for maintaining a separation between mind and body in his metaphysics. She says of the relationship between mind and body in his work, "The two remain 'parallel' and never intersect."[6] While parallelism is a well-known tenet of Spinoza's philosophy, Irigaray concludes that this parallelism is the same kind of mind/body dualism that occurs throughout the history of philosophy to the detriment of women. She says that in Spinoza's work, "thought and body have remained separate. And this leads, on the social and cultural level, to important empirical and transcendental effects: with *discourse* and *thought* being the privileges of a *male* producer.... Even today, bodily tasks remain the obligation or the duty of a female subject. The break between the two produces rootless and insane thinking as well as bodies (women and children) that are heavy and slightly 'moronic' because they lack language."[7] Irigaray suggests that parallelism in Spinoza's thought results in a dualistic split between the empirical and the transcendental. She says of Spinoza's view, "As long as our thinking is unable to limit the body, or vice versa, no sex act is possible. Nor any thought, any imaginary, or symbolic of the flesh."[8] While Spinoza does say that, as modes of the attributes of unitary substance, the mind and the body do not interact, Irigaray glosses over important nuances within his *Ethics*.

Spinoza's view of substance is an attempt to offer an alternative to Cartesian dualism. While well-known Spinoza scholars interpret Spinoza's metaphysics as dualistic, other traditional scholars such as Edwin Curley are also reading his work as nondualistic (with different degrees of emphasis on aspects of materialism in his view).[9] A nondualistic reading of his parallelism depends upon understanding Spinoza as departing from Descartes' metaphysics.

At the most basic level, contrary to Descartes' belief that thought and extension are two separate substances, Spinoza maintains that there can be only one substance, by which he understands that which "is in itself and is conceived through itself, that is, that whose concept does not require the concept of another, from which it must be formed" (E, I, Def Aff 3). Spinoza's substance is self-contained in the sense that *"two substances having different attributes have nothing in common with each other"* (E, I, Prop 2). Further, contrary to Descartes' view, substance is self-caused, but not created (E, I, Props 6–8). Substance, as self-caused, has always existed. With regard to causality, Descartes argues that his Judeo-Christian God is the incorporeal, separate, and efficient cause of the world. In *Ethics*, Book I, Spinoza argues that God is the immanent cause of the world and, thereby, everything is conceived through God. Spinoza rejects a view of substance or of God that could posit an inside and an outside to God. This view of God as an immanent cause allows Spinoza to make radical claims about thought and extension.

Spinoza employs the language of "substance," "attribute," and "mode" to describe the non-Cartesian status of thought and extension. These terms are distinguished as follows: (1) God is "a substance consisting of an infinity of attributes" (E, I, D6); (2) attributes are "what the intellect perceives of a substance, as constituting its essence" (E, I, D4); and (3) modes are "the affections of a substance, *or* that which is in another through which it is also conceived" (E, I, D5). Although Spinoza maintains a theory of singular substance, he also articulates relationships between substance, attributes, and modes that allow him to employ the language of active/passive and infinite/finite within this theory. His definitions for *natura naturans* and *natura naturata* aid him in discussing these distinctions while remaining consistent with a theory of singular substance. Spinoza says,

> By *Natura naturans* we must understand what is in itself and is conceived through itself, *or* such attributes of substance as express an eternal and infinite essence, that is (by P14C1 and P17C2), God, insofar as he is considered as a free cause. But by *Natura naturata* I understand whatever follows from the necessity of God's nature, *or* from any of God's attributes, that is, all the modes of God's attributes insofar as they are considered as things which are in God, and can neither be nor be conceived without God. (E, I, Prop 29, Schol)

Natura naturans, or nature as active, refers to God as substance and its attributes. *Natura naturata*, or nature as passive, allows Spinoza to address modes as following from the attributes while remaining logically consistent with his definitions for and propositions about substance and attributes.[10] However, Spinoza is careful to state that the distinction between *natura naturans* and *natura naturata* does not make God a remote, disconnected cause of finite things. For "all things that are, are in God, and so depend on God that they can neither be nor be conceived without him" (E, I, Prop 28, Schol 2). In his text *Spinoza and Other Heretics: The Marrano of Reason*, Yirmiyahu Yovel explores how this is possible. Yovel follows Spinoza scholars in using the language of "horizontal" and "vertical" causation to discuss the complex relationship between finite and infinite modes.¹¹ He then relates this discussion to the distinction between *natura naturans* and *natura naturata*.¹²

Yovel understands "horizontal" and "vertical" causation in the following way. The "horizontal" line expresses "the universe from the viewpoint of mechanism and finitude." In this line, finite things produce each other. The "vertical" line of causation describes how "particular things are derived from God as their immanent cause, following a *logical* principle of particularization." This line "goes from the substance through an attribute to a series of infinite modes (direct and mediated), until it is said to reach and determine the particular individual." Yovel discusses how natural laws are located in the infinite modes. He says, "Natural laws are individual entities transmitting the power and necessity of God through one of his attributes. They thereby serve as intermediary agents in engendering particulars." While mediating between *natura naturans* and *natura naturata*, natural laws and infinite laws belong to *natura naturata*. According to Yovel, horizontal and vertical lines both express the process of "cosmic particularization." Their relation is to be understood as follows: "horizontal causality realizes vertical causality by translating its inner logical character into external mechanistic terms."¹³ While mechanistic laws do not determine particular things directly, they do determine how other particular things will behave. Yovel says that the kind of complementarity demonstrated here is a typical way for Spinoza to discuss dualities and to explain dual positions as aspects of the same thing.

In a further discussion of finite modes, Yovel relates "vertical" and "horizontal" causation to *natura naturans* and *natura naturata*. Both complementary distinctions are central to comprehending why finite modes should not be understood as created by the "vertical" line of causality. To begin, Yovel describes how finite modes are dependent upon substance insofar as their essence does not imply existence; however, finite things are still eternal (and thereby not created). To capture the complementarity between both "vertical" and "horizontal" causation and *natura naturans* and *natura naturata*, Yovel says,

> Generation and destruction occur in Spinoza as particular essences are translated into concrete things in the domain of duration and external causality. Here horizontal causality takes over from the vertical, and a time-dimension is added to being. This is *natura naturata*, the world of dependent things, seen (and exist-

> ing) *sub specie durationis*. But the same system of finitude exists and can be seen also *sub specie aeternitatis*. . . . In conclusion, *natura naturans* and *natura naturata* are simultaneously eternal systems, existing irrespective of beginning or end. The system comprising the substance, the attributes, and the infinite modes, provides finite things with ontological support and with their nature and laws; it does not so much engender them (in time) as it constitutes them (timelessly).[14]

According to Yovel, entering into time is moving from a vertical relation to a horizontal one. Natural laws as infinite modes mediate between *natura naturans* and *natura naturata*.[15] Thus, finite modes are not created by, but are ontologically dependent upon, substance.

These distinctions help to clarify how Spinoza's view of thought and extension is different from Descartes'. Spinoza classifies thought and extension as two of the infinite attributes that express God's eternal and infinite essence.[16] Further, Spinoza argues that these attributes have equal value within the infinite, singular substance of God. As Deleuze says, "In terms of the Spinozean critique of all eminence, of all transcendence and equivocity, no attribute is superior to another, none is reserved for the creator, none is relegated to the created beings and to their imperfection."[17] While these attributes have equal status, and both express God's essence, Spinoza claims that these attributes never interact. He says, "*Each attribute of a substance must be conceived through itself*" (E, I, Prop 10). However, the order of ideas directly parallels the order of extended things. This parallelism is at the root of the dualist interpretations of his metaphysics. But alternate interpretations of Spinoza's parallelism depict it as more complex than this initial conclusion. For while thought and extension may not interact insofar as they are attributes, they are ultimately expressions of one and the same substance—they are both equal expressions of God.

Edwin Curley captures the unique aspect of Spinoza's parallelism in *Behind the Geometrical Method* by describing how Spinoza responds to the paradox that emerges from Descartes' view of substance. He identifies this paradox as follows: Descartes claims that the mind and body are two separate substances. However, in Meditation 6, he also claims that there is a real union between the mind and the body. This "substantial union" is incompatible with Descartes' theory of two substances. Curley believes that Spinoza seeks to resolve Descartes' paradox with his parallelism.

However, Spinoza's parallelism can only be viewed as a worthy response if the reader focuses less on the fact that Spinoza says that the attributes of mind and body never interact, and more on the identity thesis that accompanies this claim. This thesis is rooted in Spinoza's claim that *"the order and connection of ideas is the same as the order and connection of things"* (E, II, Prop 7). This thesis connects the parallel attributes of mind and body within the theory of singular substance and makes the connection necessary. Curley concludes that "if we look to the further development of Spinoza's doctrine of mind-body identity in Parts I and III of the *Ethics*, if we look to the consequences which he thinks follow from his doctrine that the mind and the body are one and the same thing, conceived in two different ways, we shall find that the fundamental thrust of Spinoza's system is anti-dualistic, that it is a form of materialistic monism."[18]

This reading takes seriously Spinoza's view that *"the mind does not know itself, except insofar as it perceives the ideas of the affections of the body"* (E, II, Prop 23). Curley says, "To understand the mind, we must understand the body, without which the mind could not function or even exist. In spite of all the parallelistic talk, the order of understanding never proceeds from mind to body."[19] While the mind and body do not interact in any direct way, Spinoza's view of singular substance and the expression of that substance through the attributes permit an interpretation of him as nondualistic.

Irigaray's (Unacknowledged) Consonance with Spinoza

Irigaray situates Spinoza within the philosophical tradition that excludes the body and values only the mind as an epistemological tool. While Spinoza is not to be touted as a seventeenth-century feminist, Irigaray overlooks his work as an early example of and possible resource for undermining dualistic thinking. Identifying such resources is especially important to her method of strategic essentialism. While miming hopelessly dualistic texts provides a useful and necessary critique of the tradition, Irigaray is most productive in introducing new ideas when a text itself contains ideas that are useful to her.[20] She does not sufficiently explore points of consonance between her view and Spinoza's with regard to the following: (1) Spinoza's valuation of extension, (2) the role of the body in attaining knowledge, and (3) the affinity between Spinoza's "imagination" and "reason" and her "imaginary" and "symbolic."

In *Ethics*, Book II, Spinoza concludes from the fact that mind cannot affect body and vice versa that the mind is not to be understood as something that controls the body, and the body has as much value as the mind. Spinoza repeatedly rejects the Cartesian view of bodies as matter that God set in motion from afar that human minds are both distinct from and intimately linked to, and that the mind can act on. According to the definitions of substance, attributes, and modes, God is expressed through the attributes of both thought and extension (*natura naturans*). Both mind and body, as modes that express the attributes of thought and extension, follow from the necessity of God's nature and attributes (*natura naturata*). *Natura naturata* is not created by *natura naturans*. Although mind and body never interact, Spinoza views the body as an epistemological tool. As he says, "*The human mind is capable of perceiving a great many things, and is the more capable, the more its body can be disposed in a great many ways*" (E, II, Prop 14). His theory of substance makes this claim possible.

Spinoza further elevates the status of extension, and marks his view as non-Cartesian, by stating that "*no attribute of a substance can be truly conceived from which it follows that the substance can be divided*" (E, I, Prop 12). Spinoza believes that insofar as extension, as an attribute of substance, expresses God's essence, it is not divisible—it is infinite. In Cartesian philosophy, only thinking substance has the status of "indivisible" and "infinite." But Spinoza must make this claim if he asserts that thought and extension are both attributes of equal value that are merely expressing God's essence in different ways. Further, according to both the distinction and relationship between *natura naturans* and *natura naturata*, Spinoza can also claim how, in some sense, the modes are not divisible.[21]

Spinoza further challenges the Cartesian view, and elevates the status of the body, when he says, "*The body cannot determine the mind to thinking, and the mind cannot determine the body to motion, to rest, or to anything else (if there is anything else)*" (E, III, Prop 2). In his explanation, Spinoza departs from a theory of knowledge that would understand the mind (in the form of active will) as acting on a body (that is passive with regard to this will); he believes that individuals who hold this view are ignorant of causes. In response to imagined objections to his view, he says, "Does not experience also teach that if . . . the body is inactive, the mind is at the same time incapable of thinking?" or "They [his objectors] do not know what the body can do, or what can be deduced from the consideration of its nature alone, and that they know from experience that a great many things happen from the laws of Nature alone which they never would have believed could happen without the direction of the mind" (E, III, Prop 2, Schol). Spinoza here emphasizes once again that the body is of equal value to that of the mind, and that thought itself could not happen without the body. In his time, Spinoza's views were interpreted as dangerously heretical and indicative of atheism. While not disputing that he can be read in a rationalist vein, one might argue that his valuation of extension undeniably departs from the dominant Cartesian, rationalist discourse.

In Irigaray's early work, her diagnosis of most major religions is that they elide the body (matter) in favor of the mind (God). While she employs the language of substance only strategically, Irigaray challenges Cartesian metaphysics and epistemology in a manner similar to that of Spinoza. Following Ludwig Feuerbach, Irigaray maintains that religion is created by humans and is designed to help individuals have an ideal with which to identify—this ideal is central to subject formation. According to Irigaray's secular interpretation of religion, the transcendent, Judeo-Christian God is a projection of the masculine valuation of mind over matter. It supports male identity to the exclusion of female identity. Irigaray says, "And the gender of God, the guardian of every subject and every discourse, is always *masculine and paternal* in the West."[22] Women, as a part of the imaginary and associated with matter, are typically excluded from the upper echelons of religious orders, and they are not considered subjects in the same way as are men. Irigaray believes that the only way to alter this situation, and break down mind/body dualism in religion, is to construct female divinities and reconfigure representations of male divinities.[23] Bracketing the complexities of this idea, both kinds of divinities must incorporate mind and matter (the sensible/transcendental).[24] While Irigaray neatly places Spinoza in the tradition of dualism that she rejects with her view, his work can be read as undermining that same dualism. Rather than underscoring Spinoza's view of a divinity that embraces, rather than fears, extension, Irigaray glosses over this aspect of his work.

The body plays a central role in Spinoza's account of the attainment of knowledge. As indicated earlier, even though Spinoza believes that the mind and body do not interact, the necessary connection between the attributes of thought and extension render this distinction, in some ways, an ultimately false one. As Spinoza says, "*The object of the idea constituting the human mind is the body, or a certain mode of extension which actually exists, and nothing else*" (E, II, Prop 13). He concludes from Part II, Prop 13 and Prop 7 that "the idea of the body and the body, that is by (P13), the mind and the body, are one and the same individual, which is conceived now under the attribute of thought, now under the attribute of extension" (E, II, Prop 21). Given this necessary identity between mind and body, one cannot attain knowledge without a body that is actively engaged with other bodies. In fact, the more interaction a body has with other bodies, the more ideas a mind has.[25] Even if we grant that Spinoza excludes a female subject from this discussion, he is still arguing that men who are not ignorant comprehend themselves as unique—and indissoluble—combinations of mind and body. This model challenges typical portrayals of the Enlightenment man of reason. The body plays a necessary role in the acquisition of knowledge. While Irigaray might argue validly that Spinoza excludes women from this picture, that criticism is distinct from her representation of his parallelism in *An Ethics of Sexual Difference*.

Finally, points of consonance exist between Spinoza's "imagination" and "reason" and Irigaray's "imaginary" and "symbolic." The unique relationship between reason and imagination in Spinoza's view is an early foreshadowing of Irigaray's concern that the history of philosophy has elided the bodily and affective in favor of the rational.[26] In order to demonstrate affinity between Irigaray and Spinoza, it is not necessary to argue that Spinoza is discussing the imagination as an unconscious, or, in Lacanian terms, as if it were structured like a language.[27] The relationship between the imagination and reason is also a key point of consonance.

In the *Ethics*, Part II, Proposition 40, Spinoza names his three levels of knowledge (imagination, reason, intuition). The first level of knowledge, imagination, encompasses inadequate and confused ideas about the body. Spinoza says of the first order of knowledge: "*Knowledge of the first kind is the only cause of falsity*" (E, II, Prop 41). At this level of knowledge, we experience reality as an onslaught of particulars—with no real understanding of either universals, or the causal order of nature. As Spinoza describes it, "I have been accustomed to call such perceptions knowledge from random experience" (E, II, Prop 40, Schol 2). For example, through imagination, we think that things are present to us that are not. We base this judgment on past experience. We err because our minds are "considered to lack an idea which excludes the existence of those things which it imagines to be present to it" (E, II, Prop 17, Schol). Further, we perceive ourselves to be acted upon rather than understanding ourselves as active (albeit both limited and dependent upon God) within nature. Both the second and the third kind of knowledge distinguish truth from falsity. Second-order knowledge is characterized by "common notions and adequate ideas of the properties of things" (see E, II, Props 38–40). Spinoza specifically calls the common notions "reason." Here we recognize adequate ideas that are common between ourselves and other people, for *"all bodies agree in certain things"* (E, II, L2). And *"those things which are common to all, and which are equally in the part and in the whole, can only be conceived adequately"* (E, II, Prop 38). According to Spinoza, these ideas must be adequate because, as ideas in both the part and the whole, they are ultimately expressions of God's essence. Ideas that follow from these adequate, common ideas are also adequate. Through the common notions, we understand more clearly the necessity inherent to the causal order of nature. However, in second-order knowing we still classify the world into ontologically discrete categories. Third-order knowing "proceeds from an adequate idea of the formal essence of certain attributes of God to the adequate knowledge of the essence of things" (E, II, Prop 40, Schol 2). Spinoza calls this intuitive knowledge. Third-order knowledge ultimately depends upon understanding the relationship between a mode and the attribute of which it is an expression. Yovel says about third-order knowledge that it is

> a change in perspective which, without addition or subtraction, provides us with a deeper insight of the same thing through a new processing, or synthesis, of the same informative ingredients. Before there were only external causes and universal laws by which to understand the particular thing, or rather, the way this thing instantiates a set of abstract common properties. Now, however, all previous information coalesces to produce a singular item, the particular essence of this thing as it follows immanently from one of God's attributes according to a logical principle of particularization.[28]

Third-order knowledge allows us to understand both the essence of a particular thing and how it is a necessary expression of one of God's attributes. In third-order knowledge, one learns that there are no real ontological distinctions and that the cause-and-effect order of nature is actually an expression of God's attributes.

Interpretations about the relationship between the three levels of knowledge have varied. Genevieve Lloyd clearly explains two opposing approaches in her *Spinoza and the Ethics*.[29] A traditional approach follows Hegel's interpretation of Spinoza as a strict rationalist. According to this view, the imagination is an inferior form of knowledge that is eclipsed by rational understanding. A second approach understands the relationship between the imagination and reason as more complex. Antonio Negri is a proponent of this approach. According to Negri, "Imagination becomes something more than a source of error, to be transcended. . . . Reason can criticize those fictions, replacing them with better ones. The goal is not to transcend and spurn imagination but to complement it and collaborate with it."[30] Negri believes that Spinoza does not abandon the imagination as an epistemological tool.

Etienne Balibar's interpretation of Spinoza, in *Spinoza and Politics*, also supports the second approach. Balibar emphasizes the unbreakable link between imagination and reason when he says: "In reality, all men live in both the world of the imagination and that of reason. In every man there is already some reason (that is, some true ideas and some joyful passions), if only because of the partial knowledge he has of his own usefulness; and in every man there is still some imagination (even when he has acquired many true ideas through science and philosophy and from his own experience), if only because of his own inability to dominate all external causes."[31] According to Balibar, all humans are enmeshed in both the realm of the imagination and that of reason. Imagination can be controlled, but never completely eclipsed from human experience.[32] If we take seriously Spinoza's idea that a person's mind is necessarily the idea of her body, and that she comes to know both her own body and the world through her bodily interactions, it is implausible for her to fully escape either the imagination or the affects. As Lloyd says, "Although Spinoza is, as a rationalist, committed to the power of reason to transcend error, this is not a matter of shedding imaginings. The imagination has a resilience which can coexist with the knowledge of its inadequacy."[33] If the imagination is taken seriously as a necessary step toward, and inevitable part of, higher forms of knowledge, then the possibility for dialogue between Spinoza and Irigaray about the relationship between the imagination and reason emerges, and the need for an alternate interpretation of Irigaray's view of Spinoza is reinforced.

The relevance of this re-reading of Irigaray's Spinoza is underscored by Spinoza's discussion of emotion in the *Ethics*.

In *Ethics*, Part III, Spinoza indicates how he incorporates emotions into his metaphysics and epistemology by explaining the relationship between adequate and inadequate ideas and the affects of joy, sadness, and desire. According to Spinoza, the affects of joy/goodness are experienced when we are the adequate cause of these affects, and sadness/evil result when we are acted upon (also known as a passion of the mind). He says, "*The actions of the mind arise from adequate ideas alone; the passions depend on inadequate ideas alone*" (E, III, Prop 3). Desire to persevere in our existence—*conatus*—is the essence of all humans. Spinoza believes that we attain higher levels of knowledge and joy by understanding the adequate causes of ideas and by having a body that is productively engaged in the world. The higher our level of knowledge and affectivity, the greater our joy.

The ability to act in such a way that we achieve great levels of joy is explained in *Ethics*, Book V when Spinoza indicates that a mind becomes an adequate cause by understanding immanent causality and the nature of God. Although mind and body remain separate, joy depends upon greater affectivity. Once a human being starts to understand that, according to God's nature, all things are necessary and determined, he or she no longer understands life as happening to him or her. This individual starts to understand that he or she is a necessary part of the order of the universe, and in that limited sense, is an active rather than a passive agent who is randomly acted upon by outside forces. If one achieves this knowledge, he or she achieves neither a state of quasi-disembodiment in life nor the promise of an afterlife for the soul (as in some ancient and Christian conceptions of the soul). Rather, this state is characterized by intense joy and love of God.[34] For Spinoza, the body and emotions are central to the ideas of the mind and, ultimately, to human knowledge of God—we do not shed them as we ascend a ladder of knowledge.

Spinoza's view of the imagination, emotions, and reason speaks to Irigaray's claims about the relationship between the imaginary and the symbolic and to her view that men and women both need to become affective beings in addition to rational ones. While Spinoza's "imagination" and "reason" help him to break down the dualism between reason and emotion, Irigaray attains a similar goal by using psychoanalytic concepts.

Trained in both Freudian and Lacanian theory, Irigaray moves fluidly, and strategically, between each theory's definitions of the unconscious and consciousness.³⁵ Irigaray's general concern with psychoanalytic understandings of the unconscious (imaginary) and consciousness (symbolic) is the following, opposed associative chains: (1) unconscious/ irrational/ body/female/pre-culture and (2) consciousness/rational/mind/male/culture. Irigaray criticizes the division between these two chains as rooted in cultural bias against the feminine. She argues not only that a new symbolic needs to emerge that reflects the repressed female imaginary, but also that the male symbolic must incorporate human characteristics relegated to the female imaginary and labeled as negative—especially emotions and the body.

Much like Spinoza's imagination and reason, for Irigaray, the imaginary realm within psychoanalytic theory is to be taken seriously as both underlying and overlapping with the symbolic realm. While the imaginary is more akin to the unconscious for Irigaray, and can thereby be subject to radically different operations from those of the symbolic order (as opposed to confused operations, as with Spinoza's "imagination"), it is still central to the symbolic. For example, in the first of two key stages toward the development of mature subjectivity, the ego emerges out of the stage in which the imaginary dominates. In the second stage, mature subjectivity hinges on the child's ability to submit to the symbolic order. However, this entrance into the symbolic order does not entail shedding the ego; the ego matures and changes through this entrance, and the subject proper is "born." The imaginary is never eclipsed out of Irigaray's theory of subjectivity as a powerful and influential force in our personal identity. The symbolic, social order also never frees itself of imaginary elements. As with Spinoza's "imagination" and "reason," an unbreakable link exists between the imaginary and symbolic. A hierarchical relationship also exists between the imaginary and the symbolic. The symbolic order holds an elevated status insofar as it is the key to mature subject formation and has a direct effect on both social and political institutions. This is not to deny that the imaginary is central to, and formative of, the symbolic. However, the symbolic is the rational and most directly intelligible representation of the imaginary.

Thus, Irigaray's imaginary and symbolic operate according to a logic akin—although not identical—to that between Spinoza's imagination and reason. The overlap between the imaginary and imagination and the symbolic and reason results in the following: (1) both the "imagination" and the "imaginary" bring the body and affectivity to the realm of reason; (2) both operate according to a logic that can be distinct from the rational realm; (3) while reasoned thought is a desirable end for knowledge, both the "imagination" and "imaginary" are productive of knowledge; (4) the interaction between the two realms (imagination/reason and imaginary/symbolic) offers an explanation for both happiness and suffering; and (5) as embodied beings, we cannot escape into a purely rational or discursive realm.

Spinoza and Contemporary Feminist Philosophy

Irigaray's critique of the history of philosophy and psychoanalytic thought undeniably shaped and advanced contemporary feminist philosophy. While not questioning this enormous contribution, I conclude by considering two of Moira Gatens's concerns in *Imaginary Bodies* about Irigaray's use of psychoanalytic concepts to the exclusion of Spinozistic concepts: the "reality"/"imagination" distinction and the prioritizing of sexual difference.[36] My goal is not to evaluate the validity of these concerns, but to use them to suggest two closely related ways in which Spinoza's work is useful to Irigaray's.

In *Imaginary Bodies*, Gatens examines how sexed bodies are represented in Western culture from a social, political, and ethical perspective. Three chapters are devoted specifically to using Spinoza's work to address contemporary issues. In chapter 4, Gatens provides the following explanation of why she turns to Spinoza: "The Spinozistic view does not lend itself to an understanding of sexual difference in terms of a consciousness/body or sex/gender distinction. For Spinoza the body is not part of passive nature ruled over by an active mind but rather the body is the ground of human action. The mind is constituted by the affirmation of the actual existence of the body, and reason is active and embodied precisely because it is the affirmation of a *particular* bodily existence."[37] Since Spinoza does not prioritize either mind or body, he challenges the traditional division between man/mind/politics and woman/body/nature. Gatens appreciates this view because it not only has profound affects for understanding personal identity, but also upsets the idea that the best political order is composed of individuals who have abstracted away from their bodies and control their bodies as if they were subduing an irrational, dangerous force. In fact, Spinoza's view suggests that a political body always depends upon the lived experience of its citizens. The most successful society provides opportunities for citizens to actualize their full potential in a noncoercive manner.

In her turn to Spinoza, Gatens incorporates both the psychoanalytic (and specifically Irigarayan) concept of the imaginary and the Spinozistic concept of the imagination.[38] However, she also indicates two ways in which Irigaray's psychoanalytic approach to addressing social and political exclusions is potentially problematic. In *Imaginary Bodies*, she defines, and limits, her use of the imaginary in the following way: "I am not concerned with the physiological, anatomical, or biological understanding of the human body but rather with what will be called *imaginary bodies*. . . . The term 'imaginary' will be used in a loose but nevertheless technical sense to refer to those images, symbols, metaphors and representations which help construct various forms of subjectivity. . . . I am not proposing a theory of the imaginary."[39] While Gatens believes that the "imaginary body," as a psychoanalytic concept, is helpful in understanding how a culture constructs both its own identity and the identity of its citizens, she distances herself from overextending its scope by developing it into a theory about a universal "social imaginary."

Speaking specifically about her belief that Irigaray has done this, Gatens indicates that "in her later work, she [Irigaray] extends her use of 'imaginary' to the social *per se*. . . . An unavoidable consequence of positing a unitary notion of *the* social imaginary is that it will come to stand in contrast to a notion of 'reality.' . . . The deployment of a 'reality'/'imagination' distinction inevitably leads to a contrast between a less than satisfactory present and an idealized future."[40] Gatens further differentiates herself from Irigaray's work by indicating a second point of concern. "Whilst agreeing that representations of sexual difference are central to social imaginaries, I do not think it helpful to reduce the complexity and variety of social imaginaries to a univocal sexual imaginary."[41] To avoid both the "reality"/"imagination" distinction and the claim that sexual difference dominates the social imaginary, Gatens does not depend solely upon psychoanalytic concepts and prefers the plural term "social imaginaries." She sees the joining of the psychoanalytic imaginary and the philosophical imagination as a unique way of approaching social and political exclusions in Western culture.[42]

Several points emerge when we apply Gatens's insights to the difference between Spinoza's imagination and reason and Irigaray's imaginary and symbolic. First, by focusing on imagination and reason within the context of his view of mind and body as modes that follow from distinct attributes of the same substance, Spinoza suggests that confusion about reality in the realm of imagination, and clarity in the realm of reason, are achieved always in the context of particular bodies and emotions. In other words, a lack of understanding is directly related to a misunderstanding about one's own body in the causal order of nature. For Spinoza, an advance in knowledge will not mean finding out that the mind is superior to the body and emotions; it will entail discovering that the more a person's body can do (and this "do" can and should be defined very broadly), or the greater its affectivity, the more knowledge. As Gatens demonstrates, this logic is useful for a critique of a culture because it emphasizes the following points: First, in order to critique a culture, one must really understand the unique, everyday interactions that make up that particular culture. Second, within a Spinozistic framework, bodily differences exist and are given different meanings according to the intersection of distinct factors, such as ignorance, fear, historical era, economics, and geography. Since the bodily composition of any given culture, and the means by which it assigns meaning to that composition, will vary across cultures, it is not possible to privilege one form of difference (for example, sexual difference) over another in the analysis of a culture. Third, while not neglecting the dominant ideas of a culture, or the aforementioned factors that are bolstering those ideas, change within a culture will depend upon altering the unique, embodied interactions that occur within that culture.

When Irigaray talks about the relationship between the imaginary and the symbolic for an individual, the logic that she employs is similar to Spinoza's use of imagination and reason. Both Irigaray and Spinoza see that powerful fantasies or points of confusion about the body often serve as the basis for a person's belief system and the social norms and political systems that govern a culture. Both acknowledge that these fantasies and confusions often result in social and political exclusions. Further, as Gatens points out, the psychoanalytic understanding of the body as a "lived" body coincides with Spinoza's similar attempt to overcome viewing the body/mind relationship in dualistic terms (either the body determines the mind or the mind determines the body). However, if Irigaray is read as asserting that the female imaginary dominates the realm of excluded other, and is exclusively that against which the male symbolic order is constructed, then this is where Irigaray and Spinoza would part ways. Applying Gatens's categories, first, this institutes a distinction between "reality" and "imagination" where the current, male-dominated symbolic order is a distorted form of reality that needs to be exchanged for some future symbolic order that includes women. This raises the question of how we can escape from inside of this distorted reality in order to institute a new reality.[43]

Second, it could result in the claim that sexual difference is the most important difference. For Spinoza, sexual difference could not be the only form of bodily difference that matters in how a person experiences his or her world. Some other factors that could matter (and it is important to note that we cannot know how they might matter unless we have a context) are physical power, ability to experience pleasure and pain, a particular body's random contact with other bodies, and the characteristics of those other bodies. With regard to the characteristics of bodies, we might consider how another person lives his or her body, the degree to which one's body increasingly enters into varied relationships with other bodies, and the social context that interprets how difference is constituted. This last consideration is important. Interpretations of difference might have a negative impact when they are guided by ignorance, injustice, selfish interests, or brute facts.

Scholars have debated whether or not Irigaray's focus on sexual difference translates into a denial that other forms of difference and exclusion are equally important.[44] In these debates, the question of whether or not sexual difference dominates the imaginary ultimately overlaps with whether or not there is a "reality"/"imagination" distinction in Irigaray's work. Irigaray's method of strategic essentialism and mimesis makes it difficult to pinpoint whether sexual difference is the most important distinction for her or whether she is strategically miming what she believes poses as a dominant myth about reality in Western culture. Whether it is the former or the latter, Spinoza's work is still relevant to Irigaray's work in at least two related ways.[45]

First, part of her method of critiquing and reworking the history of philosophy is to go back through that history and engage with what is useful. Irigaray's interpretation of Spinoza's work in *An Ethics of Sexual Difference* engages with a dualist and rationalist interpretation of Spinoza.[46] By interpreting Spinoza in this manner, she has missed an opportunity to appropriate the language to address the concerns raised by Gatens, Judith Butler, and others. Engaging with his work, and miming his language, could help her to address some of the concerns about her work listed above.

Second, Irigaray is already committed to Spinozistic principles of working for political change through action. If Irigaray and Spinoza are, indeed, working with a similar set of problems in a way that productively overlaps, then she could employ his language to align her practice with her theory. Texts such as *I Love to You, Democracy Begins Between Two*, and *To Be Two* were all inspired by and, at various moments, give accounts of Irigaray's experience with the Italian women's movement.[47] Rosi Braidotti predicts that "in the field of the philosophy of sexual difference, the conceptual alliance of Irigaray with the Italian women is going to be one of the most exciting sites of theoretical production of this end of the century."[48] In line with a Spinozistic paradigm that links knowledge and social and political organization to everyday existence, Irigaray recognizes that it is important to find ways to challenge the everyday social and economic position in which women find themselves. She asserts that Western society suffers a decrease in ethics and power because of its current economic, social, and political organization. In effect, Irigaray implements a Spinozistic link between knowledge, imagination, bodies, and emotion. Incorporating Spinoza's language might allow her to more effectively address concerns about the potential for exclusion that her psychoanalytic discourse produces when she employs it in the social and political realm.

Irigaray's most recent work focuses more concretely on how to represent women within the laws and religion of a society.[49] While Penelope Deutscher's recent text, *A Politics of Impossible Difference*, interprets this work as using both paradox and the impossibility itself of Irigaray's proposed political reforms as strategic devices for radically altering the current political and symbolic order, Spinoza might still have a role in Irigaray's work. Spinoza's valuation of the body, his challenge to the Judeo-Christian conception of God, and his analysis of power are surely useful frameworks for Irigaray to use to approach everyday social and political concerns. In the same spirit of Irigaray's own commitment to drawing from multiple frameworks (philosophical, psychoanalytic, sociological, and so on), readers invested in an Irigarayan framework might consider revisiting Spinoza's work as a substantial resource for thinking through social and political issues.

Notes

1. Luce Irigaray, *An Ethics of Sexual Difference*, trans. Carolyn Burke and Gillian C. Gill (Ithaca: Cornell University Press, 1993).

2. Luce Irigaray, *Speculum of the Other Woman*, trans. Gillian C. Gill (Ithaca: Cornell University Press, 1985).
3. Simone de Beauvoir, *The Second Sex*, trans. H. M. Parshley (New York: Vintage, 1989).
4. Irigaray, *Ethics of Sexual Difference*, 6.
5. Numerous authors have offered analyses of Irigaray's use of mimesis and strategic essentialism. See Diana Fuss, *Essentially Speaking: Feminism, Nature, and Difference* (New York: Routledge, 1989); Margaret Whitford, *Luce Irigaray: Philosophy in the Feminine* (New York: Routledge, 1991); Rosi Braidotti, *Patterns of Dissonance*, trans. Elizabeth Guild (New York: Routledge, 1991) and *Nomadic Subjects* (New York: Columbia University Press, 1994); Naomi Schor, "This Essentialism Which Is Not One," in *Engaging With Irigaray*, ed. Carolyn Burke, Naomi Schor, and Margaret Whitford (New York: Columbia University Press, 1994), 57–78; Tina Chanter, *Ethics of Eros: Irigaray's Re-writing of the Philosophers* (New York: Routledge, 1995); Tamsin Lorraine, *Irigaray and Deleuze: Experiments in Visceral Philosophy* (Ithaca: Cornell University Press, 1999).
6. Irigaray, *Ethics of Sexual Difference*, 86.
7. Ibid., 87.
8. Ibid., 89.
9. See Jonathan Bennett, *A Study of Spinoza's Ethics* (Indianapolis: Hackett, 1984), 50. Bennett says that "Spinoza's dualism involves a logical and causal split between extension and thought—between physics and psychology, as one might say." However, Bennett carefully articulates how Spinoza's dualism is distinct from Descartes' "property dualism" (see 40–50). I will soon discuss Curley's work.
10. See Edwin Curley, *Behind the Geometrical Method: A Reading of Spinoza's Ethics* (Princeton: Princeton University Press, 1988), 37. See also Julie Klein, "Aristotle and Descartes in Spinoza's Approach to Matter and Body," *Graduate Faculty Philosophy Journal* 26 (2005). Klein provides a clear gloss of the *natura naturans/natura naturata* distinction when she says, "*Natura naturans* names substance or nature as eternal, infinite, and free. These three adjectives function essentially synonymously in the *Ethics*. 'Necessary,' in the sense of enacting actuality without external limitation, is another synonym: 'That eternal and infinite being we call God, or Nature, acts from the same necessity from which he exists [*aeternum illud et infinitum Ens, quod Deum sive naturam appellamus, eadem qua existit necessitate agit*]' (E4pref). To be infinite is to be without end and, quite literally, to be indefinable, i.e., ungraspable. The passive participle *naturata* is best understood as 'natured' in the sense of being 'determined to produce an effect,' the formula that dominates the surrounding propositions and scholia. *Naturata* is, in a word, a gloss on *determinata*," 163.
11. For a fuller explanation of Yovel's view of infinite and finite modes, and the difficulties that he identifies as accompanying Spinoza's view of the infinite modes, see Yirmiyahu Yovel, "The Infinite Mode and Natural Laws in Spinoza," in *God and Nature in Spinoza's Metaphysics*, ed. Yirmiyahu Yovel (New York: E. J. Brill, 1991). Yovel says of the distinction between finite and infinite modes that "modes are defined as dependent things, entities whose essence does not involve existence; as such, they constitute *Natura naturata* and are divided into two kinds: finite and infinite. (The KV also calls them the 'particular' and the 'universal' sides of *Natura naturata*). An infinite mode is a real if dependent thing, even (as we shall see later) a kind of singular universal; as such, it serves as the metaphysical category and form of being underlying natural laws" (82). Yovel also addresses the problematic relationship between *natura naturans* and *natura naturata*; he focuses on the infinite modes as exemplar of the difficulties in this relationship. For example, he says, "The force of the argument that runs throughout the sequence Epp21–24 creates a kind of logical trap or 'imprisonment,' whereby God's infinity cannot but be transmitted onward as it is—intact—with nothing to depreciate it from the timeless to the durational. Yet Spinoza performs this depreciation in the concept of infinity, which allows him to move on, rather unaccountably, from *Natura naturans*, the timeless substance and its attributes, to duration and *Natura naturata*, the world of 'created' or dependent things" (86). While the article does not resolve the difficulties, it provides a clear outline of the problems.

12. As Yirmiyahu Yovel notes in *The Marrano of Reason*, vol. 1 of *Spinoza and Other Heretics* (Princeton: Princeton University Press, 1989), the relationship between "vertical" and "horizontal" causality and *"natura naturans"* and *"natura naturata"* is complex. Within each complementary pair, it is not entirely clear how a seamless move is made between each pair and its complement.
13. All quotations in this paragraph come from Yovel, *Spinoza and Other Heretics*, vol. 1, 157–58.
14. Ibid., 160.
15. Ibid., 161. See also Yovel, "The Infinite Modes and Natural Laws in Spinoza," 79.
16. See Gilles Deleuze, *Expressionism in Philosophy: Spinoza*, trans. Martin Joughin (New York: Zone Books, 1992), 17. Deleuze maintains, as the title suggests, that the idea of expression is central to comprehending Spinoza's system, but is sometimes neglected by his commentators.
17. Ibid., 88.
18. Curley, *Behind the Geometrical Method*, 82.
19. Ibid., 78.
20. See Luce Irigaray, *I Love to You: Sketch of a Possible Felicity in History*, trans. Alison Martin (New York: Routledge, 1996). In this text, Irigaray uses Hegel's logic of the dialectic to discuss how both men and women can develop gender identity.
21. As evinced in Yovel's earlier description of "horizontal" and "vertical" causality and *natura naturans* and *natura naturata*, the discussion about eternality and indivisibility becomes more complex once we turn to modes. Julie Klein's article "Aristotle and Descartes in Spinoza's Approach to Matter and Body" provides a clear discussion of many complex aspects of Spinoza's metaphysics. She clarifies the difficulty surrounding the extended mode when she addresses how Spinoza responds to the following criticism: corporeal substance cannot be infinite or associated with divine perfection because it consists of parts. She indicates that Spinoza views the above criticism as confusing imagining with understanding. She says, "To make the discussion concrete, Spinoza gives the example of water. 'Water, insofar as it is water, is generated and corrupted, but insofar as it is substance, it is neither generated nor corrupted.' Water qua water is a determinate mode of substance, specific configuration of nature that can be found, produced in the lab, made to flow or pool, frozen, vaporized, drunk, and so on. If some processes generate water, others destroy it by changing its structure, recombining its elements, etc. Qua substance, the water is neither generated absolutely—i.e. made from nothing—nor destroyed absolutely. Rather, the generation and corruption of modes is the very operation of substance as 'an infinite connection of causes' (E5p6)" (165). Spinoza's theory of substance, and the complexities of the relationship between *natura naturans* and *natura naturata* allow for this kind of complex statement.
22. Irigaray, *Ethics of Sexual Difference*, 6–7.
23. See Luce Irigaray, *Sexes and Genealogies*, trans. Gillian C. Gill (New York: Columbia University Press, 1993). Irigaray says that, "Divinity is what we need to become free, autonomous, sovereign. No human subjectivity, no human society, has ever been established without the help of the divine" (62). And, "But as long as woman lacks a divine made in her image she cannot establish her subjectivity or achieve a goal of her own" (63).
24. Margaret Whitford, Elizabeth Grosz, Tamsin Lorraine, and Penelope Deutscher have all written about Irigaray's understanding of divinity and her use of the term "sensible transcendental." According to Whitford's *Luce Irigaray*, the sensible transcendental remains an imprecise concept in Irigaray's work because it is merely a marker of the divine/infinite. As such, it incites her readers to think of the possibility of female-defined subjectivity—without prescribing in advance the terms of that subjectivity. Elizabeth Grosz, in *Irigaray and the Divine* (Sydney: Local Consumption, 1986), emphasizes how, for Irigaray, divinity is intended as a strategic device to help humans to recognize themselves as both finite (corporeal) and infinite (referring to the mind). In *Irigaray and Deleuze* Lorraine explains how Irigaray's sensible transcendental is intended to overturn mind/body dualism. Penelope Deutscher, in *A Politics of Impossible Difference* (Ithaca: Cornell University Press, 2002), indicates that the definition and use of the divine is multiplied in Irigaray's work because it is to be used for social and political change.

25. See Spinoza, E, II, Prop 14: "*The human mind is capable of perceiving a great many things, and is the more capable, the more its body can be disposed in a great many ways.*"

26. While I agree with popular readings of Irigaray that the imaginary in her work has multiple, historical influences (for example, Margaret Whitford's reading in *Luce Irigaray*, chapter 3 ("Rationality and the Imaginary") and Tina Chanter's *Ethics of Eros*, I refrain from reading Spinoza's view of imagination back through that lens.

27. While I have mentioned that Irigaray is influenced by both Freud and Lacan, I focus here on the consonance between Irigaray's use of the Lacanian framework and Spinoza. Of course there is no shortage of articles and books that discuss the links between Freud and Spinoza. However, the Lacanian framework is central to Irigaray's work, and I am bracketing debates about whether or not Lacan is faithfully continuing Freud's work. Fewer authors have placed Spinoza in direct dialogue with Lacanian concepts. One example is found in Osamu Ueno's essay "Desire and the Double in Spinoza" in *Desire and Affect: Spinoza as Psychologist*, ed. Yirmiyahu Yovel (New York: Little Room Press, 1999). Ueno uses Lacanian language and ideas to discuss the role of the imagination in the beginning of subject formation. Bracketing active affects, Ueno looks at passive affects in order to suggest that consciousness is initially determined by not knowing our actual bodies in a direct way. He says, "In a word, in wanting and willing, the subject is not in the center of his own thinking: in reality, he is thinking somewhere other than in his consciousness" (82). Suggesting that there is an unconscious and imaginary dimension to this initial consciousness, Ueno includes the Lacanian terms "imaginary ego" and "mirror stage" to describe his interpretation. Another example is found in Moira Gatens's *Imaginary Bodies: Ethics, Power, and Corporeality* (New York: Routledge, 1996). See also Susan James's interview with Moira Gatens and Genevieve Lloyd, "The Power of Spinoza: Feminist Conjunctions," *Hypatia* 15 (2000): 40–58. James says: "In Moira's *Imaginary Bodies* we find a deliberately hybrid notion of the imaginary which draws from Spinoza and from the psychoanalytic tradition" (53). I will turn to Gatens's view in the conclusion.

28. Yovel, *The Marrano of Reason*, 156.

29. Genevieve Lloyd, *Spinoza and the Ethics* (London: Routledge, 1996), 55–70.

30. Antonio Negri, *Savage Anomaly: The Power of Spinoza's Metaphysics and Thought*, trans. Michael Hardt (Minneapolis: University of Minnesota Press, 2000), 63.

31. Etienne Balibar, *Spinoza and Politics*, trans. Peter Snowdon (New York: Verso, 1998), 109–10.

32. Cf. Negri, *Savage Anomaly*. Negri interprets Spinoza along similar lines in *Savage Anomaly* when he says, "Spinoza presents precisely here, in the imagination, the fulcrum for the construction of the world. . . . There are no discontinuities in Spinoza's thought but an infinite number of catastrophes, which reformulate the continuity of being along the line of imagination, of a depth of productive attribution that, like the water in the earth and in bodies, circulates everywhere. Omnipresent" (225).

33. Lloyd, *Spinoza and the Ethics*, 67.

34. Yovel offers clarification on the status of finite modes in "Knowledge as Alternative Salvation," in *Marrano of Reason*. Here he says that "finite modes in Spinoza are as eternal as the substance from which they derive. The vertical line of causality should be understood not as a process of 'creation' or 'emanation' but as ontological dependence or support. Seen *sub specie aeternitatis* (through their essences), finite things are just as eternal and primordial as their sustaining substance. The difference is that the essence of finite things does not imply existence but requires the essence of the substance in order to exist. Yet this dependence is eternal; it is a logical, timeless relation by which the modes, seen as particular essences, presuppose God. They inhere in God as their ontological support and are implications of God's essence, but they are there eternally like God himself" (160).

35. However, she ultimately uses Lacan's categorizations of "Imaginary," "Symbolic," and "Real."

36. See Moira Gatens, "Modern Rationalism," in *A Companion to Feminist Philosophy*, ed. Alison Jaggar and Iris Marion Young (New York: Blackwell, 2000). She briefly addresses Irigaray's critique of Spinoza and marks the difference between her own reading of Spinoza as a resource, and Irigaray's

critique of him. She says of Irigaray's reading: "The extent to which it is appropriate to understand that as a 'reading' of Spinoza is not clear" (28)

37. Gatens, *Imaginary Bodies*, 57.

38. Gatens also cites Cornelius Castoriadis and Michèle Le Doeuff as important influences on the development of her notion of the "imaginary."

39. Gatens, *Imaginary Bodies*, viii.

40. Ibid., ix.

41. Ibid., x.

42. Among other texts, see Moira Gatens and Genevieve Lloyd, *Collective Imaginings: Spinoza, Past and Present* (London: Routledge, 1999). Both Genevieve Lloyd and Moira Gatens are engaging with Spinoza's work in a manner distinct from Irigaray's critical project. First, both are reading Spinoza as overcoming dualism, rather than supporting it. Second, they argue that we should read Spinoza's metaphysics, ethics, politics, and epistemology as continuous. Third, they adopt his idea of the imagination as a flawed understanding of causality, power, and bodies—and Gatens's *Imaginary Bodies* is particularly crucial to a discussion about Irigaray on this point. Fourth, they are influenced by and discuss Michèle Le Doeuff's work. Fifth, they use Spinoza's nondualistic discourse and logic to respond to contemporary issues affecting individuals who experience oppression of different forms (political, cultural, sexual, racial, and so on).

43. I am intentionally using the language of "inside" and "outside," since this seems to be part of Gatens's concern.

44. Some authors who have debated this include Judith Butler, *Bodies That Matter: On the Discursive Limits of Sex* (New York: Routledge, 1993); Pheng Cheah and Elizabeth Grosz, "The Future of Sexual Difference: An Interview with Judith Butler and Drucilla Cornell," *Diacritics* 28 (1998): 19–42; and Whitford, *Luce Irigaray*. Butler has expressed wariness of Irigaray's view in *Bodies That Matter*, and in unison with Drucilla Cornell in Cheah and Grosz, "Future of Sexual Difference." Grosz, Cheah, and Whitford have at various points denied that Irigaray's view multiplies exclusion.

45. While resolving the issue of whether it is the former or the latter is important, it demands a degree of attention that cannot be provided in an essay of this length.

46. One reason for this might be that alternate interpretations of Spinoza emerged in the decades following the publication of *An Ethics and Sexual Difference*. Although this is pure speculation, it only seems fair to acknowledge that two decades of recent scholarship reinterpreting Spinoza are the impetus for this essay.

47. Luce Irigaray, *Democracy Begins Between Two*, trans. Kirsteen Anderson (New York: Routledge, 2000) and *To Be Two*, trans. Monique M. Rhodes and Marco F. Cocito-Monoc (New York: Routledge, 2001).

48. Braidotti, *Nomadic Subjects*, 261.

49. While beyond the scope of this chapter, there are differences of opinion about how to interpret the connection between Irigaray's early and later work. For examples of these opinions, see Cheah and Grosz, "Future of Sexual Difference," and Deutscher, *Politics of Impossible Difference*.

10

The Politics of the Imagination

Moira Gatens

The theme of this chapter was prompted by Gilles Deleuze's claim that Spinoza's political writings allow us to think about human relations not simply in terms of "utilisations and captures" but also in terms of "sociabilities and communities." Deleuze asks: "How do individuals enter into composition with one another in order to form a higher individual, ad infinitum? How can a being take another being into its world, but while preserving or respecting the other's own relations and world? And in this regard, *what are the different types of sociabilities*, for example? *What is the difference between the society of human beings and the community of rational beings?*"[1] Spinoza's political and ethical writings present multiple forms of sociability: associations built on superstition, tyrannies grounded in fear and hope, communities of rational individuals, and societies bound by the ties of friendship. None of these forms of sociability contradicts his deceptively simple claim that the right "of every individual is coextensive with its power" (TP, II, 38). The coextension of right and power applies to bodies politic as well as to individuals. From a contemporary perspective this may seem to be an unlikely starting point for a philosopher whose major work is titled *Ethics*, because if "right" and "power" are coextensive, what, if anything, can justify the normative claim that a community of rational beings is superior to a tyrannical state?[2] Spinoza's response to this question is complex and requires an understanding of his naturalistic views on bodies, rights, and powers that, in turn, ground his account of law and ethics. In the first two sections of this chapter, I will consider Spinoza's notions of the body and law, respectively. In the third section I argue that his immanent and developmental account of knowledge implies not only different ways of knowing but also corresponding ways of being. In the final section I will draw out the implications of the previous sections for the political meanings that attach to different forms of human embodiment and the sexual and racial imaginaries to which they give rise.

What Is a Body?

The originality of Spinoza's account of the manner in which bodies are composed and decomposed can be thrown into stark relief by recalling Descartes' explanation of the distinction between death and life: "The body of a living man differs from that of a dead man just as does a watch or other automaton . . . when it is wound up . . . from the same watch or other machine when it is broken."[3] This mechanistic conception of the body led to insoluble problems at the level of accounting for that strange hybrid that is human being. According to Descartes, all that exists does so under one of two radically distinct substances, mind and matter. Human being, thus internally radically divided, is composed of a free soul whose essence is to think and a determined body whose essence is to be extended. The unity of mind and body cannot be rationally demonstrated but rather is "experienced."[4] Such "experience" involves the soul's suffering the actions of the body and the body's suffering the actions of the soul. By contrast, Spinoza argues that there is only one substance, which is single and indivisible; body and mind enjoy only a modal existence and may be understood as "expressions" or modifications of the *attributes* of substance, that is, extension and thought, respectively. Human being is conceived as part of a dynamic and interconnected whole:

> We have conceived an individual which is composed only of bodies which are distinguished from one another only by motion and rest, speed and slowness, ie., which is composed of the simplest bodies. But if we should now conceive of another, composed of a number of individuals of a different nature, we shall find that it can be affected in a great many other ways, and still preserve its nature. For since each part of it is composed of a number of bodies, each part will therefore (by L7), be able, without any change of its nature, to move now more slowly, now more quickly, and consequently communicate its motion more quickly or more slowly to the others. But if we should further conceive a third kind of individual composed of this second kind, we shall find that it can be affected in many other ways, without any change of its form. And if we proceed in this way to infinity, we shall easily conceive that the whole of nature is one individual, whose parts, ie., all bodies, vary in infinite ways without any change of the whole individual. (E, II, L7, Schol).

On this model the human body is understood to be a relatively complex individual, made up of a number of other bodies. Its identity cannot be viewed as a final or finished product, because it is a body whose constituent parts are in constant interchange with its environment. The human body is radically open to its surroundings and can be composed, recomposed, and decomposed by other bodies. Its openness is both a condition of its life, that is, of its continuance in nature as the same individual: "the human body, to be preserved, requires a great many other bodies, by which it is, as it were, continually regenerated" (E, II, Postulates on the Body, IV); and of its death, since it is bound to encounter bodies more powerful than it that will, eventually, destroy its integrity as an individual—though such destruction always and necessarily implies further compositions, distinct from the first. Such "encounters" with other bodies are good or bad depending on whether they aid or harm the characteristic constitution of a given body.

The human body, like every other animate body, does not owe its power of movement to either an inbuilt automatic mechanism or a mysterious "soul-substance" that can will movement in the body. Rather, the human mind expresses under the attribute of thought "the idea of a singular thing which actually exists," that is, "the object of the idea constituting the human mind is the body, or a certain mode of extension which actually exists, and nothing else" (E, II, Props 11 and 13). The complexity of any particular mind depends on the complexity of the body of which it is the idea. As Hans Jonas has observed, Spinoza's account of the mind and body offers, for the first time in modern theory, "a speculative means . . . for relating the degree of organization of a body to the degree of awareness belonging to it."[5] Thus, reason is not seen as a transcendent or disembodied quality of the soul or mind, but rather reason, desire, and knowledge are embodied and express, at least in the first instance, the quality and complexity of the corporeal affects. There is no question of mind/body interaction here, since "the body cannot determine the mind to thinking, and the mind cannot determine the body to motion, to rest or to anything else" (E, III, Prop 2).

Descartes' attempt to account for mind/body interaction through the "occult hypothesis" of the pineal gland (E, III, Pref) is not the only casualty of this monistic conception of human being. Spinoza also rejects outright that which this hypothesis assumes: a soul possessed of free will. He does not consider the will and the intellect to be separate faculties; rather "there is no volition, or affirmation and negation, except that which the idea involves insofar as it is an idea" (E, II, Prop 49). Necessary laws govern all of nature, including all the actions and passions of human nature. The fundamental and determined desire of any existing body is its endeavor to persevere in its existence. Spinoza names this endeavor, or striving, *conatus*.

In contrast to the Cartesian view, for Spinoza, body and mind *necessarily* suffer or act in concert. For, "in proportion as a body is more capable of doing many things at once, or being acted on in many ways at once, so its mind is more capable than others of perceiving many things at once" (E, II, Prop 13, Schol). An increase of power in the body has as its necessary correlate an increase in the power of the mind, and vice versa. Human freedom, though not free will, amounts to the power that one possesses to assert and extend oneself in the face of other (human and nonhuman) bodies that strive to do likewise. On this ethical stance, virtue cannot be reduced to the mere cultivation of "good habits," but rather concerns the power of any particular individual to continue in its existence. All bodies (including nonhuman bodies) possess this virtue, though to varying degrees. Human virtue is qualitatively distinct from the virtue of other things insofar as it concerns the endeavor to increase one's power of existing in accordance with reason, which is a specifically human power. For Spinoza, human being is determined to the exercise of such reason in pursuit of that which it thinks will increase its power.

If one examines Spinoza's view of the human individual in isolation from the rest of nature it appears to be an egocentric, even hedonistic, ethical theory. However, one cannot make sense of Spinoza's philosophy—which is deeply opposed to all forms of anthropocentrism—if one privileges the individual human body. Since a large component of the striving of any body is its necessary relations with other bodies, human striving, like all striving, seeks to join itself with that which increases its power (hence Spinoza's definition of joy) and to avoid or destroy those bodies that decrease its power of acting (hence Spinoza's definition of sadness).[6] This is why Deleuze understands Spinozistic reason, at its most fundamental level, as "the effort to organize encounters on the basis of perceived agreements and disagreements" between one body and the next.[7] This effort to select or organize our encounters leads to the formation of associations between bodies of similar or compatible powers and capacities: that is, it leads human beings to society. As will be argued below, Spinoza's account of the formation of *types* of sociability implies historically and culturally variable conceptions of "reasonable" associations. This view represents another important departure from Descartes, who applied the same method in the ethicopolitical realm that he elsewhere applied to optics and science: "the single fact of diversity among states suffices to assure us that some states are imperfect."[8] Diversity in legal and moral codes, from his perspective, is inevitably a sign of error. Spinoza, on the contrary, offers a perspective from which to think through difference and embodiment in terms other than those of error or notions of cultural superiority and inferiority.

Law as Command Versus Law as Knowledge

Spinoza does not define human being as essentially *homo socius*. He claims, on the contrary that "men are not born to be citizens, but are made so" (TP, V, 61). Human beings come to form associations not because of an inherent sociability but rather because in pursuing their own preservation and their own increase in power they come to see that by joining with or conquering other human bodies they increase their power and hence their right, since "every man has right to the extent that he has power" (TP, II, 41). Such associations, in other words, are formed indirectly (through the pursuit of something else that is perceived as good) rather than directly. It is only within such associations that human beings have the opportunity to develop their powers of reason and justice. This is because "the law of Nature forbids nothing at all except that which is not within anyone's power to do" (TP, II, 45). Hence, "a wrong cannot be conceived except in a civil condition" (TTP, XVI, 179) and justice and injustice "can be conceived only in a state" (TP, II, 47). It is only in civil society that human being can strive effectively and directly to increase its specific power, namely, understanding, which entails a power of *selecting* encounters with others. It is in civil society only that human freedom—here understood in terms of an increase in one's power to act rather than be acted upon—is possible. Human freedom, in other words, necessarily is a collective endeavor. In order to see how the Spinozistic view of sociability is tied to his notion of civil society, attention needs to be paid to his conception of law and its power to organize bodies and regulate their powers.

In *A Theologico-Political Treatise*, Spinoza distinguishes between divine (or natural) law and civil (or human) law. Each type of law can be understood differently depending on through which kind of knowledge (imagination or reason) it is grasped. Spinoza understood it to be a source of great confusion, and the cause of considerable human misery, that natural law is so frequently understood on the model of law as (divine) command or decree. He insists that natural laws, whereby "all things happen and are determined" are impossible to break, change, or disobey, since they "always involve eternal truth and necessity" (TTP, III, 36). It is the imagination only that grasps god as a lawgiver and judge. As one commentator explains: "There is no law intrinsic to nature that is not the law of god, since god is taken as coextensive with nature. . . . It is impossible to speak of events or behaviour as obeying or not obeying the natural law. Rather this law is the actual nature of the entity itself, the actual order of the occasion, which entity and occasion are manifestations of god's nature."[9] An adequate understanding of natural law involves knowledge of the second kind, or reason, and far from necessity representing a limit on our freedom, according to Spinoza, it is the very condition of such liberty. It is the illusion of free will, which is then projected onto an anthropomorphized nature, which obscures the freedom that we may attain: the freedom to understand our situation and, on the basis of such understanding, to act to maximize our power and our joys.

Civil law concerns "a rule of life which man prescribes for himself or for others for some purpose," that is, that aims "to safeguard life and the commonwealth" (TTP, IV, 48–49). Such laws will not be universal and will both reflect and contribute to the reproduction of the particular historical, religious, or national character of different peoples. Above all, the laws of any given civil body will reveal the historical and continuing basis of such complex associations. In contrast to natural law, human or civil law can be understood as command or decree but in a very particular sense. This sense concerns the virtue (or, what amounts to the same thing, the power) of the state that is, in turn, correlated with different modes of understanding.

Civil law may be understood as command but a sovereign cannot command or decree anything at all, without qualification. Spinoza conceives of the state as a complex body that must possess a degree of self-knowledge if it is to persevere in its own existence. The sense in which the state can exceed the proper exercise of its power is tied, precisely, to its continuing existence as a state. As Belaief argues: "If anything lacks the power to function according to its essential nature, it can no longer be said to participate as the SAME thing in reality. This is as true for an individual law as it is for an entire legal system, as true for an individual man as it is for the state."[10] This understanding of law has some interesting consequences for determining whether or not a sovereign or state can be said to exercise its power reasonably. As Cairns has pointed out, "Spinoza shows that there is an inescapable connection between power and its proper exercise."[11] From this basis, one may argue that a state that exercises its power to enslave, oppress, or exploit its population will be inferior in kind to a state that exercises its power in order to expand the capacities of its citizens. In this connection consider the distinction Belaief draws between Hobbes and Spinoza: "In Hobbes's view there is no distinction between force and power with respect to the sovereign; in Spinoza's view force must be guided by reason if it is to become power."[12] In this context it is important to note that Spinoza draws tight connections between power, freedom, and virtue. He writes, "Civil laws depend solely on the commonwealth's decree, and the commonwealth, to maintain its freedom, does not have to please anyone but itself and to deem nothing as good or bad other than that which it itself decides is good or bad for itself" (TP, IV, 59–60). The ambiguity in the last phrase—"and to deem nothing as good or bad other than that which it itself decides is good or bad *for itself*"—is crucial. If something is bad for it then the virtue of the state dictates its avoidance, just as every individual strives to seek that which it thinks is good and avoid that which is harmful to it. This understanding of the state posits an internal curb on state power: the avoidance of those decrees, commands, or enactments that will certainly lead to its harm or ruin. Thus, Spinoza is entitled to assert that "the ruler is bound to observe the terms of the [social] contract for exactly the same reason as a man in the state of nature, in order not to be his own enemy, is bound to take care not to kill himself" (TP, IV, 60).

The second sense in which the power of the state is limited concerns Spinoza's particular understanding of volition; that is, he denies that the intellect and the will are separate faculties. This feature of Spinoza's jurisprudence offers a method for determining the excellence, or otherwise, of any particular state, since its particular decrees or commands are manifestations of its own self-understanding. The will of the state, for Spinoza, can be no more arbitrary than the will of the individual; in both cases that which the body wills is determined by its relative virtue or ignorance. Again, Belaief makes this point succinctly: "Since [on Spinoza's account] law is held to be a product of will this is tantamount to having it as a product of thinking and judging. . . . The will of the sovereign, that is, laws, are not consecrations of the sovereign's desires but rather the ideas which he affirms. The goodness or badness of the laws will depend on whether these affirmed ideas are adequate or inadequate, true or false."[13] These "checks" on sovereign power carry some interesting consequences. First, the notion that bad governments are responsible for their own ruin takes on an extra dimension in the context of Spinoza's philosophy. Bad government also may be held "responsible" for forming bad citizens. Spinoza argues that the raison d'être for civil society and the laws it institutes concern the establishment of peace and security *in order that* both the minds and the bodies of citizens may be developed to their highest degree. Thus, one may distinguish between a "good" law and a "bad" one in terms of its tendency either to aid "an individual in the fullest development of his powers or virtues" or to fail to "aim towards aiding the development of men's powers."[14]

Those who would claim Spinoza as an early proponent of liberal political philosophy must turn a blind eye to a crucial difference between his stance and that of liberal theory. Spinoza does not allow the existence of any special rights to property or the person prior to civil life. The sovereign, on Spinoza's view, does not exist in order to enforce pre-civil moral, personal, or property rights. Consequently, Spinoza's sovereign has a much greater responsibility to, and for, its citizens than on the liberal view. Spinoza's rejection of the notion of human "natural" right or justice places responsibilities on the civil body that go much further than its acts of omission, for example, the failure to provide protection for its citizens.[15] Such a rejection places the onus of responsibility on the civil body for acts of commission also, that is, the actual behavior and values of the citizens, since their morality is largely constituted through, and dependent on, the particular laws of that state.

Second, because of this profound effect that laws have on the character of a people (TTP, XVII, 200), the ideas that the sovereign affirms, through law, become embodied in the polity and perpetuated by social institutions. Further, if the social understanding of law as command is promulgated, it will have an inhibiting effect on the development of the capacities of citizens, since obedience is not knowledge and can, at best, only imitate knowledge.[16] For Spinoza, it is the distinction between grasping law as arbitrary command and law as knowledge that marks the difference between human bondage and human freedom. If one understands the law as those ideas affirmed by the sovereign body for its preservation and if one obeys the law, not to avoid punishment but because one understands and pursues the preservation of civil society, then one acts *directly* (E, IV, Prop 67, Dem). If, however, one obeys the law from fear of punishment or hope of reward then one is under the external control of another and so in bondage. One acts only *indirectly*, in order to acquire rewards or avoid punishment. Nothing follows from the second sort of acting, which, strictly speaking, is not action at all, but a passive reaction to an outside authority that is recognized as being more powerful than oneself. Hence, a state that encourages obedience without understanding will be one whose citizens are incapable of either acting or expanding their powers of acting. Those who act in the first manner, that is, directly, would constitute a community of rational beings; those who (re)act in the second manner, that is, indirectly, can easily become a society of slaves: "it is slaves, not free men, who are assigned rewards for virtue" (TP, X, 132). This view of the law and civil society obviously begs the question in relation to those who are disadvantaged by civil arrangements, for example, indigenous peoples, slaves, women, and others. I defer consideration of this issue until the final section of this chapter.

The analysis offered above provides good reasons for understanding in its strongest sense Spinoza's claim that the state has a duty to develop the minds and bodies of its citizens. As he says, in the section on freedom of thought and speech in A *Theologico-Political Treatise*, it is not the purpose of the state "to transform men from rational beings into beasts or puppets, but rather to enable them to develop their mental and physical faculties in safety, to use their reason without restraint and to refrain from the strife and the vicious mutual abuse that are prompted by hatred, anger or deceit. Thus the purpose of the state is, in reality, freedom" (TTP, XX, 223). The contrast between obedience and knowledge is one means by which to distinguish between an association of human beings founded upon fear and hope and a community of rational beings. What would be the differences in the civil bodies and laws of each type of sociability? A state whose peace depends entirely on fear will produce a particular type of sociability—a weak sociability that is built on sad passions. Such a state is arguably not performing its ultimate function as Spinoza conceived it: the increase of the capacity of its citizens to act, that is, the collective endeavor to realize freedom. On Spinoza's view, the democratization of sovereignty should bring about an increase in the capacities and powers of its citizens. However, the democratization of sovereignty inevitably will alter the relations between the constituent parts of the sovereign body, along with the ideas that it affirms. Notions of justice and fairness that have become institutionalized in law and other social practices will demand revision as institutionally embodied traditions and orthodoxy—for example, power relations between slave and master, women and men, "black" and "white"—clash with the determined striving of all to become free.

Embodied Knowledge

Can a Spinozistic perspective help in thinking through the necessary steps in the reformation of ethical relations that were formed through past relations of domination and subordination, for example, those between the sexes and among "racialized" groups? Insofar as the political realm is concerned with the organization of our needs and resources, our rights and obligations, it is quintessentially concerned with the management of the passions and the collective imaginings through which those passions are organized. In Parts I and II of the *Ethics* Spinoza has laid the groundwork for the surprising claim that opens Part III: "I shall consider human actions and appetites just as if it were a question of lines, planes, and bodies." Of course, he does much more than this—he offers a genealogical account of how it is we become conscious of our power to affect and be affected in ways that cause joy or sadness, that is, in ways that involve an increase or decrease in our feeling of power. The more our actions emanate from within us rather than outside us then the more powerful and free we are and the more we experience joy. The capacity to act, rather than be acted on, to express one's own nature rather than merely reflect or react to the nature of another, is an expression of one's freedom, power, virtue or *conatus*. Throughout the progress of the *Ethics*, these terms come to stand in an almost synonymous relation to each other (see E, IV, D8). Spinoza's notion of power is not opposed to freedom, nor is freedom opposed to necessity. Rather, necessity is the condition of possibility for becoming conscious of our power, or put differently, "freedom does not remove the necessity of action, but imposes it" (TP, II, 42). There is, of course, a qualitative difference between the feeling of an increase in power and a genuine increase in power. Many of our affects give rise to feelings of power that may be largely imaginary. Yet these imaginary feelings of an increase in our power may indeed increase our power to act, though this is likely to be in an erratic and unreliable way. Such joyful affects may easily be reversed and hence become sad and debilitating affects.

Spinoza does not dismiss imagination or passion as unworthy of philosophical and political analysis. Human life, necessarily, involves a large and ineradicable imaginary component. His theory of the imagination is succinctly captured in the opening proposition of Part IV of the *Ethics*: "Nothing positive which a false idea has is removed by the presence of the true insofar as it is true." The scholium to this proposition reads:

> An imagination is an idea which indicates the present constitution of the human body more than the nature of an external body.... For example, when we look at the sun, we imagine it to be about 200 feet away from us. In this we are deceived so long as we are ignorant of its true distance; but when its distance is

> known, the error is removed, not the imagination, that is, the idea of the sun, *which explains its nature only so far as the body is affected by it*. . . . And so it is with the other imaginations by which the mind is deceived, whether they indicate the natural constitution of the body, or that its power of acting is increased or diminished: *they are not contrary to the true, and do not disappear on its presence.* (E, IV, Prop 1, Schol; emphasis added)

This scholium holds true for all the imaginings that arise from the affective relations between bodies of all kinds: human and nonhuman, individual and corporate, bodies. The nature of one's imaginary grasp of these bodies will depend upon the affects they engender—do they increase or diminish one's power of acting? Do they cause pleasure or pain? Just as there is a vast difference between the knowledge one may have about the sun, on the one hand, and the way the sun affects a given body, on the other (does it warm it or burn it?), so too can one distinguish between the general nature, constitution, or powers of a body and the manner in which it affects another body. However, as the above scholium makes clear, gaining adequate knowledge about another body, including the powers it possesses independently of its relation to me, does not *remove* the affect that it produces in me; that is, such understanding does not cancel out the imaginary relation that I have toward it.

The imaginary aspects of human social and political relations warrant more careful scrutiny than they usually receive in political philosophy. Spinoza's account of the imagination may assist in understanding the processes through which sexual and racial differences are made politically significant, as well as how these differences become embedded in social institutions. Differences between individuals involve *qualitative* as well as quantitative differences in power. This is one possible way in which one could describe sex and race differences. Given that, for Spinoza, the mind is the idea of the body, it is arguable that insofar as individuals are bodily different, such differences would have their parallels in the specific kinds of pleasures and pains of which each type of body is capable.[17] The "essentialism" of Spinoza's ontology, if we can call it that, pertains to the powers of action and enjoyment peculiar to each. Concerning the specificity of the joys and pains of this or that individual, he writes:

> Both the horse and the man are driven by lust to procreate; but the one is driven by an equine lust, the other by a human lust. So

also the lusts and appetites of insects, fish, and birds must vary. Therefore, though each lives content with his own nature, by which he is constituted, and is glad of it, nevertheless that life with which each one is content, and that gladness, are nothing but the idea, or soul, of the individual. And so the gladness of the one differs in nature from the gladness of the other as much as the essence of the one differs from the essence of the other. Finally, it follows that there is no small difference between the gladness by which a drunk is led and the gladness a philosopher possesses. (E, III, Prop 57, Schol)

Gladness—or the power of being affected by joy—that arises through either drinking alcohol or engaging in philosophy is a power of enjoyment that is unlikely to be markedly different simply by virtue of one's biological sex. One may acknowledge this without thereby denying that historical conditions can, and do, inhibit some and facilitate other sorts of activity purely on the basis of one's designated sex. In addition, social conditions construct different social and political significances *of the same activity* for the sexes. Such historical and sociopolitical conditions can, and do, affect the range of capacities and powers that women and men are able to express. A person's capacity to affect and to be affected is not determined solely by the body she or he is but also by everything that makes up the context in which that body is acted upon and acts. When the term *embodiment* is used in the context of Spinoza's thought it should be understood to refer to not simply an individual body but the *total* milieu of that body. The powers of action of any particular body are inescapably relational on this view.

Spinoza's "essentialism" is thus not likely to provide support for "identity politics," since individuals are as much formed by their milieu as by their own constitution. Hence, a man and a woman from a similar historical and political context may have more in common than will two women or two men from radically different contexts. This view of the complex constitution of sexed or racialized identities resists the too-easy reduction of politics to the identities of "sex" or "race." Indeed, it is arguable that these categories belong to a system of classification (genus, species, kind) that is quite foreign to Spinoza's thought. As Deleuze makes clear, Spinoza defines beings "by their *capacity for being affected*, by the affections of which they are capable, the excitations to which they react, those by which they are unaffected, and those which exceed their capacity and make them ill or cause them to die. In this way, one will obtain a classification of beings by their power; one will see which beings agree with others, and which do not agree with one another, as well as who can serve as food for whom, who is social with whom, and according to what relations."[18] Spinoza's view of embodiment and power carries with it the corollary that all human relations are ethically structured. One primary sphere of ethical relations between the sexes will be sexual relations. The view of love and the sexual relation presented in the *Ethics* is extremely interesting and deserves consideration in its own right. The two chapters by Amelie Rorty and Alexandre Matheron included in this volume offer persuasive reasons for why these views remain interesting today. Here I want to further explore the implications of the fact that these relations take place in a milieu that has a history of excluding women from political participation. What effect does this have on the ability of both, the man and the woman, to develop their capacities for freedom? What effect does this history have on the ability of each to maintain a harmonious relation, that is, a relation that involves an agreement in power?[19]

To consider this question in Spinoza's own terms, we need to place the philosophy of the *Ethics* in a political frame. One can read the *Ethics* as a philosophy of power that offers a fluid and immanent ethics of joyful and life-enhancing encounters, rather than a transcendent morality that dictates dry duties and encourages a suspicion of the body, pleasure, and laughter. However, the realization of virtue, in Spinoza's sense, assumes a particular social and political context. The *Ethics* is not addressed to those who are in a state of nature—where conceptions of justice are meaningless. Nor is it addressed to those who live under tyrannical governments. Rather, the ideal reader of the *Ethics* is a free and rational member of a democratic body politic.

Sexual and Racial Imaginaries

As Matheron points out, in Chapter 4 of this volume, Spinoza's references to sexual difference number less than a dozen. His comments on race and ethnicity do not amount to many more. As few as these comments are, it is nonetheless notable that often they arise in contexts where there is a tension in Spinoza's thought between his drive to validate democratic polities that aim to realize the powers and capacities of all, on the one hand, and his anxiety about the uneducated "multitude" and the socially destructive force of undisciplined passion, on the other.[20] Rather than castigating theorists of the past for their sexism or racism, I agree with Michael Rosenthal when he suggests that the task of contemporary theorists is not to censure the writings of past philosophers but rather to see that "the very tensions in these texts call upon us to resolve them in our philosophical endeavors."[21]

While the sexual relation has political consequences for both sexes, the history of the "political problem" posed by sexual difference is a different "problem" for women from what it is for men. The same thesis holds for the "political problem" of race and ethnicity: the problem looks different from the point of view of those who occupy the subordinate position. The power of action of excluded groups continues to be depleted through the enduring influence of the past in the present. Merely formal equality may not significantly alter the affective milieu in which subordinated identities continue to be formed and in which they act. Powerful social imaginaries, and the negative expectations they promote, continue to affect the ability of disparaged identities to realize their capacities. This is why it is important to stress that "embodiment" in the context of Spinoza's thought must be understood to refer to not simply an individual body but the *total* affective milieu of that body. But how can "imaginary" ideas about specific kinds of identity have "real" effects on the capacities to act of those identities? This problem remains a puzzle only if one insists on opposing the "imaginary" to the "real." Social and political reality, it has been suggested, largely is constituted through our imaginary relations, that is, through the first kind of knowledge. It is precisely this phenomenon that requires investigation rather than dismissal.

At the end of Part III of the *Ethics*, Spinoza contrasts the affects of pride and despondency. The despondent person imagines him- or herself as weak and disdained by others. This "imaginary" affect has the *real* consequence that he or she actually cannot realize his or her powers. Although Spinoza's own account of this passion is described in an individualistic way, when proper weight is accorded to the power of the social imaginary, the social and political dimensions of this "despondency," or "weakness," come into focus. In his explanation of despondency Spinoza writes: "For whatever a man imagines he cannot do, he necessarily imagines; and he is so disposed by this imagination that he really cannot do what he imagines he cannot do. For so long as he imagines that he cannot do this or that, he is not determined to do it, and consequently it is impossible for him to do it" (E, III, Def Aff XXVIII). From an individualistic point of view the incapacity of a subordinated individual might serve to justify his or her inferior status. But if the entire milieu in which any given individual acts is taken into consideration certain incapacities may then be seen as structural, or systemic, in nature and the relational identities that are formed within these structures can be viewed as politically constituted differences.

As Matheron points out, Spinoza sees two main problems associated with sexual passion. The first concerns the individual: sexual passion runs the risk of inhibiting one's power to act and to think. The second is political: sexual passion gives rise to competition (implicitly, competition between men) and so promotes discord in the social body. Presumably, this is why, in A *Political Treatise*, in the section on democracy, Spinoza excludes women from political participation. Given his view that "the purpose of the state is, in reality, freedom" (TTP, XX, 223) and his view that the democratic state is "the most natural form of state, approaching most closely to that freedom which nature grants to every man" (TTP, XVI, 179), this exclusion—along with the exclusion of slaves and servants—is surprising.[22] The reason Spinoza offers for such exclusion is that women, slaves, and servants are not independent beings but rather are under the authority of men and masters. Concerning women, he poses the question of "whether it is by nature or by convention that women are under the authority of men" (TP, XI, 136). He answers that women are under men's authority by nature, since "women do not naturally possess equal right with men" (TP, XI, 137). This is a perplexing view for Spinoza to uphold. Elsewhere he warns against treating entire classes of peoples as possessing intrinsic class-based traits or qualities. For example, in A *Theologico-Political Treatise*, he argues against racial or national stereotypes and says that "nature creates individuals, not nations" (TTP, XVII, 200). His point is that dispositions, ways of life, and prejudices that constitute classes of people are the historical result of specific laws and customs, not nature.[23] Moreover, national or ethnically based stereotypes are grounded not in nature but in affective relations with different others: "If someone has been affected with joy or sadness by someone of a class, or nation, different from his own, and this joy or sadness is accompanied by the idea of that person as its cause, under the universal name of the class or nation, he will love or hate, not only that person, but everyone of the same class or nation" (E, III, Prop 46). When placed within the unequal power relations that characterize politicized identities the tendency to universalize has uneven consequences depending on whether or not such generalizations receive institutional support and validation.

In the *Political Treatise* Spinoza cites the case of the Amazons from Justin's *Histories* alongside the comment that if men were ruled by women then they would be "so brought up as to be inferior in ability" (TP, XI, 137). Yet he does not note that this has been the historical situation of women. Women were brought up in a manner that inhibited their capacity to make full use of their abilities. What is the cause of Spinoza's blindness to the historical situation of women? I will venture a tentative thesis after considering a further argument he offers for the exclusion of women from citizenship. He writes: "If, furthermore, we consider human emotions, that men generally love women from mere lust, assessing their ability and their wisdom by their beauty and also resenting any favours which the women they love show to others and so on, soon we shall see that rule by men and women on equal terms is bound to involve much damage to peace" (TP, XI, 137). This argument pinpoints a tension in Spinoza's political theory. Men have all sorts of passions about all sorts of things that the body politic is not obliged to accommodate. Men may be greedy, querulous, ambitious, and so on, all of which may lead to upsetting the peace. However, in none of these cases does Spinoza consider it appropriate for the political realm to fail to regulate and govern such passions. On the contrary, if men cannot be masters of their own passions, then laws and the power of political society will serve to amend their behavior by appealing to a more fundamental passion: fear of punishment. Why is the "lust" of men for women exempted from the standard political solution to the fact that passions divide men, pull them in contrary directions, and make them enemies to one another? Why should men's desire to dominate or exploit others, for example, in slavery or other forms of servitude, be tolerated in the polity? Spinoza's exclusion of women, slaves, and servants from a democratic polity introduces a tension into his general account of the drive to form "reasonable associations."

Women, as a class, occupy an ambivalent place in the imaginary of political theory—both historically and in the present. This affects the quality of life of individual women in a multiplicity of ways: some relatively trivial (for example, "everyday" sexism) and others not so trivial (for example, the appalling treatment women often receive from the law, especially in cases of rape and domestic violence). Charles Mills has made a similar point with regard to race, arguing that the idea of the independent, free individual in modern political theory is dependent on excluded others in at least two senses. First, political conceptions of freedom derive from the practice of slavery: conceived as subhuman, "the slave establishes the norm for *humans*."[24] Second, the normative status and privilege accorded to "whiteness" allows race to be posited as a biological or natural category through its concealment of the sociopolitical construction of the "white" norm. Put differently, "whiteness is not really a color at all but a set of power relations."[25] In order to understand the ethical import of politicized identities an understanding is required of how sexual and racial imaginaries continue to structure the sociopolitical milieu in which individuals act.

One might start by acknowledging the importance of Spinoza's insight that *modes of knowing imply specific ways of being*. If knowledge implies a mode of being rather than having, and if our beliefs, opinions, and imaginings are not "possessions" of which we can take an inventory, then it is not surprising that they cannot be eradicated by purely formal means.[26] If, as Spinoza argues, nature forms individuals, not classes or nations, then the origin of the prejudices, predispositions, and peculiarities of any given society must be sought in laws and customs and particular "ways of life," that is, in embodied beliefs and habits. An ethics that is not utopian needs to consider people as they are now, historical men and women whose passions and imaginings about each other have been formed, at least in part, by past and present social and political institutions.

What would Spinoza's genealogical approach to affective life yield if it were applied to his own arguments for the differential political treatment of women, slaves, and servants? First, it is striking that racial and sexual differences are points of tension in his reasoning about democratic polities. It is precisely the fact that women, slaves, and servants were not full members of the body politic that allowed men and masters to continue to exert "natural" right within civil society. If these groups did enjoy genuine membership in a genuinely democratic polity, then equal political right would supersede individual instances of unequal natural right. This would then mean that those passions that tend to disrupt civil peace—for example, sexual passion and the desire to dominate—would be managed by the guardians of civil peace. The abolition of a priori status is, after all, precisely the kind of change that the institution of democracy promises.

These points of tension in Spinoza's reasoning are endemic to theorizations of political relations of domination and subordination. It is not peculiar to the seventeenth-century philosophical imagination. Women, and other groups (for example, the colonized, Jews), that were historically excluded from developing democracies embody the tension that lies at the heart of the major institutions of contemporary liberal democratic societies. The ethical problem concerning the legal treatment meted out to women, and others whose own "imaginings" are not represented in positions of institutional influence, is also a political problem. The effects of past historical exclusions from citizenship do not vanish once those who were excluded gain the franchise or other formal rights. Indeed, they do not vanish even when previously excluded individuals become members of Parliament! Nirmal Puwar has demonstrated the contemporary force of destructive racial imaginaries in the English Parliament. One memorable example she offers concerns a "black" MP entering an elevator in the Houses of Parliament. Mistaking him for cleaning staff, one of his "white" colleagues informs him, "Only Members [of Parliament] can go in the lift."[27] There is a multiplicity of embodied habits, customs, and laws, in the present, that continue to inhibit the ability of racialized or sexualized identities to fully realize their powers and capacities. Political subordination is not just a matter of the ideas we hold but also, and crucially, about ways of being in the world. The removal of formal bars on previously excluded groups does not amount to full participation in legal and political institutions, since the historical force of those institutions are embodied in ways that continue to deplete the powers of action of subordinated identities. How can an individual imagine him- or herself as being of equal worth to any other when that individual figures in the social imagination as fit only for menial tasks and in need of external governance? Contemporary sexual and racial imaginaries configure women and "nonwhites" as *both* free and rational members of a democratic political body *and* beings under the "natural" authority of (white) men. Critical work on the ethicopolitical consequences of this tension—especially its affective and imaginary aspects—should be part of the collective drive to realize human freedom within a "community of rational beings."

Notes

1. Gilles Deleuze, *Spinoza: Practical Philosophy*, trans. Robert Hurley (San Francisco: City Lights, 1988), 126, my emphasis.
2. Edwin Curley considers this question in "Kissinger, Spinoza, and Genghis Khan," in *The Cambridge Companion to Spinoza*, ed. Don Garrett (Cambridge: Cambridge University Press, 1996).
3. R. Descartes, *The Passions of the Soul*, in *The Philosophical Works of Descartes*, vol. 1, trans. E. S. Haldane and G. R. T. Ross (Cambridge: Cambridge University Press, 1970), 333.
4. See Descartes' letter to Princess Elisabeth in *Descartes: Philosophical Letters*, ed. A. Kenny (Oxford: Clarendon Press, 1970), 141.
5. Hans Jonas, "Spinoza and the Theory of the Organism," in *Spinoza: A Collection of Critical Essays*, ed. Marjorie Grene (Notre Dame: University of Notre Dame Press, 1979), 271.
6. Joy is "the passage from a lesser to a greater perfection" (E, III, Def Aff II). Sadness is "the passage from a greater to a lesser perfection" (E, III, Def Aff III).
7. Gilles Deleuze, *Expressionism in Philosophy: Spinoza* (New York: Zone Books, 1990), 280.
8. René Descartes, *Discourse on Method*, quoted in J. Blom, *Descartes: His Moral Philosophy and Psychology* (Brighton: Harvester Press, 1978), 43.
9. Gail Belaief, *Spinoza's Philosophy of Law* (The Hague: Mouton, 1971), 41–42.
10. Ibid., 25; emphasis in the original.
11. H. Cairns, *Legal Philosophy from Plato to Hegel* (Baltimore: Johns Hopkins University Press, 1949), 289.
12. Belaief, *Spinoza's Philosophy of Law*, 52.
13. Ibid., 106.
14. Ibid., 77, 83.
15. The one natural human right Spinoza does allow is the *right to think* (TTP, XVIII, 208).
16. For example, Spinoza argues that Moses aimed "not to convince the Israelites by *reasoned argument* . . . but to obey the Law under threat of punishment, while exhorting them thereto by promise of rewards. These are the means to promote *obedience, not to impart knowledge*" (TTP, XIV, 159; emphasis added).
17. See Genevieve Lloyd, "Woman as Other: Sex, Gender, and Subjectivity," *Australian Feminist Studies* 10 (1989), 13–22.
18. Deleuze, *Spinoza: Practical Philosophy*; emphasis in the original. See also: "In short, if we are Spinozists we will not define a thing by its form, nor by its organs and its functions, nor as a substance or a subject" (127).
19. Take the example of a man and a woman of similar capacities who desire to share an equitable and so harmonious life. If the woman fares worse professionally than the man does because of sexual discrimination, what effect will this have on the harmony that both endeavor to achieve? Contemporary arrangements concerning child care are relevant to this question.
20. Two important studies that take this theme as a central focus include Etienne Balibar, *Spinoza and Politics*, trans. Peter Snowden (London: Verso, 1998) and Antonio Negri, *The Savage Anomaly*, trans. Michael Hardt (Minneapolis: University of Minnesota Press, 1991).
21. Michael Rosenthal, "The Black, Scabby Brazilian," *Philosophy and Social Criticism* 31, no. 2 (2005): 219.
22. Women are indeed a "political problem" for Spinoza. The unfinished *Political Treatise* abruptly breaks off precisely at the point where he excludes women *as a class*. In an essay that highlights the aporetic nature of Spinoza's writings on democracy, and his ambivalence toward "the masses" and women, Etienne Balibar dares to say: "We watch him [Spinoza] die before this blank page." Etienne Balibar, "Spinoza, the Anti-Orwell: The Fear of the Masses," in *Masses, Classes, Ideas*, trans. James Swenson (New York: Routledge, 1994), 26.
23. Spinoza writes that "it is only difference of language, of laws, and of established customs that

divides individuals into nations" and that the laws and customs of a people may give rise to their "particular character, the[ir] particular mode of life" and those attitudes that mark them off from others (TTP, XVII, 200).

24. Charles Mills, *The Racial Contract* (Ithaca: Cornell University Press, 1997), 58; emphasis in the original.

25. Ibid., 127.

26. Yovel makes this point well. He writes that for Spinoza "knowledge is more a mode of being than of having, not something we possess but something we *are* or *become*." Yirmiyahu Yovel, *The Adventures of Immanence*, vol. 2 of *Spinoza and Other Heretics* (Princeton: Princeton University Press, 1989), 159; emphasis in the original.

27. N. Puwar, *Space Invaders: Race, Gender, and Bodies out of Place* (Oxford: Berg, 2004), 42.

11
Law and Sovereignty in Spinoza's Politics

Susan James

Recently, several outstandingly innovative writers have found in Spinoza's philosophy a conception of politics that speaks to many of the concerns of contemporary feminism. By focusing on what Spinoza calls imagination, they have developed an interpretation of his work that offers a way to view sexual difference as a fundamental yet variable dimension of political life, a way to theorize the ineradicability of politically significant differences of feeling and opinion, a way to understand the central role of local narratives and symbols in the construction of identity, and a way to conceive the social dimensions of affect.[1] Taken together, these interpretations contribute to a view of politics as a process in which sovereign and subjects can explore and criticize the self-understandings around which their common way of life is organized and can cooperate to enhance their freedom by devising effective forms of legislation. The overall aim of politics is thus taken to be that of preserving and increasing liberty; but each particular, embodied community needs to determine in its own case how freedom is to be lived (TTP, XX, 567).[2] Despite the fact that Spinoza himself is unexpectedly negative about the political capacities of women, feminist theorists have shown how his approach can "open up possibilities for the social critique of fictions which elude the resources of more conventional criticism."[3] As male and female subjects come to appreciate how their imaginative grasp of their situation both empowers and constrains, they strengthen their ability to assess, and where necessary revise, the laws and conventions by which they are governed.

This interpretation of politics draws support from the final chapter of the *Tractatus Theologico-Politicus*, where Spinoza examines the limits of state power. Extending a line of thought already present in Hobbes's *Leviathan*,[4] he observes that, because sovereigns cannot control the minds of their subjects, they are unable to prevent individuals from thinking and judging as they please (TTP, XX, 566–67).[5] Coercive as the state apparatus may be, it will not be able to stop subjects from forming their own feelings and opinions; and since these vary as much as tastes, any polity is bound to contain an ineliminable groundswell of conflicting affects and judgments. Furthermore, because humans are in general no better at controlling their tongues than their thoughts (TTP, XX, 566), any attempt to police the expression of ideas will run a high risk of failure. Sovereigns the world over therefore need to face up to the fact that they cannot rely on legislation to enforce or outlaw belief and must recognize that the law can at most impose a level of uniformity on what people do. Even here, however, a sovereign's power will be circumscribed by its subjects' power to resist it, so that in order to survive, a sovereign must be sensitive to what its subjects will and will not tolerate.[6]

Spinoza's stress on the limits of state power plays an important part in his political philosophy; but although he encourages his readers to note that sovereigns must be prepared to negotiate with their subjects, his commitment to a consensual image of government is nevertheless ambivalent.[7] Sovereigns, as Spinoza portrays them, must be sufficiently powerful to make and enforce the law (TTP, XIX, 557–58). In addition, they must be capable of determining what kinds of dissent amount to sedition, of punishing subjects whose opposition they regard as seditious, and of specifying the limits within which subjects may discuss and challenge their judgments. Finally, when a sovereign refuses to respond to criticism, its subjects remain bound to obey its laws, even when they believe those laws to be wrong (TTP, XX, 568). So as well as sketching the lineaments of a politics of compromise, Spinoza is a steely defender of the view that certain elements of a sovereign's power, including the ability to determine the boundaries of negotiation, should be as absolute as possible.

What should we make of this tension between the presumption that certain elements of a sovereign's power must be fixed, and the more open approach to lawmaking emphasized by many recent commentators? Does Spinoza's delineation of the incontrovertible elements of sovereign power undermine the emphasis on negotiation that feminist scholars have found so productive, or can the two be reconciled? One influential response to this question, championed by Negri and Matheron, takes up a remark in the *Tractatus Politicus* to the effect that the only absolute form of sovereignty is that held by a democratic assembly whose decisions, and hence laws, are themselves the outcome of negotiation and compromise.[8] In states where every subject plays a part in the process of making the law, and thus possesses a share of sovereign power, no one has to be coerced into obeying laws that they have not made for themselves. Laws about the non-negotiable aspects of sovereign power emerge from democratic forms of collective negotiation and decision making, and because this minimizes the threat of resistance, the sovereign's power is as absolute as possible.

This is an important and compelling line of interpretation, but I shall argue that it only partly resolves the tension with which we are concerned. To get a fuller grasp of the issue, we need to go back a bit and look again at what it takes for the sovereign of a state to achieve a near-absolute level of power. Negri and Matheron's appeal to democracy presupposes that the power of a sovereign is measured in relation to the power of other human agents (principally the multitude of subjects), and their proposed solution is designed to dissipate conflict between the sovereign's ability to make the law and its subjects' ability to resist. But for Spinoza there is also a theologicopolitical aspect of the problem. In order to assess the extent of the sovereign's power to make law, one needs to consider whether this power is limited by nonhuman agents, and in particular by God. If the deity ordains laws that humans are obliged to obey, both the sovereign's authority and a consensual politics will be framed by the non-negotiable demands of divine legislation, and both will need to be reexamined in the light of this restriction. Concentrating on this second aspect of Spinoza's discussion, I shall argue that by taking it into account we are able to cast new light on the apparent tension between the negotiable and non-negotiable aspects of sovereignty.

One of the most puzzling features of the sovereign's power, as Spinoza presents it, is the manner in which it depends on both imagination and reason. On the one hand, sovereigns must create and maintain their ability to control the law by using the interlocking resources of reason and imagination to negotiate with their subjects. On the other hand, Spinoza seems to treat the claim that a sovereign must possess certain specific powers as a finding of reason. The latter requirement not only conjures up a traditional image of a patriarchal sovereign whose word is law, but also comes as a shock in the work of a philosopher who is usually so sensitive to the interplay between imagination and reason. The abrupt transition from one to the other is uncomfortable, because the imaginative dimension of the sovereign's power, on which its effectiveness has hitherto been held to depend, seems suddenly to be laid aside.

For theorists who rejoice in the central place of imagination in Spinoza's politics, this may well be a troubling moment. However, as I shall show, tracing out the theological aspect of his conception of sovereignty allows us to reconsider whether the claim that sovereigns must possess certain fixed powers is in fact grounded in reason rather than imagination. One of the central aims of the *Tractatus Theologico-Politicus* is to undercut the view that the sovereign's ability to make the law is limited by the law of God. By examining how Spinoza argues against this position, we can arrive at a better appreciation of the pressures that prompt him to endow the sovereign with non-negotiable powers and also come to recognize that these powers are themselves indebted to imagination. At one level, the absoluteness of Spinoza's conception of sovereignty offers a challenge to a line of interpretation that revolves around imagination and has proved singularly productive for feminism. At another level, however, it can be shown to vindicate this line of interpretation, by revealing that Spinoza's appeal to imagination runs even deeper than most commentators have appreciated.

The idea that the authority of the sovereign might be limited by the law of God is alien to many contemporary readers, but it played a crucial part in early modern debates about political power.[9] Spinoza's analysis of the problem therefore needs to be seen as a contribution to a complex set of controversies and as aiming to overturn a number of established views. A crucial point of reference for understanding what is going on in the *Tractatus Theologico-Politicus* is the political theory of Thomas Hobbes, to which it is deeply indebted.[10] So much so that Spinoza's discussion of this theme can be fruitfully interpreted, so I shall suggest, as an attempt to consolidate and extend Hobbes's arguments. Broadly speaking, both Hobbes and Spinoza address themselves to readers who hold that God has made laws that human beings are obliged to obey, and which they can come to know in two ways.[11] The natural light of reason enables them to discover what the law of nature requires of them; and through scripture they can learn the content of the law revealed to the prophets. The obligatory force of divine law in both its forms gave rise to a difficulty that is lucidly stated in Hobbes's *Leviathan*. Without a knowledge of divine law, Hobbes explains, "a man knows not, when he is commanded anything by the civil power, whether it is contrary to the law of God or not; and so, either by too much civil obedience, offends the divine majesty, or through fear of offending God transgresses the commands of the commonwealth."[12] In two of his three political works, *De cive* and *Leviathan*, Hobbes offers a series of arguments designed to resolve this uncertainty by establishing that the law of God, whether natural or revealed, is only binding when promulgated by a human being and that the power to promulgate the divine law lies solely with the sovereigns of states. The authority of sovereigns is thus not limited by any countervailing legal duty to God, and nothing can override their subjects' obligation to obey them. In the *Tractatus Theologico-Politicus* Spinoza develops this controversial claim and integrates the resulting view into his broader philosophical position. Drawing on a metaphysical conception of the deity that Hobbes explicitly rejects, and an analysis of prophecy that goes beyond anything to be found in *De cive* or *Leviathan*, he arrives at a conception of law as a purely human phenomenon.[13]

Because Hobbes and Spinoza are aiming to discredit the authority of two different types of divine law, their argument proceeds in stages, and both begin by criticizing the view that the law of nature poses a challenge to the sovereign. Their discussion is organized around Hobbes's etymological claim that a law in the strict sense of the term is a command. "Law," Hobbes asserts, "is not advice (*consilium*) but command (*mandatum*)." It derives "from one who has power over those whom he instructs," and it generates obligations, so that "to do what one is instructed by law is a matter of duty."[14] To discover whether the so-called laws of nature are really laws at all, one therefore has to consider whether they are commands. If we consider them as made by God, Hobbes concedes (introducing a possibility to which he will return later on) this may indeed be the case. However, if we consider them as "proceeding from nature," we find that rational investigation of humans and their circumstances does not yield commands, but only what Hobbes describes as theorems or dictates of reason. "What we call the laws of nature are nothing other than certain conclusions, understood by reason, on what is to be done and not to be done; and a law, properly and precisely speaking, is an utterance by one who by right commands others to do or not to do. Hence, properly speaking, the natural laws are not laws, insofar as they proceed from nature."[15]

As Hobbes goes on to explain, the law of nature is constituted by theorems about our conservation and defense and deals both with the relations between individual human beings and with the honor or worship due to God.[16] Theorems on the first of these topics tell us to uphold various virtues such as "justice and equity and all habits of the mind that conduce to peace and charity" and make up what is generally referred to as the moral law.[17] Thus, in accordance with what he takes to be a widely shared view, Hobbes holds that "the natural law is the same as the moral law" and, by appealing to the status of the law of nature, he infers that what is usually described as the moral law is in fact not a law in the proper sense of the term.[18] While it tells us what it is good for us to do and possesses an authority "legible to all men that have use of natural reason," it does not consist of commands and therefore does not oblige us.[19]

When Spinoza comes to discuss the same issue, he adopts Hobbes's definition. "The word 'law,'" he reiterates, "is simply used to mean a command which men can either obey or disobey" (TTP, IV, 426). However, because his conception of the law of nature differs from the Hobbesian one, his argument about its status proceeds along different lines. Putting aside Hobbes's conception of the laws of nature as normative precepts, he first points out that the term is also applied more widely to describe the behavior of things that act for a fixed and determined reason (TTP, IV, 426).[20] For example, "the fact that all bodies, on colliding with smaller bodies, lose as much of their own motion as they impart" is in this sense a law about bodies, and "the fact that a man, in remembering one thing, forthwith calls to mind another like it . . . is a law that necessarily follows from the nature of man" (TTP, IV, 426). On the assumption that laws are commands (TTP, IV, 427),[21] it immediately becomes evident that these so-called laws of nature can only be laws in a metaphorical sense (TTP, IV, 427).[22] Since we have rational grounds for believing that all laws of this sort are necessary and eternal, we have no choice but to be governed by them, and it makes no sense to think of them as edicts that can be obeyed or disobeyed.[23] The language of command simply cannot get a grip on a deterministic universe.

Spinoza consolidates the conclusion that our talk about the laws of nature is merely metaphorical by drawing still more deeply on distinctive features of his metaphysics. One of the insights we can arrive at through rational philosophical inquiry, he claims, is that nature and God are one and the same and thus that the more we learn about nature, the more we learn about God.[24] As he puts it, "The whole of our knowledge, that is, our supreme good, not merely depends on our knowledge of God but consists entirely therein," so that "we acquire a greater and more perfect knowledge of God as we gain more knowledge of natural phenomena" (TTP, IV, 428). Once we appreciate that this is the case, we can recognize that the immutable laws of nature are the workings of God's mind, and we can shake off an anthropomorphic conception of God as a king or ruler who issues commands. This set of claims both opens up a sense in which natural laws are divine and simultaneously reveals that a true idea of the deity is incompatible with a conception of him as a legislator. It therefore offers further support for the view that the law of nature is not a law in the sense of a set of commands.

For Hobbes, as we have seen, the natural law is simultaneously a moral law by virtue of its content. It consists of precepts specifying what we ought to do and forebear from doing. Furthermore, Hobbes goes on to claim, both the natural and moral laws are also divine because, in creating nature, the deity determined that this particular set of eternal precepts articulates the good for human beings. Since Spinoza does not conceive of God as the creator of nature, this argument is not available to him, and he accordingly provides a different account of the relationships between natural, moral, and divine law. As we investigate nature, we acquire knowledge of a great variety of causal regularities, of which those concerning human good and harm are a subset; but while the process of coming to understand what is good for us by this means gives us knowledge of our own condition, it is not a matter of recognizing commands that oblige us to act in a certain way. By reasoning, we come to see that without an understanding of the natural world, including ourselves, we shall be incapable of working out either what ends are most beneficial to us or how to set about achieving them. This insight in turn enables us to infer that our supreme good, and the goal for which we should above all strive, is understanding. If we then consider the status of the precept "The way for humans to achieve their supreme good is to pursue understanding," we find that, insofar as it is an immutable truth about nature, it is a natural law in the metaphorical sense; but insofar as it concerns human good, it is simultaneously a moral law. Furthermore, since nature and God are one and the same, this moral recommendation can equivalently be expressed as "Love God"—that is to say, love God by devoting yourself to understanding him. Reformulating the recommendation in this fashion brings home to us that the object of the moral law is God, and that it is appropriate to describe the moral law as divine, since it is simultaneously about the good for human beings and about their relationship to the deity (TTP, IV, 428).[25] The recommendation "Pursue understanding," which flows from both the natural and moral laws, is therefore equivalent to the key precept of the divine law, "Love God."

By merging the three types of legislation, Spinoza is able to apply his account of the status of the natural and moral laws to their divine counterpart and to conclude that the divine law is not strictly speaking a law at all. Since, as we have already seen, God is not the kind of being who issues commands, loving him cannot be a matter of obeying his decrees, and the divine law can therefore be a law only in a metaphorical sense.[26] It offers us a set of recommendations that are in fact for our good, but it does not oblige us to follow them.

It remains to consider how knowledge of the recommendations we can derive from our understanding of God and nature can be turned into laws in the proper sense of the term, that is to say, into commands. How can a recommendation that tells us how to achieve our own good become a law that we are obliged to obey? Hobbes's answer to the question hinges on three central claims. First, the law of nature is not transparent and therefore stands in need of interpretation. Before its precepts can be turned into commands, some authority has to determine what it recommends.[27] Second, a law in the sense of a command must be promulgated in such a way that those who are bound by it are aware of their duties. For example, "the command of the commonwealth is law only to those who have means to take notice of it," and so it must be written and publicized.[28] Finally, an utterance only has the force of a command when the agent who utters it has the power to ensure that it is obeyed. In the state of nature no one is capable of interpreting, promulgating, and imposing the recommendations that constitute the natural law, thus turning them into binding commands; in the state, the only figure that possesses these powers is the sovereign. Hence, laws of nature can be transformed into commands only by a sovereign, and although they are "naturally reasonable," it is only by virtue of sovereign power that they become laws.[29]

Hobbes's argument is based on the assumption, defended elsewhere in his political works, that it is possible for human beings to create circumstances in which a sovereign has the power to issue commands that its subjects are under an obligation to obey. But before Spinoza can adopt this starting point he needs to go more deeply into its presuppositions and engineer a compromise with his own conception of nature as a closed causal system. Philosophical inquiry tells us, he insists, that all natural events, including human actions, are determined by their causes and that what we regard as contingency is simply an effect of our ignorance. In that case, however, a strictly philosophical account of nature will allow no room for the idea that human beings can choose whether or not to obey commands and no room for laws conceived as commands that can be obeyed or disobeyed. Instead, antecedent causes will determine everything people do, including the way they understand and respond to laws. Spinoza unblinkingly embraces this inference. "I grant that all things are determined by the universal laws of nature to exist and to act in accordance with a definite and determined reason" (TTP, IV, 426).[30] However, he immediately goes on to argue that we are usually unable to make much use of it in nonphilosophical contexts. Because "generalisations concerning fate and the interconnection of causes can be of no service to us in forming and ordering our thoughts concerning particular things," and because we have no knowledge of "the way things are in actual fact ordered and connected" (TTP, IV, 426–27), we are for practical purposes justified in viewing events as contingent and explaining some of them by an appeal to human agreement or decision (TTP, IV, 426).[31]

This transition from a strictly rational conception of nature to the more familiar outlook on the world that Spinoza attributes to human imagination enables him to accommodate both the idea that people can choose whether or not to issue commands and the idea that they can choose whether or not to obey them.[32] It thus makes room for our ordinary notion of a law and simultaneously opens up space for a new definition. A law, Spinoza now explains, is "a rule of conduct, which men lay down for themselves or others for some end" (TTP, IV, 427). So in order to turn an understanding of what is metaphorically described as the moral or divine law into a law in this narrower sense of the term, some human agent must lay down the relevant claims as rules of conduct. If we add to this the background assumption that a law is a command, we can introduce the further stipulation that the agent in question must possess enough power to be capable of issuing orders that others will obey.

Although he does not particularly draw attention to it, Spinoza's explicit provision that laws are laid down by humans is highly significant. As we have seen, God is not in his view the kind of being who is capable of issuing commands (though we may still imagine him as doing so). Only human agents, whether individual or collective, can impose rules of conduct on one another, and in fact they can make laws of two different kinds. On the one hand, they can create human laws, or rules of conduct designed to safeguard life and the state. On the other hand, they can make divine laws concerned with the supreme good, namely, the knowledge and love of God (TTP, IV, 427). So for the divine law to become law in the ordinary sense of the term, it has to be legislated by a human agent and imposed by human power. As Spinoza will go on to explain in more detail, the divine law may be realized by a wise sovereign who sees how to translate its recommendations into specific decrees that subjects are capable of obeying; and there is also, in his view, a derivative sense in which subjects may legislate the divine law for themselves by willingly obeying the sovereign's commands. In both cases, however, the law is a human creation and consists entirely of human decrees.[33]

While he defends this conclusion in his own way, Spinoza is basically in agreement with Hobbes's view that only human agents can transform either the law of nature or the moral law into commands. Nature itself does not impose legal obligations on human beings, and we must construct them for ourselves. This is a radical and provocative conclusion; but before they can guarantee that there are no nonhuman sources of legal authority capable of challenging the sovereign's power, both theorists need to dispose of the further claim that, even if the law of nature does not consist of divine commands, the revealed law certainly does.[34]

In *De cive* and in *Leviathan*, Hobbes draws a sharp distinction between the laws of nature insofar as they proceed from nature (when, as we have seen, they are not laws in the proper sense) and the same laws insofar as "they have been legislated by God in the Holy Scriptures." In the latter case, he allows, "they are very properly called by the name of laws; for

Holy Scripture is the utterance of God, who issues commands in all things by the highest right."[35] This concession seems to sit uncomfortably with the rest of his position. If scripture gives us access to divine laws that we are obliged to obey, these laws must surely derive from a source of authority that is independent of sovereigns and may at least in principle restrict or oppose their edicts. Moreover, in a society where biblical revelation is taken seriously, such a division of authority may become a source of faction and have destructive political consequences.[36]

Hobbes's response to this objection is intricate. Before God gave Moses the Ten Commandments, he argues, the only divine law was the law of nature. However, since we know from scripture that the Commandments were subsequently handed down by God himself, we need to ask, "Who was it that gave to these written tables the obligatory force of laws?"[37] In order to be bound by a command one has to know that it was issued by a suitable authority and understand what it requires of one; but where prophecy is concerned, this raises an epistemological problem. A prophet such as Moses, who receives a direct revelation, knows that God has spoken and what he has demanded. By contrast, ordinary people to whom the prophet recounts his revelation cannot possess the same assurance, since both the Bible and everyday experience warn us that prophetic claims can be mistaken or insincere.[38] The mere fact that Moses told the Jewish people that he had received the tables of the law from God consequently did not enable them to know that his testimony was accurate and could not oblige them to conform. Instead, what obliged them was the fact that, when Moses promulgated the law, he was already their sovereign and they had already agreed to obey him. Revealed laws therefore only become binding when imposed by a human sovereign, and "all subjects are bound to obey that for divine law which is declared to be so by the laws of the commonwealth."[39]

Once again Spinoza endorses this conclusion, but once again his argument for it constitutes an even deeper attack on Christian theology than anything Hobbes articulates. As we have seen, Hobbes's main reason for denying that subjects are bound by laws known through revelation is epistemological; unless one receives a revelation, one cannot be sure whether God has issued a command. Whatever Hobbes may privately have believed, he does not explicitly challenge the view that God sometimes issues commands to prophets, but focuses instead on the problem of how we can know what these commands are. By contrast, Spinoza's argument takes a yet more unorthodox step. What the Bible represents as laws, he explains, are not in fact commands made by a deity. Contrary to an established outlook, God cannot be the source of our legal obligations, and in fact there *are* no divine laws of a kind that can form a counterweight to the legal authority of sovereigns.[40]

This stretch of the *Tractatus Theologico-Politicus* treads on dangerous theological ground, and Spinoza begins concessively by allowing that the Mosaic law "can be termed the law of God, since we believe it to have been sanctioned by prophetic insight." At first glance, this seems to imply that Moses did indeed articulate laws made by the deity and to echo Hobbes's position; but on closer inspection it becomes clear that this is not what Spinoza is saying. Prophets, he proposes, possess outstanding imaginative gifts and, through narratives, images, and metaphors are able to grasp the significance of situations in ways that elude ordinary people. However, since there is nothing exceptional about their intellects, we should not expect them to provide philosophical insights into the nature of the divine law or the supreme good. This conclusion is supported by the Old Testament, in which it is obvious that prophets, along with other key figures, often failed to understand the true nature of the deity. For example, we can see from the conversation between God and Adam, as it is narrated in Genesis, that even the first man did not appreciate that the law of nature is entirely determined. If he had realized this, he would have understood that it was not simply his own will that caused him to eat the apple offered to him by Eve and would not have described his action as a choice (TTP, II, 410; IV, 430). However, we can also see that the narrative represents the situation as Adam imagined it, or to put the point differently, as it was revealed to him. He imagined God as a being who commanded him to act in a certain way and gave him the option of obeying or disobeying. In short, he conceived of God as a lawmaker; and the same applies to the prophets, including Moses, whose experience of God was of a deity who gave him a set of commandments and told him how to impose them on the citizens of the ancient state of Israel (TTP, II, 411–13; IV, 431). Such imaginative powers can be immensely productive as a means of persuading a people to cooperate for their mutual benefit; but insofar as they represent God as the source of commands, they rest on a misconception.

In taking a stand on the character and status of revealed law, Hobbes and Spinoza were entering into a sequence of fierce theological debates and challenging those biblical commentators and religious authorities who regarded the commandments contained in scripture as obligations distinct from the civil law. Both authors approach this fraught discussion by arguing that a correct reading of the Old Testament shows that the Ten Commandments were part of an elaborate legal code imposed by Moses when he became the ruler of the Jews (TTP, V, 436), and both insist that the obligation to adhere to them derived from Moses's sovereign power, which enabled him to enforce the law through threats and punishments. The Ten Commandments were therefore part of Jewish civil law and are nowadays only laws in jurisdictions where the sovereign makes them so.[41]

Turning to the laws supposedly taught by Jesus Christ, Spinoza again develops a line of argument defended in *Leviathan*.[42] Unlike Moses, who saw how the divine law applied to the predicament of the Jews, and expressed his insight in a civil code that was exceptionally effective in maintaining a historically specific state, Christ was able to understand the tenets of the divine law in their universal or philosophical form. As we have seen, these tenets are not laws, but recommendations about how to achieve the supreme human good. So Christ was not a lawmaker, and if he occasionally presented his insights as commands, this was simply a concession to the intellectual limitations of his audience (TTP, IV, 431–32). The New Testament therefore does not contain anything that purports to be a revealed law and presents no challenge to the rule of earthly sovereigns.

Looking back, we can see that the fulcrum of Hobbes's case for the absolute power of sovereigns is his skeptical attitude to revealed law. While he does not explicitly deny that God reveals himself to man, he insists that the workings of revelation are too mysterious and uncertain to ground laws that impose obligations on communities of ordinary human beings. Biblical evidence does indeed suggest that God sometimes reveals specific commandments through his prophets; but individuals who are not themselves the beneficiaries of revelation can never be sure that prophetic testimony is veracious and can therefore never have sufficient reason to regard it as binding. Unlike Hobbes, Spinoza takes a more anthropological approach and, rather than simply putting prophecy aside as epistemologically deficient, offers to explain it. When the prophets describe themselves as articulating laws decreed by God, they are interpreting a situation they only partly understand, and although they sincerely believe that they are communicating decrees made by a deity for human beings, there *is* no deity of the kind they imagine. Thus, they themselves are the true authors of the law. Just as individuals who possess great intellectual gifts can grasp the content of the divine law in its natural and moral guises by philosophical means, so prophets can come to appreciate it by imagination. But whereas a philosopher who understands it will recognize that it is not a law in the strict sense of the term, the prophets erroneously imagined it as a set of divine commands that humans are under an obligation to follow. In truth, however, what is known as the divine law merely identifies our supreme good and recommends us to pursue it. To become a law that fits Spinoza's definition ("a rule of conduct laid down by men, for themselves or others, for some end") it must be interpreted and legislated by human beings.

Spinoza has now put in place two sets of arguments, each designed to undercut a particular conception of the laws made and enforced by God. The first, which appeals to our capacity for philosophical understanding, claims to show that, although reason gives us access to what are called laws of nature and to what is called the divine law, it also enables us to see that these are not commands. Instead, the natural and divine laws consist of truths and recommendations, which possess no legal status and do not impose any legal obligations. The second set of arguments then aims to discredit the view that a number of divine commands are recorded in scripture. It counters this position by claiming that the lawmaking God described in the Bible is the fruit of imagination. The prophets and their peoples may have conceived God as a legislator who would reward the obedient and punish sinners; but no such being in fact exists, and the laws attributed to him were ordained and enforced by human beings. Taken together, the two arguments comprehensively slough off the widespread early modern assumption that political life is shaped and limited by divine commands and banish even the shadowy figure of a divine lawmaker who continues to haunt the pages of Hobbes's philosophy.[43] Law, it emerges, is never something to be discovered, but always something that humans have to use their reason and imagination to construct.[44]

Can this reading of Spinoza's analysis of sovereignty help us to reconcile the consensual aspects of his politics with his insistence that sovereigns must possess the power to determine the boundaries of negotiation and criticism within the state? To put the point another way, does the argument we have been tracing help us to see why Spinoza might impose these limits on the imaginative process of negotiation and compromise through which diverse individuals are able to understand themselves as citizens who compose "as it were one mind and one body"? To sustain his account of politics, Spinoza has to accord real force to civil legislation, since it is now the sole source of political order. Yet if law is to be effective, a number of conditions must be met, among them the basic requirements that sovereigns are able to understand themselves as issuing commands, and citizens to conceive of themselves as obeying freely. As we have seen, Spinoza has identified a sense in which these self-conceptions, on which the idea of law rests, are the fruit of imagination, since the conviction that humans are capable of commanding and obeying is a consequence of our inability to understand the multiple causes that determine our actions. For practical purposes, this imaginary perspective is the only one available to us, and insofar as it enables us to represent ourselves as loci of power, it is undoubtedly productive. However, while we cannot overcome the limitation inherent in this way of imagining ourselves, we are nevertheless capable of understanding the nature of its shortcomings. Like Spinoza himself, we can appreciate that, from a philosophical point of view, law embodies a misconception about our own capacities. Thus construed, it appears as doubly human: the self-understandings on which law rests are the fruit of an unavoidable yet inadequate perspective deriving from human imagination; and the laws built on this imaginary basis are entirely constructed by human beings. Without imagination there would therefore be no law, and no politics.

It is easy to see why this analysis might have shaken the confidence of Spinoza and his contemporaries. The sovereign, previously subject to the law of God, now appears as a fragile and isolated entity whose task is to create law in the face of a series of challenges: from its subjects, from a lack of the quasi-prophetic imagination that will enable it to make its commands acceptable, and from the recognition that the legal framework on which its power rests ultimately derives from a lack of understanding. Whereas the traditional picture had portrayed God as the preeminent lawmaker, and had represented human sovereigns as small-scale inheritors of his legislative power, Spinoza shatters this image. God does not issue commands and, but for imagination, what humans inherit is his incapacity to do so.

Insofar as this dramatically more exposed conception of sovereignty is rooted in imagination, the tension between consensual government and non-negotiable sovereign power from which we began is not, after all, a tension between imagination and reason, but rather a tension between imagination's more and less malleable features. While the identities that we construct for ourselves alter with individual and collective experience, there is something peculiarly immovable about our sense that some of our actions are voluntary and thus about those aspects of our political practices that depend on it. As one of these, law is a resilient notion, capable of functioning as the organizing category of political life. Nonetheless, Spinoza questions the depth of its authority by making it the creation of a human sovereign, who first employs the deeply rooted imaginative vocabulary of command and obedience, and then draws on imagination once again to devise a narrative capable of persuading its subject to accept the laws it makes. If we now consider why the *Tractatus Theologico-Politicus* places such emphasis on the absoluteness of sovereignty, this fragility may be part of the answer. Political order consists in the law made by an inherently precarious sovereign who is, as we have found, challenged from many directions. The power to limit negotiation therefore serves not so much as a vehicle for tyranny, but more as an attempt to counteract the sovereign's vulnerability by giving it the means to protect its subjects and promote their freedom.

The analysis offered here of Spinoza's grounds for holding that a sovereign must possess certain non-negotiable powers is not complete. Along with Hobbes, Spinoza has additional psychological and political reasons for favoring such an arrangement. Underlying them, however, is the challenging claim that the sovereign's power to make law is the fruit of imagination and thus of a pervasive kind of misunderstanding. An appreciation of this conclusion allows us to reconsider and reject the view from which we began, that the absolute aspects of sovereignty run counter to the emphasis on imagination that plays such a vital part in feminist readings of Spinoza's political philosophy. This, we can now see, is at best a half-truth. To understand Spinoza's account of sovereignty, we need to appreciate the ways in which it depends on and emerges from imagination.

Notes

I have benefited from many helpful comments on earlier drafts of this chapter and am grateful for them all. I particularly want to thank Maria Aristodemou, Alex Douglas, Peter Fitzpatrick, Moira Gatens, Eric Schliesser, Quentin Skinner, and Theo Verbeek for numerous constructive suggestions, which I have done my best to take into account.

1. These interpretations are to some extent indebted to Gilles Deleuze. His *Expressionism in Philosophy: Spinoza*, trans. Martin Joughin (New York: Zone Books, 1990), published in French in 1968, and *Spinoza: Practical Philosophy*, trans. Robert Hurley (San Francisco: City Lights, 1988), published in French in 1983, have had an enormous influence, as has Louis Althusser's discussion of

Spinoza as a theorist of ideology. See especially Althusser, *Essays in Self-Criticism* (London: New Left Books, 1976), chap. 4. Some of the most important examinations and elaborations of the themes identified above, not always directly applied to feminism, are to be found in Etienne Balibar, *Spinoza and Politics* (London: Verso, 1998) and *Masses, Classes, Ideas* (London: Routledge, 1994); Moira Gatens and Genevieve Lloyd, *Collective Imaginings: Spinoza, Past and Present* (London: Routledge, 1999); Moira Gatens, "Feminism as Password: Re-thinking the 'Possible' with Spinoza and Deleuze," *Hypatia* 15, no. 2 (2000): 59–75; Warren Montag, *Bodies, Masses, Power: Spinoza and His Contemporaries* (London: Verso, 1999); Gillian Howie, *Deleuze and Spinoza: Aura of Expressionism* (Basingstoke: Palgrave Macmillan, 2002).

2. The translation used in this chapter is Benedict de Spinoza, *Tractatus Theologico-Politicus*, in *Complete Works*, ed. Michael L. Morgan, trans. Samuel Shirley (Indianapolis: Hackett, 2002).

3. Gatens and Lloyd, *Collective Imaginings*, 5.

4. Thomas Hobbes, *Leviathan*, ed. Richard Tuck (Cambridge: Cambridge University Press, 1991), 256.

5. For Hobbes's discussion of the same point, see *Leviathan*, 198–99.

6. Gatens and Lloyd, *Collective Imaginings*, chap. 5; Balibar, *Spinoza and Politics*, 110; Hilail Gildin, "Spinoza and the Political Problem," in *Spinoza: A Collection of Critical Essays*, ed. Marjorie Grene (Notre Dame: University of Notre Dame Press, 1979), 377–87.

7. See Balibar, "Jus-Pactum-Lex," in *Masses, Classes, Ideas*, 174f; Gatens and Lloyd, *Collective Imaginings*, 67–70.

8. Antonio Negri, "Reliqua Desiderantur: A Conjecture for a Definition of Democracy in the Final Spinoza," in *The New Spinoza*, ed. Warren Montag and Ted Stolze (Minneapolis: University of Minnesota Press, 1997), 219–47; Alexandre Matheron, "Spinoza and Hobbes," in *The New Spinoza*, ed. Montag and Stolze, 207–16 and Alexandre Matheron, *Individu et communauté chez Spinoza* (Paris: Minuit, 1969), 330ff.

9. See, for example, Richard Hooker: "Being so prone as we are to fawn upon ourselves, and to be ignorant of as much as may be of our own deformities, without the feeling sense whereof we are most wretched . . . how should our festered sores be cured but that God hath delivered a law as sharp as the two-edged sword, piercing the very closest and most unsearchable corners of the heart unto which the law of nature can hardly, human laws by no means possible, reach unto?" *Of the Laws of Ecclesiastical Polity*, ed. Arthur Stephen McGrade (Cambridge: Cambridge University Press, 1989), bk.1, chap. 12, 108–9.

10. On the relation between Spinoza and Hobbes, see Edwin Curley, "The State of Nature and Its Law in Hobbes and Spinoza," *Philosophical Topics* 19, no. 1 (1991): 97–117; Theo Verbeek, *Spinoza's "Theologico-Political Treatise": Exploring the Will of God* (Aldershot: Ashgate, 2003).

11. Hobbes argues that divine law does not bind atheists. Hobbes, *Leviathan*, 246.

12. Ibid., chap. 31, 245.

13. "Those Philosophers who sayd that the World, or the Soule of the World, was God, spake unworthily of Him; and denyed his existence: For by God is understood the cause of the World; and to say the World is God, is to say there is no cause of it, that is, no God." Ibid., 250.

14. Thomas Hobbes, *On the Citizen*, ed. Richard Tuck (Cambridge: Cambridge University Press, 1998), 153–4.

15. Ibid., 56. Compare "These dictates of Reason, men use to call by the name of Lawes, but improperly: for they are but Conclusions or Theoremes concerning what conduceth to the conservation and defence of themselves; whereas Law, properly is the word of him that, by right hath command over others." Hobbes, *Leviathan*, 111.

16. Hobbes, *Leviathan*, 248.

17. Ibid., 197.

18. Hobbes, *On the Citizen*, 55.

19. Hobbes, *Leviathan*, 268.

20. Translation modified. The Latin text reads "*una eademque certa ac determinata ratione agunt.*" *Spinoza: Oeuvres*, vol. 3, ed. Pierre Francois Moreau (Paris: Presses Universitaire de France, 1999), 180.

21. In the Latin original, "per legem nihil aliud intelligitur quam mandatum, quod homines et perficere et negligere possunt," *Spinoza*, ed. Moreau, 182.

22. Translation modified. "Verum enimvero quoniam nomen legis per translationem ad res naturales applicatur videtur." Ibid.

23. E. Curley, "Spinoza's Moral Philosophy," in *Spinoza: A Collection of Critical Essays*, ed. Marjorie Grene (Notre Dame: University of Notre Dame Press, 1979), 371.

24. This conception of God is explicitly rejected by Hobbes. *Leviathan*, 250.

25. For a somewhat different account of Spinoza's view of the relation between natural and civil law, see Gail Belaief, *Spinoza's Philosophy of Law* (The Hague: Mouton, 1971), 42.

26. "When one conceives God's freedom . . . as that of a tyrant or legislator, one ties it to physical contingency or to logical possibility. One thus attributes inconstancy to God's power since he could have created something else—or worse still, powerlessness, since his power is limited by models of possibility." Deleuze, *Spinoza: Practical Philosophy*, 69.

27. Hobbes, *Leviathan*, 191.

28. Ibid., 187.

29. Ibid., 191.

30. Translation modified. "Et quamvis absolute concedam omnia ex legibus universalibus naturae determinari ad existendum et operandum certa ac determinata ratione." *Spinoza*, ed. Moreau, 180.

31. Translation modified. "Quia homo, quatenus pars est naturae, eatenus partem potentiae naturae constituit; quae igitur ex necessitate naturae humanae sequuntur, hoc est, ex natura ipsa, quatenus eam per naturam humanam determinatam concipimus, ea, etiamsi necessario, sequuntur tamen ab humana potentia, quare sanctionem istarum legum ex hominum placito pendere optime dici potest." Ibid., 182.

32. "All that one needs in order to moralise is to fail to understand. It is clear that we only have to misunderstand a law for it to appear to us in the form of a moral 'You must.' If we do not understand the rule of three, we will apply it, we will adhere to it, as a duty. Adam does not understand the rule of the relation of his body to the fruit, so he interprets God's word as a prohibition." Deleuze, *Spinoza: Practical Philosophy*, 23.

33. See Miguel Vatter, "Strauss and Schmitt as Readers of Hobbes and Spinoza," *New Centennial Review* 4, no. 3 (2004): 186–91.

34. See Douglas Den Uyl, *Power, State, and Freedom: An Interpretation of Spinoza's Political Philosophy* (Assen: Van Gorcum, 1983), 10ff.

35. Hobbes, *On the Citizen*, 66–7. Compare "But yet if we consider the same Theoremes, as delivered in the word of God, that by right commandeth all things; then are they properly called Lawes." Hobbes, *Leviathan*, 111.

36. See Leo Strauss, *Spinoza's Critique of Religion*, trans. E. M. Sinclair (New York: Schocken Books, 1965), 101–4.

37. Hobbes, *Leviathan*, 356–57.

38. Ibid., 257–59, 292–97.

39. Ibid., 199.

40. See Gatens and Lloyd, *Collective Imaginings*, 95–100.

41. Hobbes, *Leviathan*, 341, 359–60.

42. While Spinoza explicitly draws this conclusion in the *Theological-Political Treatise*, Hobbes is more circumspect. See *Leviathan*, 358–60.

43. See Leo Strauss, *Philosophy and Law* (Albany: State University of New York Press, 1995), 32; Carl Schmitt, *Leviathan in the State Theory of Thomas Hobbes*, trans. George Schwab (Westport, Conn.: Greenwood Press, 1996), 57.

44. See Deleuze, *Expressionism in Philosophy*, 259.

Further Reading

Damasio, Antonio. *Looking for Spinoza: Joy, Sorrow, and the Feeling Brain*. New York: Harcourt, 2003.
Deleuze, Gilles. *Spinoza: Practical Philosophy*. Trans. R. Hurley. San Francisco: City Lights, 1988.
Dobbs-Weinstein, Idit. "Thinking Desire in Gersonides and Spinoza." In *Women and Gender in Jewish Philosophy*, ed. Hava Tirosh-Samuelson, 51–77. Bloomington: Indiana University Press, 2004.
Gatens, Moira. "Feminism as Password: Re-thinking the 'Possible' with Spinoza and Deleuze." *Hypatia* 15, no. 2 (2000): 59–75.
———. *Imaginary Bodies: Ethics, Power, and Corporeality*. New York: Routledge, 1996.
Gatens, Moira, and Genevieve Lloyd. *Collective Imaginings: Spinoza, Past and Present*. London: Routledge, 1999.
Gullan-Whur, Margaret. *Within Reason: A Life of Spinoza*. London: Pimlico, 2000.
Howie, Gillian. *Deleuze and Spinoza: Aura of Expressionism*. Basingstoke: Palgrave Macmillan, 2002.
James, Susan. "Power and Difference: Spinoza's Conception of Freedom." *Journal of Political Philosophy* 4 (1996): 206–28.
———. "The Power of Spinoza: Feminist Conjunctions." *Hypatia* 15, no. 2 (2000): 40–58.
Kent, Bonnie. *Virtues of the Will: The Transformation of Ethics in the Late Thirteenth Century*. Washington, D.C.: Catholic University of America Press, 1995.
Lloyd, Genevieve. *Part of Nature: Self-Knowledge in Spinoza's "Ethics."* Ithaca: Cornell University Press, 1994.
———. *Spinoza and the Ethics*. London: Routledge, 1996.
———, ed. *Spinoza: Critical Assessments of Leading Philosophers*. 5 vols. New York: Routledge, 2001.
———. "Woman as Other: Sex, Gender, and Subjectivity." *Australian Feminist Studies* 10 (1989): 13–22.
Montag, Warren. *Bodies, Masses, Power: Spinoza and His Contemporaries*. London: Verso, 1999.
Montag, Warren, and Ted Stolze, eds. *The New Spinoza*. Minneapolis: University of Minnesota Press, 1997.
Nadler, Steven. *Spinoza: A Life*. Cambridge: Cambridge University Press, 1999.

Ravven, Heidi M. "Spinoza and the Education of Desire." *Neuro-Psychoanalysis* 5, no. 2 (2003): 218–29.
———. "Spinoza's Ethics of the Liberation of Desire." In *Women and Gender in Jewish Philosophy*, ed. Hava Tirosh-Samuelson, 78–105. Bloomington: Indiana University Press, 2004.
Rosenthal, Michael. "The Black, Scabby Brazilian." *Philosophy and Social Criticism* 31, no. 2 (2005): 211–21.

List of Contributors

AURELIA ARMSTRONG teaches philosophy at the University of Queensland. She has published essays on Spinoza, Deleuze, Foucault, and feminism. She is currently working on two projects: a book on Spinoza, immanence, and agency and a related project on Spinoza's theory of emotion and imagination.

SARAH K. DONOVAN is an assistant professor of philosophy at Wagner College. Her research and teaching interests include feminist, social, moral, and Continental philosophy. She has published, on Luce Irigaray and Judith Butler, "Overcoming Oedipal Exclusions" in *Philosophy Today* 42 (2002), and has a forthcoming article on philosophical pedagogy and a forthcoming book chapter on philosophy and popular culture.

MOIRA GATENS is professor of philosophy at the University of Sydney. She is an Australian Research Council professorial fellow, 2006–10, and was a fellow at Wissenschaftskolleg zu Berlin, 2007–8. She is author of *Imaginary Bodies: Power, Ethics, and Corporeality* (1996) and (with Genevieve Lloyd) *Collective Imaginings: Spinoza, Past and Present* (1999). Her present research project is on Spinoza, Feuerbach, and George Eliot.

PAOLA TERESA GRASSI lives and works in Milan. She graduated from the University of Milan in 1998 with a thesis on the subject of Spinoza and the concept of the imaginary. She received her Ph.D. from the University of Padua in 2003 on the subject of Spinoza and Freud. She has taught courses on Spinoza, the imaginary, and philosophical practice.

LUCE IRIGARAY has held many posts in the United Kingdom and continental Europe. She is currently visiting professor at the Department of Philosophy, University of Liverpool, and at the Department of Theology, Liverpool Hope University (2008–9). She is author of *Speculum of the Other Woman*, *An Ethics of Sexual Difference*, *Democracy Begins Between Two*, *The Way of Love*, and several other books.

SUSAN JAMES is professor of philosophy at Birkbeck College, University of London. Among her books is *Passion and Action: The Emotions in Seventeenth-Century Philosophy* (1997) and she is the editor of *Margaret Cavendish: Political Writings* (2003). A book on Spinoza's political philosophy is forthcoming.

GENEVIEVE LLOYD is professor emerita in philosophy at the University of New South Wales and a research associate in philosophy at Macquarie University in Sydney. Her publications include *The Man of Reason: "Male" and "Female" in Western Philosophy* (second edition, 1993); *Part of Nature: Self-Knowledge in Spinoza's Ethics* (1994); *Spinoza and the Ethics* (1996); and (with Moira Gatens) *Collective Imaginings: Spinoza, Past and Present* (1999). She has edited *Spinoza: Critical Assessments* (2001) and *Feminism and History of Philosophy* (2002).

ALEXANDRE MATHERON is author of *Individu et communauté chez Spinoza*, *Anthropologie et politique au XVIIe siècle: Études sur Spinoza*, and many articles on Spinoza. He is now retired and lives in Paris.

HEIDI MORRISON RAVVEN is professor of religious studies at Hamilton College. She has published extensively on Spinoza and also on the medieval Jewish philosopher Moses Maimonides. She has secondary interests in Jewish feminism and the philosopher G. W. F. Hegel. Her work on Spinoza has led her to explore how contemporary neuroscience, especially the neuroscience of the emotions, forces us to rethink what it means for a person to be ethical. Ravven has a four-year grant from the Ford Foundation to write a book titled *What Happened to Ethics?*

AMELIE OKSENBERG RORTY teaches social medicine at Harvard Medical School. She has held posts in philosophy and the history of ideas at Yale and Brandeis universities. She is author of *Mind in Action* and editor of several books on Aristotle, ethics, personal identity, and many other topics. She has published many journal articles on Spinoza.

DAVID WEST studied philosophy at the University of Cambridge before teaching at the universities of Bradford and Liverpool. He is currently reader in political theory at the Australian National University in Canberra. His publications include *Authenticity and Empowerment: A Theory of Liberation* (1990); *An Introduction to Continental Philosophy* (1996); and, most recently, *Reason and Sexuality in Western Thought* (2005).

Index

activity and passivity: appearances and, 70–79; relational individuality and, 55–61; in Spinoza's *Ethics*, 7–8
adamah, 148–50, 153n.7
affect, Spinoza's theory of, 14, 63n.26, 147–48; appearances and, 66–70; law and sovereignty and, 211–26; lust and, 89–90, 105n.3; relational individuality and, 56–61
After Virtue (MacIntyre), 134
Agency. *See also* autonomy: autonomy and, 49–50; law and sovereignty and, 220–26
Alfarabi, 133, 139n.8
amor erga faeminam, 98–99
amor meretricius, Spinoza's concept of, 94, 96–97, 105n.8; jealousy and, 99–100
Anglo-American philosophy, Spinoza's legacy and, 11
Anscombe, Elizabeth, 126, 134–35
anthropocentrism, Spinoza's opposition to, 193
appearance, Spinoza's discussion of: freedom of activity and, 70–79; passivity, idolatry, and partiality and, 66–70
Appiah, Kwame Anthony, 139n.7
Aquinas, St. Thomas, 19, 89, 103, 108
Ariadne-Echo legend, 66–85
Aristotle: Christian view of, 133; Judeo-Islamic thought and, 21, 130; on love (*philia*), 119; naturalism of, 127–28, 139n.8; on reason, 121; Spinoza's knowledge of, 4; "supreme good" of, 111; on women, 161
"Aristotle and Descartes in Spinoza's Approach to Matter and Body," 185n.21
Armstrong, Aurelia, 13–15, 43–61
ascetic idealism, Spinoza's departure from, 19–20, 108–9

atheism, Spinoza and, 8–10
atomic individuality: autonomy and, 46–50; free will and, 134
Augustine, St., 19, 108, 126, 132, 140n.12, 141n.20, 142n.29
authenticity, autonomy and, 45–50
autonomy, 13–15. *See also* agency: relational individuality and, 43–61; social self and feminism and, 45–50
avarice, lust and, 101–2
Averroes, 133

Bacon, Francis, 108
Balibar, Etienne, 60–61, 176
baptism, Christian identity defined by, 129–30
beauty, sexuality and, 94
Behind the Geometrical Method (Curley), 170–71
Belaief, Gail, 195–96
Bennett, Jonathan, 61n.1, 184n.9
Bentham, Jeremy, 19, 108
Bible. *See also* specific books, e.g. Leviticus, Book of: law and sovereignty in, 220–26
biology, love and, 74–79
"blessedness," in Spinoza's *Ethics*, 7–8
body: gender and, 11; politics of imagination and, 190–93; role in attainment of knowledge of, 171–79; sexuality and, 87–105; in Spinoza's philosophy, 24–25, 179–83, 185n.21
Braidotti, Rosi, 183
Broad, C. D., 133–34, 142n.26
Buell, Denise Kimber, 140n.14
Butler, Judith, 187n.44

Cairns, H., 195
Campbell, Joseph Keim, 135–36, 143n.34

234 Index

care ethics, autonomy and, 46–47, 62n.6
Catholic Church, free will and, 133–38
causality, Yovel's discussion of, 168–70, 185n.21, 186n.34
cherem (ostracism) of Spinoza, 3–4
Christianity. *See also* Judeo-Islamic thought: ethics of pleasure, sexuality, and love and, 114; free will and ethics of, 127–38, 141n.20; idealism within, 108–9; identity formation and, 125–26; Irigaray's discussion of, 165–67; law and sovereignty and, 221–26
civil law, 194–98; political order and, 225–26
Code, Lorraine, 62n.10
command, law as, 193–98
common notions, in Spinoza's *Ethics*, 7
communitarianism: freedom and, 63n.30; repudiation of autonomy and, 48–50
compatibilism, free will and, 136–37
conatus. *See* essence (*conatus*)
Condemnations of 1277, 129, 133
conflict, relational autonomy and, 51–61
Continental philosophy, Spinoza's legacy and, 11
conversion, baptism as symbol of, 129–30
conversos (Jewish converts to Christianity), 3
Cornell, Drucilla, 187n.44
corpora simplicissima, Spinoza's concept of, 304; love, vulgarity and learning and, 79–85; love and appearance and, 75–79
Creating the Kingdom of Ends, 128
Crescas, 133
Curley, Edwin, 4, 8, 85n.1, 142n.26, 167, 170–71

de Beauvoir, Simone, 15, 166
debility, love and, 69–70
De cive (Hobbes), 215, 220–21
Deleuze, Gilles, 59, 170, 185n.16, 189–90, 193, 201–2, 208n.18
De Libero Arbitrio (Augustine), 141n.20
democracy, law and sovereignty and role of, 213–14
Democracy Begins Between Two (Irigaray), 183
de Sade, Donatien Alphonse (Marquis), 108
Descartes, Rene: on activity and nature, 139n.8; dualism of, 30–32, 167, 172; on free will, 127–28, 132–34; on life/death distinctions, 190–91; "occult hypothesis" concept of, 192; on passions, 89; Platonic-Christian philosophy and, 21; rationalism of, 110–11; relational individuality and *res cogitans* of, 55–61; sexual difference in work of, 34–41; Spinoza's discussion of, 4–5, 11–13, 132, 170
desire: self-recognition and deferral of, 149–52; sexuality and, 89–105, 117
"Desire and the Double in Spinoza" (Ueno), 186n.27
despotism, Spinoza's attack on, 9
determinism, free will and, 133–37, 143nn.34, 36
Deutscher, Penelope, 183, 185n.24
de Witt, Johan and Cornelius, 8
difference, dominance and recognition of, 31–34
Discourse on Method (Descartes), 34–35
divinity: divine and civil law and, 194–98; Irigaray's discussion of, 155–64, 166–83, 185nn.23–24; law and sovereignty and, 214–26
Dobbs-Weinstein, Idit, 139nn.5, 7, 9
dominance: ambition of, 100; knowledge and, 29–34
Donovan, Sarah, 23–24, 165–83
dualism: affects and emotions and, 15–17; autonomy and, 44–45; beauty and, 94–95, 105n.6; *corpora simplicissima* and, 75–79; ethics of pleasure and, 116–23; gender issues and, 2; Irigaray's critique of, 166–67, 187n.42; knowledge and dominance and, 30–34; life/death distinctions and, 190–93; of reason and sexuality, 109–13; relational individuality and, 54–61; sexual difference and, 35–41; Spinoza's discussion of, 11–13, 19–20, 31–34, 172–83
Duns Scotus, John, 140n.12

elation, Spinoza's discussion of, 67–68
Elements (Euclid), 4
embodied knowledge, 198–202
emotion, Spinoza's discussion of, 176–79
Enlightenment philosophy, ascetic realism and, 108
"envelope" metaphor, Irigaray's discussion of Spinoza and, 23, 155–64
envy, Spinoza's discussion of, 98–99
Epicureans, Spinoza and, 19, 116; ascetic idealism and, 108
essence (*conatus*): embodied knowledge in, 199–202; lust and, 93–94; morality and, 111–13; "occult hypothesis" concept and, 192–93;

relational individuality and, 53–61; sexuality and, 89–91, 117–18; in Spinoza's *Ethics*, 6–7, 19; structure of appearances and, 77–79
"essentialism": embodied knowledge and, 201–2; rationality and, 113
"eternity of mind," in Spinoza's *Ethics*, 7–8
ethics: embodiment and naturalization of, 125–38; human-centered ethics, 33–34; individuality and, 53–61; sexuality and, 102–5
Ethics, politics of imagination and, 189–90
Ethics of Sexual Difference, An (Irigaray), 165–67, 182–83
Ethics (Spinoza): autonomy and relational individual in, 45–61; body discussed in, 190–93; Donovan's discussion of, 24; embodied knowledge in, 199–202; fall of Adam in, 145–52; free will in, 131–32, 141nn.22–23; imagination discussed in, 199–202; individuality discussed in, 52–61; Irigaray's comments on, 22–23, 155–64; love and elation in, 15–17; mind-body dualism in, 172–79; overview of, 4–8; philosophy of the body in, 24–25; sexual difference in, 36–41; sexuality in, 18–19, 88–105, 114–15
Euclid, 4
exteriority, relational individuality and, 55–61

fall of Adam and Eve: free will and, 132; sexuality and moral of, 95–96, 106n.9; Spinoza's discussion of, 19–20, 22–23, 36–37, 145–52
feminist theory: autonomy and, 13–14, 43–61; Donovan's discussion of Irigaray and, 165–83, 187n.46; free will and, 126–38; law and sovereignty and, 211–26; love in, 15–17; mind-body dualism and, 11–13; naturalistic ethics of Spinoza and, 20–21; relational individual and, 43–61; sexual difference and, 40–41; social self and autonomy and, 45–50; Spinoza and, 1–2, 179–83
Feuerbach, Ludwig, 173
fictional aptitude, concept of, 147–48, 152
"final causes" doctrine, Spinoza's rejection of, 5
Firestone, Shulamith, 15, 124n.27
Five Types of Ethical Theory, 133
Flanagan, Owen, 126
fluctuatio animi, 100
Foot, Phillipa, 126
Freedom and Determinism, 136
free will (freedom): Augustinian concept of, 126; community and, 63n.30; divine and civil law and, 194–98; ethics and, 126–38; Judeo-Islamic thought and, 129; knowledge of affects and, 14; knowledge of good and evil and, 36–37; love and, 83–85; metaphysics of, 109–13; naturalistic ethics of Spinoza and, 20–21; nature and, 11; relational individuality and, 57–61; sexuality and, 97–105; Spinoza's rejection of, 4–8; truth and, 82–85; Western concepts of, 19–20
Freud, Sigmund, 82, 165, 177–78, 186n.27
Friedman, Marilyn, 63n.31
friendship, Spinoza on, 119–20, 124n.23

Gatens, Moira, 24–25, 117, 121–22, 179–83, 186nn.27, 36, 187n.42, 189–207
Gebhardt, Carl, 105n.2, 106n.10
gender: love and asymmetry of, 120–22; mind-body dualism and, 11–13; Spinoza's conceptualization of difference and, 34–41
Genesis, Book of, 150, 163
Gersonides: on free will, 133, 140n.18, 142n.27; Spinoza's knowledge of, 4
glory, Spinoza's discussion of, 98
"God or Nature" (*Deus sive Natura*), 109–13, 123, 155–64
Grassi, Paola, 22–23, 145–52
Grosz, Elizabeth, 185n.24

Hampshire, Stuart, 112
Harvey, Zeev, 140n.18, 142n.27
health, sexuality and, 94–95
hedonistic self: materialism and, 110–13; rationality and sexuality and, 108–9; Spinoza's discussion of, 19–20, 115–23
Hegel, G. F. W., 176, 185n.20
Heidegger, Martin, 158, 165
highest good, Spinoza's concept of, 10
hilarity (*hilaritus*) of love, Spinoza's discussion of, 84–85
Histories (Justin), 205
history, free will and, 128–38
Hobbes, Thomas, 19, 25–26; on law and sovereignty, 195–96, 212, 215–26; moral ontology of, 111; philosophy of, 108; on sexuality, 90, 117
holism, relational individuality and, 53–54
Holland, political struggles in, 8
homosexuality: Judeo-Christian condemnation of, 114; Spinoza's concept of nature and, 19–20; Spinoza's ethics and, 118–20, 124n.23

Hooker, Richard, 227n.9
human foolishness, Spinoza's concept of, 147–48
human nature: dominance and knowledge and, 29–34; Spinoza's discussion of, 11–12
Hume, David, 19, 108

idealism, reason and, 107–9
identity: Christian anthropology of, 125–26, 129–30, 140n.14; classical individualism and, 47; ethics and, 139n.7; relational individuality and, 56–61
idolatry: appearances and, 66–70; Spinoza on true love vs., 65–85
I Love To You (Irigaray), 183
Imaginary Bodies (Gatens), 179, 186n.27, 187n.37
imagination: Gatens on politics of, 189–207; Irigaray's consonance with Spinoza on, 171–83, 186n.26; law and sovereignty and, 211–26; love and, 74–79; political analysis and, 199–202; sex and race differences and, 202–7; Spinoza's theory of, 22–24, 26, 146–52, 186n.27
individuality: love and, 71–79; morality and, 111–13; Spinoza's autonomy and, 14–15, 51–61; Spinoza's particularism and, 15–17; Spinoza's relational view of, 45–61
Inquisition, Jewish expulsions and, 3
intellectual love, Spinoza's discussion of, 122–23
interiority, relational individuality and, 55–61
internality, freedom and rationality and, 111–13
interpersonal relationships, autonomy and, 47–50
intuition (*scientia intuitiva*), 175–79; love with vulgarity and, 81–85; Spinoza's discussion of, 16–17
Irigaray, Luce, 22–24, 155–64; consonance with Spinoza of, 171–79; contemporary feminist theory and, 179–83; Donovan's discussion of, 165–83; Gatens' discussion of, 179–83
Irigaray and Deleuze (Lorraine), 185n.24
Irigaray and the Divine (Grosz), 185n.24
Islam. *See* Judeo-Islamic thought
Italian women's movement, 183

James, Susan, 25–26, 63n.30, 186n.27, 211–26
jealousy, Spinoza's discussion of, 97–100
Jewish philosophy: free will and, 140n.18; Irigaray's discussion of, 165–67; *virtus imaginandi* (virtue of imagining) and, 146–52

Jonas, Hans, 54–56, 192
joy: embodied knowledge and, 201–2; of love, 82–85; sexuality and, 89–105; in Spinoza's *Ethics*, 6–7, 119, 177–79
Judeo-Islamic thought. *See also* Jewish philosophy: determinism and, 137–38; naturalistic ethics of Spinoza and, 20–21, 127–30, 139nn.8–9; Spinoza's knowledge of, 4, 22
Justin, 205

Kant, Immanuel: on free will and ethics, 126–28, 134, 143n.36; Platonic-Christian philosophy and, 21
Kent, Bonnie, 140n.12
Klein, Julie, 127, 139n.8, 141n.25, 142n.27, 184n.10, 185n.21
knowledge: dominance and, 29–34; embodied knowledge, 198–202; law as, 193–98; love and, 81–85; sex and race differences and, 206–7; in Spinoza's *Ethics*, 6, 22–23, 172–79; Spinoza's three levels of, 175–79
Korsgaard, Christine, 128

Lacan, Jacques, 165, 174, 177–78, 186n.27
laetitia, Spinoza's discussion of, 85n.1
La Mettrie, Julien Offray de, 108
law: divine vs. civil law, 193–98; sovereignty and, 211–26
Laws, The (Plato), 114
learning, love with vulgarity and, 79–85
Le Doeuff, Michèle, 187n.42
Leviathan (Hobbes), 212, 215, 220–21, 223
Leviticus, Book of, 114
liberal theory, Spinoza and, 196–98
libido generandi, Spinoza and, 85
Literal Commentary on Genesis, The (Augustine), 142n.29
Lloyd, Genevieve, 5, 11–13, 29–42, 176, 187n.42
Lorraine, Tasmin, 185n.24
love: ethics of, 113–23; lust and, 92–93; sexuality and, in Spinoza's work, 17–19, 89–105; Spinoza on idolatry and true love, 65–85; Spinoza's theory of the passions and, 15–17
Luce Irigaray (Whitford), 185n.24, 186n.26
lust, Spinoza's discussion of, 17–19, 89–91; object of, 92–93

MacIntyre, Alasdair, 21, 134–35
Mackenzie, Catriona, 48
madness, love and, 100–101

Mahdi, Muhsin S., 139n.8
Maimonides, 133, 147; Spinoza's knowledge of, 4, 22
male sexuality, in Spinoza's work, 99–100
marriage, Spinoza's discussion of, 103–5, 106n.22
materialism, 110–13; science and, 137–38
mathematical physics: love and, 74–79; love with vulgarity and, 79–85
Matheron, Alexandre, 17–19, 87–105, 105nn.2–3, 106n.10, 117, 202–4, 213
metaphysics: of autonomy, 46–50; of freedom, 109–13; Irigaray's challenge to, 173–79; of Spinoza, 23–24, 185n.21
Mills, Charles, 206
mimesis, Irigaray's discussion of, 166–67
mind-body dualism. See dualism
mob mentality, in Spinoza's Ethics, 8
modernity, free will and, 131
monism, Spinoza's concept of, 116–17; in Ethics, 4–5; Irigaray's discussion of, 23; "occult hypothesis" concept and, 192–93; Western traditions and, 19
Moore, G. E., 132–34, 141n.24
moral community of humans, 12
morality, Spinoza's critique of, 19–20
Mosaic law, 102; ethics of pleasure, sexuality and love and, 114; Spinoza's discussion of, 10, 221–22

Nadler, Stephen, 3
naturalistic ethics of Spinoza, 20–21, 125–38, 143n.36
"naturalistic fallacy," free will and, 133
natura naturans/natura naturata distinction, 109, 168–72, 184nn.10–11, 185nn.13, 22
nature. See also human nature: divine and civil law and, 194–98; fall of Adam and role of, 150–52; free will and, 128–38; in Judeo-Islamic thought, 20–21; sexuality and, 95–96, 109–13; sovereignty and laws of, 216–26; in Spinoza's Ethics, 5, 168–69, 172; in Spinoza's political writings, 9–11, 33–34
Negri, Antonio, 176, 186n.32, 213
Nicomachean Ethics, 121
Nietzsche, Friedrich: ascetic idealism of, 108, 110; on Christianity, 126; Spinoza's work and, 27n.5
"occult hypothesis" concept of Descartes, 192
Oldenburg, Spinoza's letter to, 14, 50–52

Opera (Spinoza), fall of Adam and, 148–52
Orangist party (Holland), 8
Origen, 141n.20
O'Rourke, Michael, 136
Ovid, 108

panentheism, 110
parallelism: Irigaray's discussion of, 166–67; in Spinoza's philosophy, 23, 170–71
partiality, appearances and, 66–70
particularity: love with vulgarity and, 81–85; in Spinoza's philosophy, 66
Pascal, Blaise, 29–30
passions: imagination and, 202–7; political analysis and, 199–202; sexuality and, 88–90, 101–5; Spinoza's discussion of, 15–19, 66–70
passivity and activity: appearances and, 66–79; in Spinoza's Ethics, 7–8
patriarchy, sexuality and, 120
Philo, 130
Plato, 19, 114; eros of, 117–18; on ethics, 127; idealism of, 107–8, 119–20
pleasure: ethics of, 102–5, 113–23; sexuality and, 91–92
Political Treatise (Tractatus Politicus) (Spinoza): law and sovereignty in, 213; overview of, 8–10; role of women in, 120; sexual and racial exclusion in, 204–7; theology discussed in, 146
politics: feminism and, 43–61; Gatens on imagination and, 189–207; law and sovereignty and, 211–26; natural vs. civil law and, 24–25; sex and race differences and, 202–7; of Spinoza, 10–11
Politics of Impossible Difference, A (Deutscher), 183, 185n.24
power: embodied knowledge and, 199–202; law and sovereignty and, 211–26; love and, 71–79; mind-body dualism and, 32–34; relational individuality and, 59; sexuality and, 91; state despotism and, 10
Principles of Philosophy (Descartes), 4
procreation: marriage and, 103–5; sexuality and, 92–93
prophecy, lawmaking and, 26
psychoanalysis: Gatens' discussion of, 179–83; Irigaray's discussion of, 177–79, 186n.27
psycho-historical knowledge, love with vulgarity and, 80–81

psychological theory, structure of appearances and, 77–79
psychology, soul and, 126
Puwar, Nirmal, 207

racial difference: embodied knowledge and, 198–202; imagination and, 202–7
rationality: freedom and, 111–13; idealism of, 107–9; law and sovereignty and, 216–26; in Spinoza's *Ethics*, 6–8, 176–79
Ravven, Heidi, 20–22, 63n.24, 125–38
reason: freedom and, 37–41; gender and, 39–41; Irigaray's consonance with Spinoza on, 174–79; law and sovereignty and role of, 214–26; natural *vs.* civil law and, 25; passion *vs.*, 18–19; Spinoza's discussion of, 107–9, 122–23
relational autonomy, feminist theory and, 46–50
relational individual, autonomy and, 43–61
religion: free will and, 129–30, 140n.14; law and sovereignty and, 221–26; Spinoza's discussion of, 9–10, 109–13, 115–23
Republican party (Holland), 8
res cogitans, relational individuality and, 55–61
Rist, John, 142n.29
Romanticism, love and, 119–21, 123
Rorty, Amelie Oksenberg, 15–17, 20, 57, 65–85, 122–23, 202
Rosenthal, Michael, 203

Savage Anomaly (Negri), 186n.32
Schlegel, Friedrich, 120
science, determinism and, 137–38, 143n.35
scientia intuitiva, 122–23; love with vulgarity and, 81–85; Spinoza's concept of, 16–17
scientific thought: Spinoza's philosophy and, 2; structure of appearances and, 76–79
Scruton, Roger, 120
Second Sex, The (de Beauvoir), 166
self-determination: deferral of desire and, 149–52; Irigaray's discussion of, 158–64; Spinoza's discussion of, 51–61, 62n.10
self-governance, autonomy and, 45–50
sexual difference: comparisons of Irigaray and Spinoza on, 181–83; embodied knowledge and, 198–202, 208n.19; imagination and, 202–7; Irigaray's "envelope" of, 155–64; Spinoza's conceptualization of, 34–41
sexuality: ethics of, 102–5, 113–23; freedom and, 19–20; jealousy and, 97–100; reason and the self in Spinoza and, 107–23; Spinoza's discussion of, 17–19, 87–105
sexual realism, 108
Shier, David, 136
Shirley, Samuel, 85n.1
Shumate, Nancy, 140n.14
sin: freedom and Western concepts of, 19–20; Spinoza's discussion of, 22–23, 146–52
socialization: autonomy and, 48–50, 58–61; freedom and, 37–41
social norms: politics of imagination and, 189–90; sexuality and, 101–2
social self, feminism, autonomy, and, 45–50
Socratic thought, Spinoza's philosophy and, 82
sovereignty: law and, 211–26; power and, 195–96
Speculum of the Other Woman (Irigaray), 166
Spinoza, Baruch (Benedict): early life and thought, 2–4; Wolfson's discussion of, 130
Spinoza and Other Heretics: The Marrano of Reason (Yovel), 168–70
Spinoza and Politics (Balibar), 176
Spinoza and the Ethics (Lloyd), 176
state: divine and civil law and, 196–98; law and sovereignty and role of, 211–26; regulation of sexuality by, 118–19; Spinoza on character of, 10
Stoic philosophy: Christian condemnation of, 133; Judeo-Islamic naturalism and, 21, 130; knowledge and, 82; Spinoza's knowledge of, 4
Stoljar, Natalie, 48
strategic essentialism, Irigaray's discussion of, 166–67
Substance (*Deus sive Natura*), Spinoza's redefinition of, 3–4; discussion in *Ethics* of, 5–6, 172–79; mind-body dualism and, 11; "soul-substance" and, 192–93
suffering: freedom and, 82–85; sexuality and, 90–91; Spinoza's concept of, 149–52
superstition, Spinoza's discussion of, 9–10
"supreme good" (Aristotle), 111
symbolism, comparisons of Irigaray and Spinoza on, 179–83

Taylor, Charles, 130, 134
teleology, Spinoza's repudiation of, 19
telos, Spinoza's rejection of, 5
Ten Commandments, Hobbes's discussion of, 221

Theologico-Political Treatise (Tractatus Theologico-Politicus)(Spinoza): divine and civil law in, 194–98; ethics of pleasure, sexuality and love and, 113–14; law and sovereignty in, 212–26; natural vs. civil law in, 24–25, 33–34; overview of, 8–10; religion discussed in, 149–50, 152; sexual and racial exclusion in, 204–7; social organization in, 37–41

theology: free will and, 126–30, 132–38; law and sovereignty and, 221–26; Spinoza on illusion of, 26–27, 109–13

Thoughts (Pascal), 29–30

titillation (titillatio), 85n.1; sexuality and, 91–92, 118–19

To Be Two (Irigaray), 183

Treatise on the Emendation of the Intellect (Spinoza), 115–16, 152

Ueno, Osamu, 186n.27

uncertainty principle, determinism and, 136

utilitarianism: ascetic idealism and, 108; sexuality and, 119–20

van den Enden, Claire, 106n.22

virtue: mind-body dualism and, 32–34; Spinoza's discussion of, 24–25

Virtues of the Will, 140n.12

virtus imaginandi (virtue of imagining), Spinoza's concept of, 146–52

voluntarist concept of free will, 128, 142n.27

vulgarity: appearances and, 66–70; learning and love with, 79–85; love and, 73–79

"vulgus" (masses), Spinoza's discussion of, 9

West, David, 19–20, 107–23

Western philosophy: free will in, 126–38; idealist and hedonist traditions in, 19–20; Irigaray's critique of, 166

Whitford, Margaret, 185n.24, 186n.26

Wolfson, Harry Austryn, 130

women: imagination and role of, 205–7; in Judeo-Christian ideology, 173–79; sexuality and, 17–19, 96–105; Spinoza on role of, 36–41, 120; Spinoza's exclusion from government of, 12–13, 205–7, 208n.22

"worm in the blood" analogy, Spinoza's use of, 14, 50–52

Yitzchaki, Rabbi Shlomo "Rashi," 150, 153n.8

Yovel, Yirmiyahu, 168–70, 184n.11, 185n.13, 186n.34, 209n.26

www.ingramcontent.com/pod-product-compliance
Lightning Source LLC
Chambersburg PA
CBHW031548300426
44111CB00006BA/226